Hands-On MLOps on Azure

Automate, secure, and scale ML workflows with the Azure ML
CLI, GitHub, and LLMOps

Banibrata De

Hands-On MLOps on Azure

Portfolio Director: Kartikey Pandey

Relationship Lead: Prachi Rana

Project Manager: Sonam Pandey

Content Engineer: Apramit Bhattacharya

Technical Editor: Simran Ali

Copy Editor: Safis Editing

Indexer: Hemangini Bari

Proofreader: Apramit Bhattacharya

Production Designer: Ganesh Bhadwalkar

Growth Lead: Amit Ramadas

First published: August 2025

Production reference: 1210725

Published by Packt Publishing Ltd.

Grosvenor House

11 St Paul's Square

Birmingham

B3 1RB, UK.

ISBN 978-1-83620-033-8

www.packtpub.com

To my mother, Arati De, and to the memory of my father, Narahari De—for their sacrifices and for exemplifying the power of determination.

To my wife, Anuja, for being my loving partner throughout our shared journey of life.

To my sons, Rishik and Adwik, for sharing in my joy of creativity and unbounded energy.

– Banibrata De

Contributors

About the author

Banibrata De is a lead software engineer at Microsoft. Over the years, he has contributed in various capacities, including application performance engineering, backend architecture, and frontend development. He has been part of the Azure Machine Learning CLI team since its inception and played a key role in shaping the developer experience. He has also been an active contributor to the Azure ML SDK v2 open source project since its early days.

Currently, Banibrata works on AI Foundry, Microsoft's flagship platform for enabling large language models and agentic workflows. Prior to Microsoft, he worked at Tata Consultancy Services and PricewaterhouseCoopers, helping a wide range of clients solve complex engineering challenges across industries.

He holds a Bachelor of Engineering degree from Jadavpur University, Kolkata, India.

I want to thank the people who have been close to me and supported me, especially my wife, Anuja.

About the reviewers

Tapas Roy is a data leader passionate about unlocking the potential of data to drive strategic decisions and growth. With a rich background in data platforms, BI, and AI, he has led cross-functional teams globally, driving success across healthcare, financial services, retail, and consumer products. He fosters high-performance, collaborative cultures that tackle complex challenges while enabling continuous learning. An entrepreneur at heart, he is also passionate about blockchain innovation and future possibilities at the intersection of tech and business.

Sriram Panyam is a seasoned engineering leader with deep expertise in distributed systems, cloud platforms, and AI. He has held key roles at Google, LinkedIn, and Amazon, where he shaped large-scale systems powering global platforms. Sriram has led initiatives in systems architecture, cloud optimization, and data infrastructure while developing engineering talent and high-performing teams. His strengths include microservices, performance tuning, scalable data processing, and cloud-native design. He has driven major technical transformations and set best practices for resilient infrastructure, earning recognition as a trusted advisor and respected voice in the engineering community.

Nicola Farquharson has over 20 years of experience in networking infrastructure and Microsoft technologies, including AI, MS-SQL, Power BI, Data Science, Dynamics 365, Machine Learning, Azure, and Azure DevOps. She is the author of Exam Ref DP-900 Microsoft Azure Data Fundamentals, 2nd Edition, and has trained hundreds as a Microsoft Certified Trainer and part-time professor. Her background spans roles in cybersecurity and infrastructure analysis, with a focus on risk management and data governance. She brings a multidisciplinary perspective to architecting secure, scalable, and intelligent cloud solutions.

Table of Contents

Part 2: Implementing MLOps 63

Chapter 3: Reproducible and Reusable ML 65

Chapter 7: Monitoring the ML Model   141

Chapter 8: Notification and Alerting in MLOps   159

Part 3: MLOps and Beyond 175

Chapter 9: Automating the ML Lifecycle with ML Pipelines and GitHub Workflows 177

Chapter 10: Using Models in Real-world Applications 195

Preface

Machine Learning Operations (**MLOps**) is an emerging discipline that brings together machine learning, DevOps, and data engineering to streamline and automate the end-to-end lifecycle of machine learning models—from development and experimentation to deployment and monitoring. This book introduces MLOps in a practical, scenario-driven way, with real-world examples using Azure ML, GitHub Actions, and cloud-native services. It aims to help you operationalize machine learning models efficiently and reliably in enterprise environments. The book concludes by exploring the latest trends in LLMOps—applying MLOps to large language models such as GPTs.

Who this book is for

This book is written for DevOps engineers, cloud engineers, SREs, and technical leads who are involved in deploying and managing machine learning systems. It also serves project managers and decision-makers looking to understand MLOps processes and best practices. You are expected to have a working knowledge of the following:

- Machine learning concepts (model training, evaluation, data preparation)
- Cloud computing (Azure, AWS, or GCP)
- Software development tools such as version control, testing, and CI/CD
- Python programming

A background in DevOps is especially helpful, as this book builds on DevOps principles and extends them to ML workflows.

What this book covers

Chapter 1, Understanding DevOps to MLOps, introduces DevOps fundamentals and transitions into MLOps practices such as faster experimentation, deployment, and model governance across cloud platforms.

Chapter 2, *Training and Experimentation*, guides you through creating ML workspaces, tracking experiments, and optimizing models using hyperparameter tuning.

Chapter 3, *Reproducible and Reusable ML*, focuses on building repeatable ML pipelines and managing environments to ensure consistent and efficient ML development.

Chapter 4, *Model Management (Registration and Packaging)*, covers model registration, packaging, versioning, and deployment strategies to support the full model lifecycle.

Chapter 5, *Model Deployment: Batch Scoring and Real-Time Web Services*, explores how to implement scoring jobs for batch processing and real-time prediction using scalable cloud services.

Chapter 6, *Capturing and Securing Governance Data for MLOps*, delves into governance, lineage tracking, compliance, and security of ML workflows.

Chapter 7, *Monitoring the ML Model*, shows how to track model performance, detect data drift, monitor resource usage, and conduct controlled rollouts.

Chapter 8, *Notification and Alerting in MLOps*, teaches you how to use event-driven alerts (e.g., via Event Grid) to detect anomalies and trigger automated responses.

Chapter 9, *Automating the ML Lifecycle with ML Pipelines and GitHub Workflows*, details how to orchestrate model deployment using GitHub Actions and infrastructure-as-code practices.

Chapter 10, *Using Models in Real-world Applications*, presents three cloud-based case studies (Azure, GCP, AWS) to demonstrate MLOps in practical industry settings.

Chapter 11, *Exploring Next-Gen MLOps*, introduces LLMOps, showing how to work with **large language models (LLMs)**, **Retrieval-Augmented Generation (RAG)**, and responsible AI practices.

To get the most out of this book

The following table outlines the key software and tools covered in this book, along with the recommended operating systems to ensure optimal compatibility and performance.

Software/hardware covered in the book	Operating system requirements
Azure ML CLI v2 (latest version)	Windows, macOS, or Linux

The installation instructions are already part of the book.

If you are using the digital version of this book, we advise you to type the code yourself. Doing so will help you avoid any potential errors related to the copying and pasting of code.

After reading this book, you will be equipped to design reproducible ML pipelines that automate data preparation, training, and scoring; register, package, and deploy models using industry-grade practices; and implement governance, monitoring, and alerting to ensure transparency and compliance. You'll learn how to orchestrate the ML lifecycle using Azure ML CLI v2 and GitHub Actions with an infrastructure-as-code approach, apply MLOps principles across real-world cloud scenarios, and take your first steps into LLMOps—operationalizing large language models with a focus on safety, ethics, and performance.

The author acknowledges the use of cutting-edge AI with the sole aim of enhancing the language and clarity within the book, thereby ensuring a smooth reading experience for readers. It's important to note that the content itself has been crafted by the author and edited by a professional publishing team.

Conventions used

There are a number of text conventions used throughout this book.

`Code in text`: Indicates code words in text, database table names, folder names, filenames, file extensions, pathnames, dummy URLs, user input, and Twitter handles. For example: "In this example, job.yaml contains the schema of the job. Azure ML CLI v2 supports extensive use of YAML files to specify complex schemas for different command-line inputs."

A block of code is set as follows:

```
name: mygreat_registry
location: eastus
description: "My Azure ML Registry"
tags:
"Awesome : Great"
"ML is" : "Fun"
```

Any command-line input or output is written as follows:

```
az ml job create --file pipeline.yml
az ml schedule create --file pipeline.yml
```

Bold: Indicates a new term, an important word, or words that you see on the screen. For instance, words in menus or dialog boxes appear in the text like this. For example: "Notice the rich metadata in *Figure 4.4*, along with the **Created by job** section."

Tips or important notes

Appear like this.

Get in touch

Feedback from our readers is always welcome.

General feedback: If you have questions about any aspect of this book, email us at customercare@ packtpub.com and mention the book title in the subject of your message.

Errata: Although we have taken every care to ensure the accuracy of our content, mistakes do happen. If you have found a mistake in this book, we would be grateful if you would report this to us. Please visit www.packtpub.com/support/errata and fill in the form.

Piracy: If you come across any illegal copies of our works in any form on the internet, we would be grateful if you would provide us with the location address or website name. Please contact us at copyright@packt.com with a link to the material.

If you are interested in becoming an author: If there is a topic that you have expertise in and you are interested in either writing or contributing to a book, please visit authors.packtpub.com.

Share your thoughts

Once you've read *Hands-On MLOps on Azure*, we'd love to hear your thoughts! Scan the QR code below to go straight to the Amazon review page for this book and share your feedback.

https://packt.link/r/1836200331

Your review is important to us and the tech community and will help us make sure we're delivering excellent quality content.

Stay Sharp in Cloud and DevOps – Join 44,000+ Subscribers of CloudPro

CloudPro is a weekly newsletter for cloud professionals who want to stay current on the fast-evolving world of cloud computing, DevOps, and infrastructure engineering.

Every issue delivers focused, high-signal content on topics like:

- AWS, GCP & multi-cloud architecture
- Containers, Kubernetes & orchestration
- **Infrastructure as Code (IaC)** with Terraform, Pulumi, etc.
- Platform engineering & automation workflows
- Observability, performance tuning, and reliability best practices

Whether you're a cloud engineer, SRE, DevOps practitioner, or platform lead, CloudPro helps you stay on top of what matters, without the noise.

Scan the QR code to join for free and get weekly insights straight to your inbox:

https://packt.link/cloudpro

Download a free PDF copy of this book

Thanks for purchasing this book!

Do you like to read on the go but are unable to carry your print books everywhere?

Is your eBook purchase not compatible with the device of your choice?

Don't worry, now with every Packt book you get a DRM-free PDF version of that book at no cost.

Read anywhere, any place, on any device. Search, copy, and paste code from your favorite technical books directly into your application.

The perks don't stop there, you can get exclusive access to discounts, newsletters, and great free content in your inbox daily.

Follow these simple steps to get the benefits:

1. Scan the QR code or visit the link below:

https://packt.link/free-ebook/9781836200338

2. Submit your proof of purchase.
3. That's it! We'll send your free PDF and other benefits to your email directly.

Part 1

Foundations of MLOps

This part lays the groundwork for your MLOps journey, guiding you through the transition from DevOps to MLOps while establishing core principles, practices, and workflows. You will learn how to manage **machine learning** (**ML**) workspaces, prepare and track data, design experiments, and implement training pipelines using cloud-native tools. By focusing on reproducibility, reusability, and automation, this section equips you with the practical knowledge needed to efficiently develop and manage ML models, ensuring that your solutions are robust, scalable, and ready for production.

This part has the following chapters:

- *Chapter 1, Understanding DevOps to MLOps*
- *Chapter 2, Training and Experimentation*

1

Understanding DevOps to MLOps

In the dynamic intersection of technology and innovation, the disciplines of DevOps and **Machine Learning Operations (MLOps)**, represent transformative approaches to software and ML lifecycle management, respectively. This chapter explores how DevOps, a set of practices for faster software development, lays the groundwork for MLOps. MLOps is a similar approach specifically designed for the unique challenges of building and managing ML models.

Through a detailed exploration, we will uncover how the core principles of DevOps are not only applicable but essential to the effective management of ML processes. Because ML models can change their output for the same data, MLOps uses continuous monitoring, version control, and testing to keep them working well in real-world use.

As we progress, the chapter will break down the integration of DevOps into MLOps, highlighting key practices, such as infrastructure as code and continuous delivery, that have been adapted to meet the needs of ML workflows. Each section is designed to build upon the last, weaving a comprehensive narrative that not only educates but also empowers you to implement these practices in your own ML projects.

This journey through the foundational elements of MLOps will equip you with the knowledge to enhance efficiency, improve model reliability, and foster a culture of innovation within your teams. As we explore the crucial role of MLOps in the AI era, you will gain insights into managing the complexities of ML, ultimately leading to a mastery of technologies that drive the future of intelligent systems.

This chapter will cover the following topics:

- Understanding DevOps to MLOps
- Principles and practices of MLOps
- Quality assurance and end-to-end lineage tracking
- MLOps toolkits

Focus on the journey, not the destination (yet).

As this is an introductory chapter, we'll be laying the groundwork for MLOps without diving deep into every technical detail. Concepts and acronyms related to MLOps will be thoroughly explored in dedicated chapters later in the book.

Our primary focus here is understanding the natural progression from DevOps practices to MLOps. We'll establish the core principles and their application to the unique world of ML models.

By the end of this chapter, you'll have a foundational understanding of MLOps and its role in the AI era. This will empower you to embark on your own MLOps journey, and future chapters will equip you with the specific tools and techniques to navigate the complexities of ML workflows.

From DevOps to MLOps: Bridging the operational gap

The software development landscape has undergone a significant transformation. Traditional workflows, often characterized by siloed teams and manual processes, have given way to more collaborative and automated approaches. At the forefront of this revolution lies DevOps, a set of practices that emphasize collaboration, automation, and continuous improvement throughout the software development lifecycle.

DevOps: A foundation for MLOps

DevOps bridges development and operations through shared responsibility and automation. Its principles of continuous integration, delivery, and infrastructure as code provide the foundation for MLOps in ML.

The following are the core principles of DevOps:

- **Continuous Integration (CI)**: Frequent merging of code changes from developers into a central repository. This allows for early detection and resolution of integration issues.

- **Continuous Delivery (CD)**: Automating the delivery pipeline to reliably and quickly deploy software updates to production environments.

- **Infrastructure as Code (IaC)**: Managing and provisioning infrastructure through machine-readable definition files instead of manual configuration. This ensures consistency and reduces errors.

- **Microservices**: Building applications as a suite of small, independent services that communicate with each other. This improves modularity, scalability, and maintainability.

Along with these, the immediate effect of following DevOps principles revolutionized the development process which further paved the way for MLOps.

Revolutionizing software development

DevOps has revolutionized software development through the following:

- **Increased speed and efficiency**: Automating tasks and streamlining workflows significantly reduces development and deployment times

- **Improved quality and reliability**: Early detection of issues through CI and frequent deployments lead to more reliable software

- **Enhanced collaboration**: DevOps fosters a culture of collaboration between developers and operations, breaking down silos and improving communication

- **Greater scalability**: It adapts to microservices, which allows for easier scaling of applications to meet growing demands

By focusing on automation, collaboration, and continuous improvement, DevOps has not only revolutionized software development but also laid the groundwork for the application of similar principles in the complex world of ML. This paves the way for MLOps, a specialized set of practices designed to address the unique challenges of building, deploying, and managing ML models.

The following diagram illustrates the core principles and impact of DevOps, showcasing how it revolutionizes software development through its emphasis on collaboration, automation, and continuous improvement.

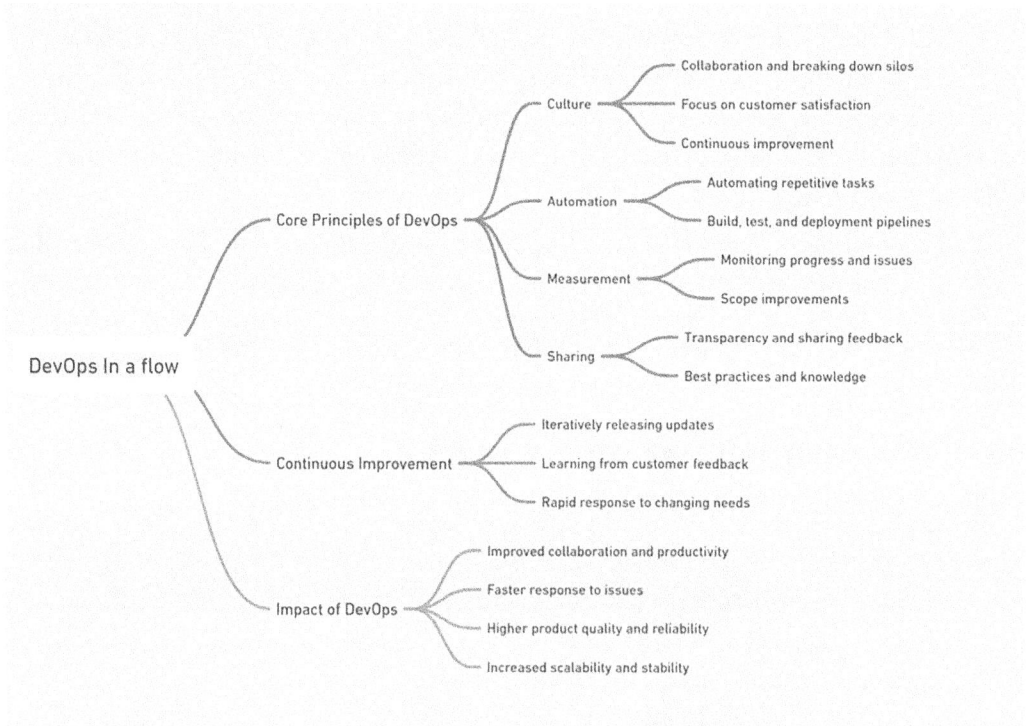

Figure 1.1 – Core principles and impact of DevOps

In summary, DevOps has not only transformed the landscape of software development but has also set the stage for a new paradigm in managing complex ML workflows. By emphasizing automation, collaboration, and continuous improvement, DevOps offers critical lessons that are directly applicable to the burgeoning field of MLOps.

The DevOps–MLOps connection

MLOps emerges as a specialized extension of the foundational DevOps practices, tailor-made to address the unique challenges of ML systems. Building upon the solid framework provided by DevOps, MLOps not only borrows core principles such as CI, CD, and IaC but also extends them to tackle the unique complexities of ML, as will be described in the *Principles and practices of MLOps* section. This section explores how MLOps adapts and extends the DevOps principles, described in the previous section, to ensure that ML models are developed, deployed, and maintained with precision in dynamic environments.

Unlike traditional software, ML models are non-deterministic. This means they can produce different outputs for the same input data depending on the training data they were exposed to. This **non-deterministic nature** necessitates ongoing monitoring of model performance in production to ensure they remain accurate and effective. Additionally, as data evolves over time, models may experience **concept drift**, where their performance degrades due to a mismatch between the training data and real-world data. This necessitates retraining and updating models to maintain optimal performance.

Another challenge specific to MLOps is model versioning and reproducibility, both of which will be explained in the *Key DevOps concepts in MLOps* section. Version control for code ensures developers can recreate past versions of software. However, in MLOps, both the code and the data used to train a model need to be versioned for true reproducibility. This means managing and tracking changes not only to the code but also to the training data and model parameters.

While these complexities add an extra layer to the MLOps process, the core DevOps principles remain a strong foundation. By adapting them to the world of ML, MLOps helps streamline the ML lifecycle, from development and deployment to monitoring and maintenance.

As we have seen, the integration of DevOps principles into the ML lifecycle introduces a framework that accommodates the non-deterministic nature of ML models and the evolving data they learn from. This framework is crucial for the sustainable and efficient operation of ML systems in production environments.

Key DevOps concepts in MLOps

With a clear understanding of how DevOps principles underpin MLOps, we can now delve deeper into specific DevOps practices that are crucial for MLOps. This section will focus on CI, CD, and IaC, explaining how these practices are adapted to meet the needs of ML workflows.

CI/CD for the ML lifecycle

MLOps leverages core DevOps principles to streamline the ML lifecycle. Let's explore how CI/CD and IaC play a crucial role:

- **CI**: CI in MLOps automates and manages key tasks that:
    - Automates tasks such as code linting, unit testing, and data validation to ensure code quality and catch issues early
    - Integrates changes from data scientists/ML engineers into a central repository, facilitating collaboration and version control

- Automates data preprocessing and feature engineering steps as part of the CI pipeline, ensuring consistency and reducing errors. We will learn more about these in *Chapter 2*.

- **CD**: CD in MLOps enables processes that:

  - Enables automated model training and retraining based on new data or code changes

  - Streamlines model deployment to various environments (testing, staging, production) for validation and monitoring

  - Facilitates A/B testing of different models to compare performance and select the best candidate for deployment. We will look at this in greater detail in *Chapter 2*.

- **IaC for ML infrastructure**: IaC for ML infrastructure defines practices that:

  - Defines infrastructure components such as data pipelines, compute resources (CPUs and GPUs), and deployment environments in machine-readable code (for example, YAML)

  - Enables consistent and automated provisioning of infrastructure across different environments, reducing configuration errors and manual setup time

  - Allows for easy scaling of resources as model training requirements or data volumes grow

  - Facilitates disaster recovery by enabling quick infrastructure rebuild based on IaC definitions.

By applying these CI/CD and IaC practices, MLOps ensures a reliable, efficient, and scalable ML development process.

By adapting CI/CD and IaC to the ML domain, MLOps not only enhances the efficiency and reliability of ML systems but also ensures that these systems can scale and evolve in response to new data and computational demands. These adaptations are critical for maintaining the robustness of ML operations.

The importance of MLOps in the AI era

Think of MLOps as your AI project's safety net and accelerator. Just as DevOps transformed software delivery, MLOps is revolutionizing how we build and maintain AI systems. Without MLOps, organizations often face "model disasters"—from degraded performance going unnoticed for months to the inability to reproduce successful models when needed.

MLOps solves these challenges through automation and standardization. It transforms manual, error-prone processes into streamlined workflows that automatically validate data, test models, and monitor performance. This means faster deployment of models, early detection of issues, and the ability to scale AI projects confidently. Most importantly, when problems occur (and they will), MLOps provides the tools to quickly identify root causes and roll back to stable versions—turning potential crises into minor hiccups while maintaining compliance and governance standards.

The following figure is a mind map for the MLOps process in a nutshell:

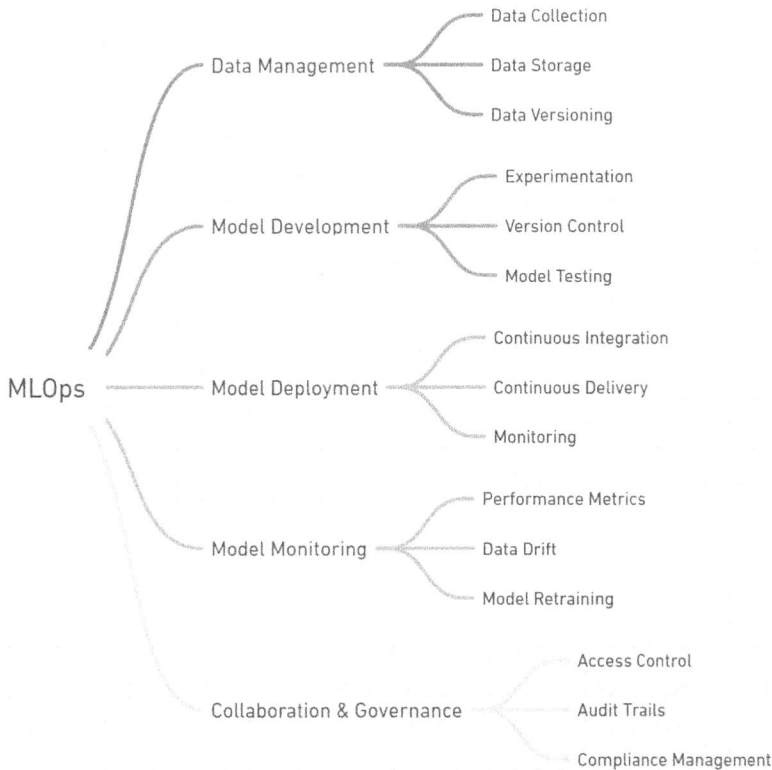

Figure 1.2 – MLOps process mind map

The mind map provides a high-level overview of the MLOps process, highlighting the key areas involved in managing ML workflows. Let's dive deeper into these areas to understand the principles and practices that make MLOps essential in addressing the unique challenges of ML.

Principles and practices of MLOps

This section dives deeper into the specific practices employed in MLOps to address the unique challenges of ML. Here's a breakdown of key areas in the following sections.

Data management in MLOps

Effective data management is a cornerstone of successful MLOps practices. By implementing robust systems for data versioning, quality assurance, and feature engineering, we can ensure that our data is reliable and ready for advanced analytical processes. The following key practices are essential for managing data in MLOps:

- **Data versioning**: Tracks changes to data used in training, ensuring that models can be reproduced with the same data for comparison or troubleshooting.

- **Data quality**: Ensures that data used for training is accurate, complete, and free from biases. Techniques include data validation, cleaning, and anomaly detection.

- **Feature engineering**: The process of transforming raw data into meaningful features for model training. MLOps practices involve versioning feature engineering pipelines and tracking their impact on model performance.

With robust systems in place for managing data versioning, quality, and feature engineering, we ensure that our foundational datasets are primed for advanced analytical processes. These management practices not only safeguard the integrity of data but also set the stage for effective experimentation.

Experiment tracking

Moving from the structured management of data, we now turn our focus toward experiment tracking, a critical component that builds upon our curated data to optimize and refine ML models. Experiment tracking involves systematically recording and comparing different ML experiments, including variations in model architectures, hyperparameters, and training datasets. This practice is essential for learning from past experiments and identifying the best-performing models. To fully grasp the significance of experiment tracking in MLOps, it's essential to understand its core aspects, including its importance, the tools used, and the benefits it brings to ML workflows:

- **Importance**: It tracks and compares different ML experiments, including model architectures, hyperparameters, and training data. This facilitates learning from past experiments and identifying the best-performing models.

- **Tools**: Several tools (such as MLflow, Neptune, and Weights & Biases) help manage experiment metadata, code, and model artifacts for easy comparison and analysis.

- **Benefits**: It enables collaboration among data scientists by sharing and reproducing experiments, leading to faster development cycles and improved model performance.

Having established a rigorous system for tracking and comparing ML experiments, we've set a benchmark for model development and iterative refinement. This framework is essential for identifying the most promising models ready for the next critical phase—deployment.

Model deployment challenges

As we transition from the laboratory settings of model training to the real-world applications of model deployment, new challenges emerge. This section delves into the complexities of deploying ML models, ensuring they perform reliably in production environments and interact seamlessly with existing systems. Successfully deploying ML models requires addressing several key challenges to ensure compatibility, performance, and interpretability:

- **Compatibility**: Ensuring models trained in specific environments are compatible with production infrastructure and can interact with other systems seamlessly.

- **Performance**: Monitoring model performance in production to identify degradation (concept drift) and ensure models meet latency and resource constraints.

- **Interpretability**: Crucial in ML to ensure that stakeholders can understand and trust the decisions made by AI systems. This becomes especially important in regulated industries such as healthcare and finance, where knowing the "why" behind a decision can be as critical as the decision itself.

With our models strategically deployed to handle real-world data and demands, the imperative shifts toward safeguarding these systems. The next frontier is ensuring that our deployment strategies not only perform efficiently but also comply with stringent security standards and regulatory requirements.

Security and compliance in MLOps

Security and compliance are paramount in the lifecycle of any ML model, particularly when handling sensitive data. This section will outline the essential practices for embedding robust security measures and ensuring regulatory compliance, from GDPR to CCPA, safeguarding your models and the data they process.

Incorporating comprehensive security and compliance measures involves several critical practices:

- **Data privacy**: Protecting sensitive data used in training models is critical. MLOps practices involve data anonymization, encryption, and access control mechanisms.

- **Encryption**: Encrypting data at rest and in transit ensures its confidentiality and prevents unauthorized access.

- **Regulations**: Following regulations such as GDPR and CCPA (which govern data privacy and security) is crucial for businesses using ML models.

After fortifying our models against security breaches and ensuring compliance with international standards, our attention must now turn to the ongoing performance and maintenance of these systems. It's crucial that they not only start strong but also sustain their accuracy and reliability over time.

Model performance and maintenance

Maintaining optimal model performance in production requires vigilant monitoring and periodic updates. This next section covers the strategies for managing model performance and the techniques for continuous performance evaluation, ensuring that our models remain effective as new data and scenarios arise. Effective model performance and maintenance involve several key strategies:

- **Model drift**: The phenomenon where a model's performance degrades over time due to changes in the underlying data distribution (data drift), or changes in how the input data relates to the target variable (concept drift). It is managed by monitoring for drift indicators and retraining models with updated data to maintain accuracy.

- **Monitoring**: Continuously monitoring model performance in production to detect drift and ensure model effectiveness.

- **Retraining**: Periodically retraining models with new data to mitigate concept drift and maintain optimal performance.

Through vigilant monitoring and periodic retraining, we can maintain the robustness of our models against the inevitable changes in data over time. Ensuring continuous model performance and mitigating concept drift are critical to the long-term success of any ML system.

MLOps tools and technologies

While maintaining model performance forms the backbone of operational success, the tools and technologies deployed throughout the ML lifecycle are the gears that keep this backbone strong and flexible. This next section explores a variety of tools—from version control systems such as Git to monitoring solutions such as Prometheus—that not only facilitate these maintenance tasks but also enhance every stage of the ML development process.

A wide range of tools exists to support different stages of the ML lifecycle, including the following:

- Version control systems (Git) for code and data versioning
- CI/CD pipelines (Jenkins and GitLab CI/CD) for automating model training and deployment
- Experiment tracking tools (MLflow and Neptune) for managing and comparing experiments
- Model deployment platforms (Kubeflow and TensorFlow Serving) for packaging and deploying models in production
- Monitoring tools (Prometheus and Grafana) for tracking model performance and health

With a comprehensive toolkit that supports every phase of the ML lifecycle, from initial data handling to ongoing model monitoring, the next step involves assembling a team capable of effectively wielding these tools. The efficacy of these technologies hinges not only on their robust capabilities but also on the skills and collaboration of the team that employs them.

Building an MLOps team

As we shift our focus from the tools that facilitate MLOps to the architects of its application, it becomes clear that a successful MLOps operation requires more than just advanced technologies. This section delves into the roles and skills necessary for an effective MLOps team, emphasizing how critical the human element is in harmonizing these technologies to unlock their full potential and drive innovation. To build a robust MLOps team, several key roles and skills are essential:

- **Roles**: Data scientists, ML engineers, DevOps engineers, data engineers, and MLOps specialists work together in an MLOps team
- **Skills**: Team members require expertise in ML, software engineering, data engineering, DevOps practices, and collaboration
- **Collaboration**: Effective communication and collaboration between team members are essential for the success of MLOps initiatives

By implementing these principles and practices, organizations can establish a robust MLOps framework to streamline the machine learning lifecycle, ensure model quality, and unlock the true potential of AI.

The following figure highlights the key differences between DevOps and MLOps:

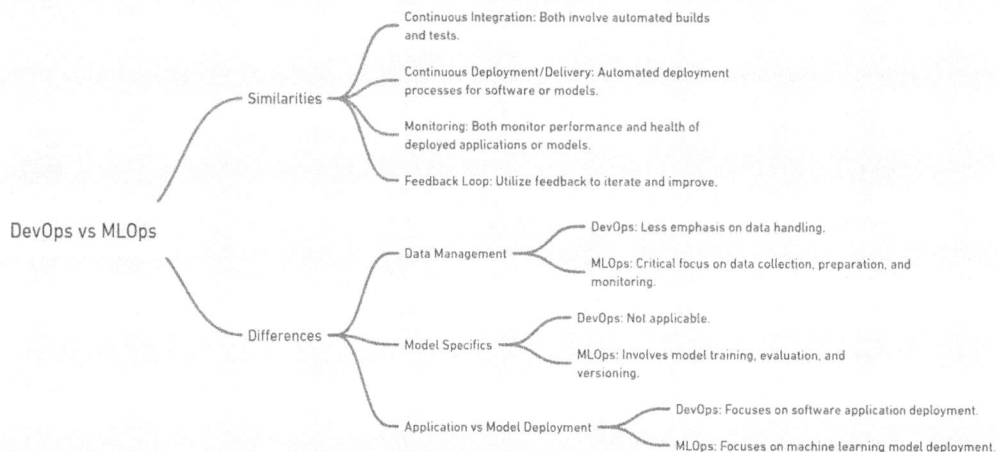

Figure 1.3 – A comparison between DevOps and MLOps

The figure highlights their similarities and differences. Similarities include continuous integration, continuous deployment/delivery, monitoring, and feedback loops. Differences are found in data management, model specifics, and the focus on application versus model deployment.

Building on the foundational differences and similarities between DevOps and MLOps, we now turn our attention to how MLOps specifically accelerates the experimentation and development of ML models. The traditional ML workflow can be slow and iterative. The next section dives into how MLOps accelerates this process by exploring core concepts such as automation, version control, and containerization.

Faster experimentation and development of models

This section dives into how MLOps accelerates the experimentation and development of models. We'll explore core concepts such as automation, version control, and containerization that streamline the process. We'll also delve into techniques like hyperparameter tuning and rapid prototyping frameworks that empower data scientists to iterate quickly and efficiently.

By embracing these MLOps practices, you'll unlock faster development cycles and ultimately deliver high-performing models in a shorter time frame:

- **Core concepts**: Faster experimentation in MLOps is built upon several core concepts that remove bottlenecks and streamline the workflow, including:

  - **Automation**: This is the key driver for faster experimentation. Automating tasks such as data preprocessing, feature engineering, model training, hyperparameter tuning, and evaluation frees up data scientists to focus on more strategic work. Tools such as ML pipelines and CI/CD systems can streamline this process. We will learn more about these in *Chapter 2*.

  - **Version control**: Tracking changes in code, data, and models allows for easy rollbacks and comparisons between experiments. Version control systems such as Git are essential for managing the ML lifecycle.

  - **Experiment tracking and reproducibility**: Record and visualize experiment details (hyperparameters, metrics, etc.) for easy comparison and analysis. Tools such as Neptune, MLflow, and Weights & Biases help track experiments and ensure reproducibility, enabling you to iterate quickly on successful approaches.

  - **Containerization**: Package models and their dependencies into containers (for example, Docker) for consistent and portable execution across different environments. This speeds up experimentation by eliminating environment setup issues.

  - **Lightweight infrastructure**: Leverage cloud-based platforms such as Azure Machine Learning, Amazon SageMaker, and the Google AI platform to access scalable compute resources for training models without managing infrastructure yourself. This allows data scientists to experiment more freely without worrying about resource limitations.

- **Techniques for faster experimentation**: In addition to these foundational concepts, specific techniques further accelerate experimentation and iteration, such as:

  - **Hyperparameter tuning**: Utilize automated hyperparameter tuning tools (for example, Hyperopt or Ray Tune) to efficiently find the best hyperparameter values for your model, improving performance without manual trial-and-error.

  - **Early stopping**: Stop model training when performance plateaus or degrades, saving time and resources by not overtraining models.

  - **Rapid prototyping frameworks**: Explore frameworks such as TensorFlow.js, PyTorch Lightning, and scikit-learn for quick model prototyping and iteration, allowing you to test out new ideas quickly.

- **Feature engineering automation**: Automate feature engineering steps with tools such as Featuretools or Federação AutoML to reduce manual effort and accelerate feature exploration.

- **Data versioning**: Version control your data to ensure consistency across experiments and allow for easy rollbacks if needed.

- **Additional considerations**: To complement these core practices and techniques, the following additional considerations enhance collaboration and effective model evaluation during rapid experimentation:

  - **Collaboration tools**: Utilize tools such as Jupyter notebooks or cloud-based notebooks to facilitate knowledge sharing, code reuse, and collaboration between data scientists.

  - **A/B testing**: Integrate A/B testing frameworks to compare different model versions in production and identify the best-performing models.

With models now being developed and refined at a much faster pace, the next critical step in the MLOps lifecycle is ensuring these models can be reliably deployed into production environments, where they can deliver real-world value.

Deployment of models into production

This section dives into the exciting world of deploying models into production using MLOps practices, so they can be used in real-world scenarios. We'll explore packaging strategies, serving infrastructure options, and best practices for API design. We'll also unveil different rollout strategies and the crucial aspects of monitoring, versioning, and security to ensure a smooth and successful transition from development to real-world impact.

- **Key considerations**: Deploying ML models from development environments to production systems requires careful planning and execution across multiple technical domains. To successfully deploy models into production, it's essential to address several key considerations that form the backbone of an effective deployment strategy. Here, we'll discuss the critical aspects that you need to focus on for a seamless transition:

  - **Packaging and serialization**: Model packaging involves converting trained models into formats suitable for production deployment. Common serialization formats include pickle for Python-based models, ONNX for cross-platform compatibility, and PMML for standardized model exchange. When packaging models, consider size optimization through techniques like model pruning or quantization to reduce memory footprint and improve inference speed.

Ensure compatibility with your chosen serving framework—for instance, TensorFlow models work seamlessly with TensorFlow Serving, while scikit-learn models might require custom serving solutions. Container technologies like Docker provide an excellent way to package models with their entire dependency stack, ensuring consistent behavior across different environments.

- **Serving infrastructure**: The choice of serving infrastructure depends on your scalability, latency, and cost requirements. Cloud-based platforms like AWS SageMaker, Azure ML, and Google AI Platform offer managed serving solutions with built-in auto-scaling and monitoring capabilities. For organizations requiring more control, container orchestration platforms such as Kubernetes provide flexibility to deploy models as microservices with custom scaling policies. On-premise deployments might be necessary for data sovereignty or security reasons, though they require more operational overhead. Consider factors like expected traffic patterns, latency requirements, budget constraints, and existing infrastructure when making your decision.

- **Model API design**: Well-designed APIs are crucial for seamless model integration with applications. Follow RESTful design principles with clear endpoint naming, appropriate HTTP methods, and consistent response formats. Implement proper input validation to handle malformed requests gracefully and return meaningful error messages. Version your APIs using URL paths (e.g., /v1/predict) or headers to maintain backward compatibility as models evolve. Document your APIs thoroughly using tools like OpenAPI/Swagger, including request/response schemas, authentication requirements, and rate limiting policies. Implement proper authentication and authorization mechanisms to control access to your models.

- **Model rollout strategies**: Different deployment strategies offer varying levels of risk and complexity. Blue-green deployments maintain two identical production environments, allowing instant switching between old and new model versions with zero downtime but requiring double the infrastructure resources. Canary deployments gradually route a small percentage of traffic to the new model version, enabling real-world performance validation with minimal risk, ideal for testing model improvements before full rollout. A/B testing compares multiple model versions simultaneously by splitting traffic, providing statistical confidence in performance differences but requiring more complex traffic management and analysis capabilities.

- **Additional considerations**: Beyond the core deployment components, several additional considerations are essential to ensure your models operate reliably, securely, and efficiently in production:

  - **Model monitoring**: Production models require continuous monitoring to detect performance degradation over time. Track key metrics including prediction accuracy, response latency, throughput, and error rates. Monitor for data drift by comparing incoming data distributions with training data using statistical tests or similarity metrics. Implement alerting systems using tools like Prometheus and Grafana to notify teams when metrics exceed predefined thresholds. Consider business-specific metrics alongside technical ones—for example, conversion rates for recommendation models or false positive rates for fraud detection systems.

  - **Versioning and rollbacks**: Maintain a comprehensive versioning system that tracks not just model versions but also the data, code, and configuration used to create each model. Use semantic versioning (e.g., v1.2.1) to clearly communicate the nature of changes. Implement automated rollback mechanisms that can quickly revert to previous model versions when issues are detected. Store model artifacts in versioned repositories with proper metadata including performance metrics, training datasets, and deployment notes to facilitate troubleshooting and rollback decisions.

  - **Scalability and performance**: Design your deployment architecture to handle varying workloads efficiently. Implement horizontal scaling using load balancers to distribute requests across multiple model instances. Use auto-scaling policies based on metrics like CPU utilization or request queue length to automatically adjust capacity. Consider model caching strategies for frequently requested predictions and batch processing for scenarios where real-time inference isn't required. Optimize model inference performance through techniques like model quantization, GPU acceleration, or specialized inference frameworks like TensorRT or Intel OpenVINO.

  - **Security**: Secure your model deployments against various attack vectors. Implement robust input validation to prevent adversarial attacks and injection attempts. Use authentication tokens or API keys to control access and implement rate limiting to prevent abuse. Encrypt data in transit using HTTPS/TLS and consider encryption at rest for sensitive model artifacts. Regularly audit access logs and implement network segmentation to isolate model serving infrastructure. Be aware of model-specific security risks like model inversion attacks or membership inference attacks, particularly when dealing with sensitive data.

Having a robust deployment strategy in place sets the stage for reliable model performance in the real world. Now, let's shift our focus to ensuring the quality and trustworthiness of those deployed models. This is where quality assurance and end-to-end lineage tracking come into play.

Quality assurance and end-to-end lineage tracking

Ensuring the quality and trustworthiness of your ML models is paramount. This section delves into the critical practices of **quality assurance** (**QA**) and end-to-end lineage tracking within MLOps. We'll explore how QA helps identify and mitigate potential issues in your models, while lineage tracking provides transparency into the entire ML lifecycle. By understanding these practices, you'll be empowered to build robust and reliable models that deliver consistent value.

- **QA in ML**: Ensuring the quality and trustworthiness of your models goes beyond just their technical accuracy. To achieve this, we need to employ a robust QA process specifically designed for the world of ML. This process encompasses several key areas:

  - **Data quality**: High-quality data forms the foundation of reliable ML models, making data validation a critical first step in the QA process. Implement automated data profiling to identify missing values, outliers, and inconsistent formats before they impact model training. Use statistical techniques like z-score analysis or interquartile range methods to detect anomalies that could skew model performance. Establish data validation pipelines using tools like Great Expectations or Apache Griffin to continuously monitor data quality metrics such as completeness, uniqueness, and validity. Create data cleaning workflows that handle common issues like duplicate records, inconsistent categorical values, and temporal inconsistencies while maintaining audit trails of all transformations applied.

  - **Model evaluation metrics**: Selecting appropriate evaluation metrics is crucial for accurately assessing model performance across different use cases. For classification problems, use accuracy for balanced datasets, but rely on precision and recall when dealing with imbalanced classes—precision measures the correctness of positive predictions while recall captures the model's ability to find all positive instances. The F1-score provides a balanced view by combining precision and recall, while AUC-ROC curves help evaluate performance across different classification thresholds. For regression tasks, **Root Mean Squared Error** (**RMSE**) penalizes large errors more heavily, making it suitable for applications where outliers are costly, while **Mean Absolute Error** (**MAE**) provides a more intuitive measure of average prediction error. Always validate metrics using cross-validation techniques to ensure robust performance estimates.

- **Bias and fairness**: Addressing bias in ML models is essential for building ethical and legally compliant systems, particularly in high-stakes applications like hiring, lending, or criminal justice. Implement fairness metrics such as demographic parity (ensuring equal positive prediction rates across groups), equalized odds (equal true positive and false positive rates), and individual fairness (similar individuals receive similar predictions). Use bias detection tools like AI Fairness 360 or Fairlearn to systematically evaluate model fairness across different demographic groups. Apply debiasing techniques including pre-processing methods (data augmentation or re-sampling), in-processing approaches (fairness-constrained optimization), and post-processing adjustments (threshold optimization per group) to mitigate identified biases.

- **Explainability and interpretability**: Model interpretability becomes critical when stakeholders need to understand and trust AI-driven decisions, especially in regulated industries like healthcare and finance. Implement **Local Interpretable Model-agnostic Explanations (LIME)** to generate local explanations for individual predictions by learning simple, interpretable models around specific instances. Use **SHapley Additive exPlanations (SHAP)** values to provide consistent feature importance scores that sum to the difference between prediction and baseline. For tree-based models, leverage built-in feature importance measures, while for neural networks, consider attention mechanisms or gradient-based attribution methods. Create explanation dashboards that present model decisions in business-friendly terms to facilitate stakeholder understanding and regulatory compliance.

- **Testing strategies**: Comprehensive testing ensures model reliability across different scenarios and use cases. Implement unit tests for individual components like data preprocessing functions, feature engineering pipelines, and model inference code using frameworks like pytest. Develop integration tests that validate end-to-end workflows from data ingestion through model prediction, ensuring all components work together correctly. Design A/B testing frameworks to compare model versions in production environments, using statistical significance testing to validate performance improvements. Include stress testing to evaluate model behavior under high load conditions and edge case testing to verify model responses to unusual or adversarial inputs.

- **End-to-end lineage tracking**: Comprehensive lineage tracking provides transparency and accountability throughout the ML lifecycle, enabling teams to understand how models were created and how they impact business outcomes:

- **Benefits**: Lineage tracking transforms debugging from guesswork into systematic investigation by providing complete visibility into data flows, model dependencies, and transformation steps. When models underperform, teams can quickly trace back through the pipeline to identify root causes, whether they stem from data quality issues, feature engineering problems, or model configuration changes. For impact analysis, lineage tracking enables teams to assess downstream effects of changes—understanding which models, dashboards, or applications might be affected by modifying a particular dataset or feature. This capability becomes invaluable for model governance, providing audit trails that demonstrate compliance with regulatory requirements and internal policies. Organizations can prove data usage authorization, model validation processes, and decision-making transparency to regulators and stakeholders.

- **Techniques**: Implement automated lineage capture through code parsing tools that analyze data science notebooks and scripts to extract data dependencies and transformation logic. Use data tagging strategies with metadata management systems like Apache Atlas or DataHub to track data origins, transformations, and usage patterns across the organization. Deploy purpose-built MLOps platforms such as MLflow for experiment and model tracking, Neptune for comprehensive ML metadata management, or Kubeflow Pipelines for workflow orchestration with built-in lineage capture. These tools automatically record model training runs, hyperparameters, datasets used, and resulting artifacts, creating comprehensive audit trails without requiring manual intervention from data scientists.

- **Version control and reproducibility**: Establish comprehensive version control practices that extend beyond traditional code management to encompass the entire ML ecosystem. Use Git for source code versioning combined with Git **Large File Storage** (**LFS**) for managing large model files and datasets. Implement data versioning using tools like **Data Version Control** (**DVC**) or Pachyderm to track changes in training datasets and ensure experiments remain reproducible over time. Create reproducible environments using containerization (Docker) or environment management tools (Conda) to capture exact dependency versions and system configurations. Maintain model registries that store not just trained models but also the complete context needed for reproduction, including training data versions, hyperparameters, and evaluation metrics.

- **Additional considerations:** In addition to core QA and lineage practices, several additional considerations further enhance the reliability, maintainability, and compliance of your ML systems:

  - **Documentation:** Comprehensive documentation serves as the foundation for knowledge transfer, troubleshooting, and regulatory compliance throughout the ML lifecycle. Create data documentation that describes collection methodologies, data sources, known limitations, and quality issues to help future users understand dataset characteristics and appropriate usage. Documentation should feature engineering processes with clear explanations of transformation logic, business rationale, and validation methods to ensure features can be correctly reproduced in production. Maintain model cards that summarize model purpose, performance characteristics, training data, evaluation results, and known limitations following frameworks like Google's Model Cards or similar industry standards. Use automated documentation tools like Sphinx or GitBook to generate and maintain up-to-date technical documentation from code comments and docstrings.

  - **Monitoring and alerting:** Proactive monitoring prevents model degradation from impacting business outcomes by detecting issues before they become critical problems. Implement performance monitoring that tracks key metrics like prediction accuracy, precision, recall, and business-specific KPIs using dashboards built with tools like Grafana or custom solutions. Deploy data drift detection using statistical tests (Kolmogorov-Smirnov, Chi-square) or machine learning-based approaches to identify when incoming data distributions deviate significantly from training data. Set up concept drift monitoring by comparing model performance on recent data against historical benchmarks, triggering retraining workflows when performance drops below acceptable thresholds. Create intelligent alerting systems that distinguish between normal fluctuations and genuine issues, using techniques like anomaly detection and trend analysis to reduce false alarms while ensuring rapid response to real problems.

Now that we've established a foundation for building high-quality and trustworthy models, let's transition to the practical tools that help us manage the entire ML lifecycle. These tools embody the MLOps principles we've discussed and empower data scientists and DevOps engineers to collaborate effectively.

MLOps toolkits: Streamlining the ML lifecycle with ML CLIs

As we conclude our exploration of MLOps foundations, let's turn to the practical tools that bring these concepts to life—specifically, the **command-line interfaces (CLIs)** that power modern ML workflows. Think of CLIs as the control center for your ML operations, providing direct, scriptable control over everything from data management to model deployment. Whether you're training models locally or orchestrating complex distributed systems, these interfaces form the backbone of efficient MLOps practices.

Modern ML CLIs, offered by platforms such as TensorFlow, PyTorch, and major cloud providers (Azure, AWS, and GCP), transform repetitive tasks into automated workflows while ensuring reproducibility and version control. They act as a universal language for MLOps, allowing teams to standardize their processes across different environments and scales. By mastering these tools, you'll be able to automate workflows, track experiments consistently, and manage ML systems with the precision and reliability demanded by production environments.

Types of ML CLIs

Having a good understanding of the different types of ML CLIs available equips you to make an informed decision when choosing the right tool for your project. Let's explore the three main categories of ML CLIs:

- **Open source ML frameworks**: Tools such as TensorFlow and PyTorch offer built-in CLIs for training models, managing data, and deploying them.
- **Standalone MLOps tools**: Platforms such as Kubeflow Pipelines and MLflow provide dedicated CLIs for experiment tracking, model registry, and serving.
- **Cloud-specific tools**: Major cloud providers—Azure, AWS, and GCP—each offer their own ML services and corresponding CLIs for seamless integration.

By understanding the strengths of each type of ML CLI, you can select the tool that best aligns with your project's needs and existing infrastructure.

Choosing the right ML CLI

Selecting the ideal CLI for your project depends on several factors:

- **Existing infrastructure**: Consider the frameworks, tools, and cloud platforms your team is already familiar with.

- **Project requirements**: Match the CLI features with your project's needs for experiment tracking, model registry, deployment, and monitoring.

- **Ease of use**: Evaluate the learning curve and user-friendliness of the CLI for your team's skill sets.

- **Community and support**: A vibrant community and accessible documentation are invaluable for effective tool utilization.

By thoughtfully selecting and utilizing an ML CLI, you can significantly accelerate development, enhance model quality, and streamline the transition from experimentation to production environments.

This section provides a high-level overview of ML CLIs offered by major cloud providers: Azure ML, Amazon SageMaker, and GCP gcloud. Each platform offers a CLI specifically designed to streamline the ML workflow.

Common management tasks with ML CLIs

ML CLIs empower you to manage various aspects of your ML projects through commands. Here are some general categories of tasks you can perform:

- **Job creation**: Initiate ML training or execution.

- **Compute resource management**: Provision and configure computing resources for your projects.

- **Data management**: Manage datasets used for training and evaluation.

- **Model management**: Register, track, and deploy ML models.

- **Endpoint management**: Create and configure endpoints for serving models in production.

- **Deployment management**: Deploy models to production environments.

While we haven't explored specific commands yet, detailed documentation links are provided for each platform in the upcoming subsections. These resources will guide you through the installation, setup, and in-depth usage of the respective ML CLIs.

In subsequent chapters, we'll delve deeper into these concepts and provide practical examples using a chosen ML CLI. This initial introduction lays the groundwork for understanding the power and functionality of ML CLIs in managing your ML projects.

Exploring ML CLIs for different cloud providers

This section explores the ML CLIs offered by major cloud providers: **Azure ML (AML)**, Amazon SageMaker, and GCP gcloud. Each subsection showcases sample commands for common tasks such as creating jobs, compute resources, data, models, and then deploying models. Links to detailed installation and setup documentation are provided for each platform under each command section.

Azure ML CLI v2

This section shows how the **Azure ML CLI** can be used to perform a basic AML workflow. Let's begin!

To create an ML job, run the following command:

```bash
az ml job create --name my-job --file job.yaml
```

In this example, job.yaml contains the schema of the job. Azure ML CLI v2 supports extensive use of YAML files to specify complex schemas for different command-line inputs. From *Chapter 2* onward, we will use more of this syntax. Documentation on this CLI schema is available at https://learn. microsoft.com/en-us/azure/machine-learning/reference-yaml-overview?view=azureml-api-2.

To manage compute resources, run this command:

```bash
az ml compute create --name my-compute --type amlcompute --min-instances 0
--max-instances 4
```

To manage datasets, run this command:

```bash
az ml data create --name my-dataset --path path/to/data --type file
```

To manage models, run this command:

```bash
az ml model create --name my-model --path path/to/model.pkl --type custom_
model
```

To manage endpoints, run this command:

```bash
az ml online-endpoint create --name my-endpoint
```

To manage deployments, run this command:

```bash
az ml online-deployment create --name blue --endpoint my-endpoint --model
my-model:1 --instance-type Standard_DS3_v2 --instance-count 1
```

The following is the installation and setup documentation or the Azure ML CLI documentation: https://docs.microsoft.com/en-us/azure/machine-learning/how-to-configure-cli.

AWS CLI with SageMaker

This section shows how the **AWS CLI with SageMaker** can be used to perform a basic AML workflow. Let's begin!

To create an ML job, run this command:

```bash
aws sagemaker create-training-job --training-job-name <job-
name> --algorithm-specification TrainingImage=<training-image-
uri>,TrainingInputMode=File --role-arn <role-arn> --input-data-config
<input-data-config> --output-data-config S3OutputPath=<s3-output-path>
--resource-config InstanceType=<instance-type>,InstanceCount=<instance-
count>,VolumeSizeInGB=<volume-size> --stopping-condition
MaxRuntimeInSeconds=<max-runtime>
```

To manage compute resources, run this command:

```bash
aws sagemaker create-notebook-instance --notebook-instance-name <instance-
name> --instance-type <instance-type> --role-arn <role-arn>```
```

To manage datasets, run this command:

```bash
aws sagemaker create-dataset --dataset-name <dataset-name> --dataset-type
<dataset-type> --dataset-source DataSourceArn=<data-source-arn>
```

To manage models, run this command:

```bash
aws sagemaker create-model --model-name <model-name> --primary-container
Image=<container-image>,ModelDataUrl=<model-data-url> --execution-role-arn
<role-arn>
```

To manage endpoints, run this command:

```bash
aws sagemaker create-endpoint-config --endpoint-config-name <config-
name> --production-variants VariantName=<variant-name>,ModelName=<model-
name>,InstanceType=<instance-type>,InitialInstanceCount=<instance-count>
aws sagemaker create-endpoint --endpoint-name <endpoint-name> --endpoint-
config-name <config-name>
```

To manage deployments, run this command:

```bash
aws sagemaker create-model-package --model-package-name <package-name>
--inference-specification ContainerDefinitions=[{Image=<container-image>}]
--source-algorithm-specification SourceAlgorithms=[{AlgorithmName=<algorit
hm-name>,ModelDataUrl=<model-data-url>}]
```

To learn about the installation and setup of the Amazon SageMaker CLI, you can visit https://
docs.aws.amazon.com/cli/latest/userguide/cli-chap-welcome.html.

GCP gcloud CLI

This section shows how the **GCP gcloud CLI** can be used to perform a basic AML workflow. Let's
begin!

To create an ML job, run the following command:

```bash
gcloud ai-platform jobs submit training <job-name> --region <region>
--module-name <module-name> --package-path <package-path> --job-dir <job-
dir>
```

To managing compute resources, run the following command:

```bash
gcloud ai-platform instances create <instance-name> --zone <zone>
--machine-type <machine-type> --accelerator type=<accelerator-
type>,count=<accelerator-count>
```

To manage datasets, run the following command:

```bash
gcloud ai-platform datasets create <dataset-name> --region <region>
--metadata-file <metadata-file-path>
```

To manage models, run the following command:

```bash
gcloud ai-platform models create <model-name> --regions <region>
--description "<model-description>"
```

To manage endpoints, run the following command:

```bash
gcloud ai-platform endpoints create <endpoint-name> --model <model-name>
--region <region>
```

To manage deployments, run the following command:

```bash
gcloud ai-platform versions create <version-name> --model <model-name>
--origin <model-dir> --runtime-version <runtime-version> --framework
<framework>
```

To learn more about the installation and setup of the GCP gcloud CLI, you can go to https://cloud.google.com/sdk/gcloud.

Benefits of organized structure

By examining the preceding commands across different providers, readers gain valuable insights:

- **Similarities and differences**: You should be able to identify how each platform approaches the ML project lifecycle.

- **Instructional content**: The clear examples demonstrate command usage for practical application, which you will benefit from.

- **Informed tool selection**: You will be able to understand how platform familiarity and project requirements influence tool choice.

- **Comprehensive learning**: From the links to detailed documentation, you can gain an in-depth exploration of specific commands and installation processes.

For ease of understanding and implementation, subsequent chapters will primarily utilize Azure CLI commands. *Chapter 2* will delve deeper into workspace and CLI usage, establishing the fundamental building blocks for future chapters.

Summary

This chapter has demystified MLOps, showing how it bridges the gap between ML development and real-world deployment. Building on DevOps foundations, MLOps addresses the unique challenges of managing non-deterministic models and evolving data landscapes through automation, version control, and continuous monitoring.

We explored the entire ML lifecycle through an MLOps lens, from data management and experiment tracking to model deployment and security. These practices, combined with powerful command-line tools, enable organizations to build reliable, scalable ML systems that can evolve with business needs. At its heart, MLOps is about creating a culture of collaboration between data scientists, ML engineers, and operations teams to transform promising models into production-ready intelligent systems.

In the next chapter, we'll dive into practical MLOps, beginning with the model training process.

2

Training and Experimentation

This chapter equips you with the skills to navigate the training phase of ML projects within Azure. We will cover the foundational elements of **Azure Machine Learning** (**AML**) that are crucial for both data scientists and DevOps engineers. This includes the **AML workspace**, which serves as the central hub for collaboration and managing machine learning workflows, and the **AML CLI**, a powerful toolkit that enables you to interact with AML resources efficiently through command-line operations.

We'll also guide you through the entire training process, from data preparation to model selection to ensure high-quality data for your models. The chapter will cover testing different algorithms and configurations to identify patterns and develop models. You'll learn how to use the CLI to efficiently manage experiments and jobs. It will also break down techniques for selecting the best model based on **key performance indicators** (**KPIs**). We'll guide you through making data-driven decisions to choose the most effective model.

Mastering these skills is essential for streamlining your ML workflows, reducing development time, and increasing collaboration across teams. By understanding how to efficiently train and manage models in Azure, you'll be better equipped to scale your solutions, improve model quality, and accelerate time-to-value in real-world projects.

In this chapter, we are going to cover the following main topics:

- Key stages in building an ML model
- AML workspace
- AML CLI
- Jobs and experiments in AML
- Data preparation

Key stages in building an ML model

Let's understand the iterative nature of the ML workflow and the key processes involved in building models:

1. **Prepare data**: Any ML problem statement starts with preparing data. This step involves collecting relevant data, cleaning it to remove inconsistencies or errors, and formatting it in a way that can be easily processed by ML algorithms.

2. **Train**: In this step, you choose an appropriate ML algorithm or model for your task. You then train the algorithm on the prepared data, allowing it to learn patterns and relationships in the data. This results in the creation of a trained model that can make predictions or take actions based on new data.

3. **Score**: Once your model is trained, you evaluate its performance by testing it on new data with known outcomes. This step helps you understand how well your model generalizes to unseen data and can identify areas for improvement.

4. **Evaluate**: In the evaluation step, you compare the outcomes predicted by your model with the known outcomes of the test data. You can then measure the quality of your model's performance using relevant KPIs such as accuracy, precision, recall, or F1 score.

5. **Decide**: Based on the evaluation results, you decide about your model. If it meets your performance criteria, you can deploy it into production for real-world use. Otherwise, you may need to go back and tweak any of the previous steps, such as collecting more data, trying a different algorithm, or adjusting your model's parameters.

The following figure captures the essence of the process. This diagram is important as we will refer to this multiple times throughout our journey during the other chapters as well:

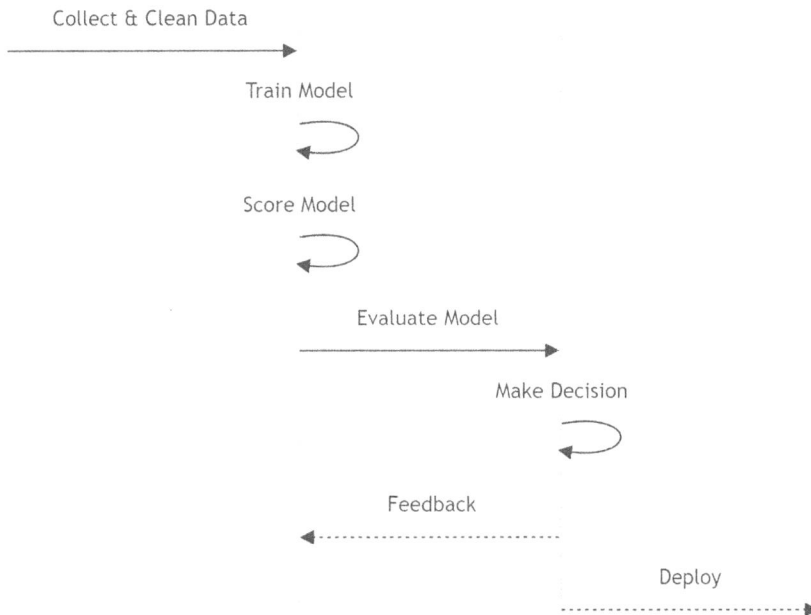

Figure 2.1 – The high-level steps to build an ML model

Now that we've established the basic process of the ML workflow, let's discuss the core AML component that facilitates these activities.

AML workspace

An **AML workspace** is a centralized environment where you can manage all the components of your ML projects. It acts as a hub for data scientists, developers, and IT professionals to collaborate and manage MLOps. The workspace provides a secure and scalable environment to work with ML models, data, and compute resources.

Key features of an AML workspace

Some salient features of the **AML workspace** are as follows:

- **Resource management**: The workspace allows you to manage various resources such as compute instances, data stores, and pipelines. It provides a structured way to organize and access these resources across different projects and teams.

- **Collaboration, access control, and cost management:** Workspaces enhance collaboration by implementing role-based access control, ensuring that only authorized personnel can access sensitive data and operations, which is a cornerstone of DevOps' best practices for managing permissions and roles. For team leads and administrators, these workspaces act as central hubs for managing access, controlling costs, and isolating data. Organizational best practices suggest using specific user roles to manage permissions effectively, assigning access based on user groups, and creating separate workspaces for each project to improve cost reporting and configuration management. Additionally, sharing Azure resources across workspaces can optimize setup time and resource utilization, further streamlining the management process.

- **Integration with DevOps practices: AML workspaces** integrate seamlessly with existing DevOps tools and practices. This includes **continuous integration/continuous deployment (CI/CD)** pipelines, enabling automated testing and deployment of ML models.

- **Monitoring and tracking:** The workspace includes capabilities for monitoring and tracking experiments, models, and deployments. This is crucial for understanding model performance, data drift, and operational metrics, which are key for maintaining reliable ML systems in production.

- **Scalability and security:** Azure ensures that the workspace is scalable to handle large datasets and compute workloads. It also provides built-in security features to protect data and resources, which is a critical aspect of any DevOps-oriented environment.

Now that we have explored the core features and benefits of an **AML workspace**, let's take a closer look at the key components that make up the workspace and how they support your machine learning workflows.

Key components of a workspace

Let's understand the essential components of an **AML workspace**, including compute resources, data stores, environments, models, and reusable code components. This section explains how each component contributes to the overall workflow:

- **Compute resources:**

    - **Compute instances:** These are preconfigured cloud computing resources that you can use to run Jupyter notebooks, training scripts, and other ML operations. They are essential for developing and testing ML models directly in the cloud.

    - **Compute clusters:** For larger workloads and training more complex models, compute clusters provide scalable cloud computing power that can be adjusted based on your needs.

- **Data stores and data**:

  - **Data stores**: These are storage accounts attached to your workspace, used to store the data your models need for training and prediction. AML supports various types of data stores, including Azure Blob Storage and Azure File Storage.

  - **Data**: Managed versions of data can be easily shared and reused across various experiments. Data ensures that every model training run is traceable and reproducible by keeping track of data versions.

- **Environments**: Environments specify the Python packages, environment variables, and software settings required to run your training scripts or host your models. They ensure that your experiments are reproducible by maintaining consistent software configurations.

- **Models**: Trained ML models are stored as assets within the workspace. You can manage model versions, track their performance, and deploy them to production environments directly from the workspace.

- **Components**: These are reusable pieces of code that define a step in your ML pipeline, such as data preparation, model training, or inference. Components help standardize processes and improve efficiency by enabling reuse across different projects and pipelines.

Having grasped the core components of your **AML workspace**, it's time to understand how to effectively manage these resources. Each component plays a vital role in your ML workflow, and efficiently managing them is key to streamlining your development process.

In the next section, we'll delve into the practicalities of managing workspace resources. We'll explore how to leverage the Azure portal and Azure CLI to create, configure, and utilize these components within your workspace. This will equip you with the skills to set up your workspace, add compute resources, connect data stores, register data, and configure environments—all essential steps for building a robust foundation for your ML projects.

Managing workspace resources

Creating and managing these resources is straightforward in AML. You can use the Azure portal, Azure CLI, or AML SDK to create and configure workspaces and their associated resources. Here's how you might typically set up a workspace and its resources:

1. **Create a workspace**: You can create a workspace directly from the AML studio, the Azure portal, or using the CLI. This workspace acts as a container for all your ML assets.

2. **Add compute resources**: Once your workspace is set up, you can add compute instances or clusters depending on your processing needs. These resources can be scaled up or down based on the workload.

3. **Connect data stores**: Attach or create new data stores to your workspace to ensure that your data is accessible for training and inference tasks.

4. **Register data**: Import and register datasets to your workspace to make them easily accessible for your experiments and ensure that data versioning is maintained.

5. **Configure environments**: Define and configure environments that can be reused across different experiments to ensure consistency in your training and deployment phases.

By effectively managing these resources, you can streamline your ML workflows, enhance collaboration among team members, and accelerate the time from experimentation to production. Now, as we mentioned in the previous chapter, let's get into the specific examples of how to use the **AML CLI** to get started.

AML CLI

Creating a robust ML workspace starts with setting up a dedicated environment that isolates your project dependencies from global settings. This is crucial for maintaining consistency across different development stages and among various team members. In this section, we will look at how to set up and install the necessary packages in the **AML CLI** and then understand its fundamental structure and usage.

Setting up a virtual environment

Here's a step-by-step guide to setting up a virtual environment and installing the necessary packages:

1. **Choose your environment manager**: For Python-based projects, tools such as conda or venv are popular choices. conda is preferred for managing environments that require complex dependencies, while venv is suitable for simpler Python dependencies.

2. **Create a virtual environment:**

    *   Use this for conda:

```
```
conda create -n myenv python=3.11
conda activate myenv
```
```

- Use this for venv:

```
```
python -m venv myenv
source myenv/bin/activate # On Windows use `myenv\Scripts\
activate`
```
```

3. **Install the AML CLI package:**

```
pip install azure-cli
az extension add -n ml
```

4. **Test the installation:** Ensure all packages are installed correctly and can be imported into your Python environment without errors:

```
az  --version
```

Check that `azure-cli` and the `ml` extensions are installed and the versions are as shown here:

```
(myenv) banibrata [ ~ ]$ az --version
azure-cli                     2.60.0

core                          2.60.0
telemetry                     1.1.0

Extensions:
ml                            2.25.1

Dependencies:
msal                          1.28.0
azure-mgmt-resource           23.1.0b2

Python location '/home/banibrata/myenv/bin/python'
Extensions directory '/home/banibrata/.azure/cliextensions'

Python (Linux) 3.9.19 (main, Mar 28 2024, 18:56:59)
[GCC 11.2.0]

Legal docs and information: aka.ms/AzureCliLegal


Your CLI is up-to-date.
(myenv) banibrata [ ~ ]$
```

Figure 2.2 – Installation of CLI

A quick help on the main command shows the subgroups that support the different parts of MLOps:

```
(myenv) banibrata [ ~ ]$ az ml -h

Group
    az ml : Manage Azure Machine Learning resources with the Azure CLI ML extension v2.
        Install Azure CLI ML extension v2
        https://docs.microsoft.com/azure/machine-learning/how-to-configure-cli.

Subgroups:
    batch-deployment              : Manage Azure ML batch deployments.
    batch-endpoint                : Manage Azure ML batch endpoints.
    component                     : Manage Azure ML components.
    compute                       : Manage Azure ML compute resources.
    connection     [Preview] : Manage Azure ML workspace connection.
    data                          : Manage Azure ML data assets.
    datastore                     : Manage Azure ML datastores.
    environment                   : Manage Azure ML environments.
    feature-set                   : Manage Azure ML feature sets.
    feature-store                 : Manage Azure ML feature stores.
    feature-store-entity          : Manage Azure ML feature store entities.
    job                           : Manage Azure ML jobs.
    model                         : Manage Azure ML models.
    online-deployment             : Manage Azure ML online deployments.
    online-endpoint               : Manage Azure ML online endpoints.
    registry                      : Manage Azure ML registries.
    schedule                      : Manage Azure ML schedule resources.
    workspace                     : Manage Azure ML workspaces.
    workspace-hub [Preview] : Manage Azure ML WorkspaceHub.

To search AI knowledge base for examples, use: az find "az ml"
```

Figure 2.3 – Basic subgroups of the CLI

To update the ml extension to the latest version, use the following:

```
az extension update -n ml
```

With your environment set up and the AML CLI installed, you are now ready to explore the basic structure and usage of the **AML CLI** to begin managing your machine learning workflows efficiently.

Basic structure and usage of the AML CLI

The **AML CLI** is structured around a set of commands that correspond to different aspects of ML workflows. Here are a few of the basic commands and their purposes:

- **Creating a workspace**: Before running any ML jobs, you need a workspace. It can be created using the following:

```
az ml workspace create --name <your-workspace-name> --resource-group
<your-resource-group>  --subscription-name <your-subscription-name>
```

- **Setting defaults**: To avoid repeatedly specifying common parameters such as workspace and resource group, you can set defaults:

```
az account set --subscription-name <your-subscription-name>
az configure --defaults group=<your-resource-group> workspace=<your-workspace-name>
```

- **Creating a new workspace**: While you can create a workspace using direct CLI parameters, you can also create a new workspace using a YAML configuration file for a more structured and reusable setup, which is especially useful for consistent workspace management in DevOps workflows. To create a new workspace using Azure CLI v2, you can utilize the following command structure. This command allows you to specify the workspace details in a YAML file, which includes configurations such as the workspace name, location, and other descriptive information:

```
az ml workspace create --name my_workspace
```

This setup will help you understand the foundational commands necessary to start running ML training jobs on Azure using the **AML CLI**. It's important to familiarize oneself with these commands to effectively manage and execute ML workflows in the cloud.

Workspace: A closer look

Now with a basic understanding of the usage of the CLI, let's suppose you create your first workspace using the CLI command in the last section. The following figures shows how the workspace created is presented both in the CLI and AML Studio (web interface to interact with MLOps):

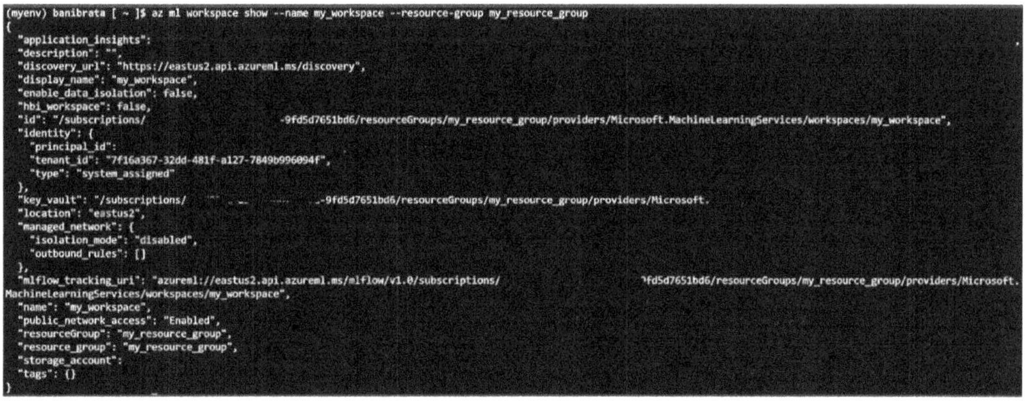

Figure 2.4 – Workspace from the CLI, first look

While the CLI provides a straightforward, scriptable way to view and manage your workspace, many teams also use the Azure portal for a visual overview and easier navigation through workspace resources. The Azure portal complements the CLI by offering an intuitive interface to explore and manage your **AML workspace** interactively:

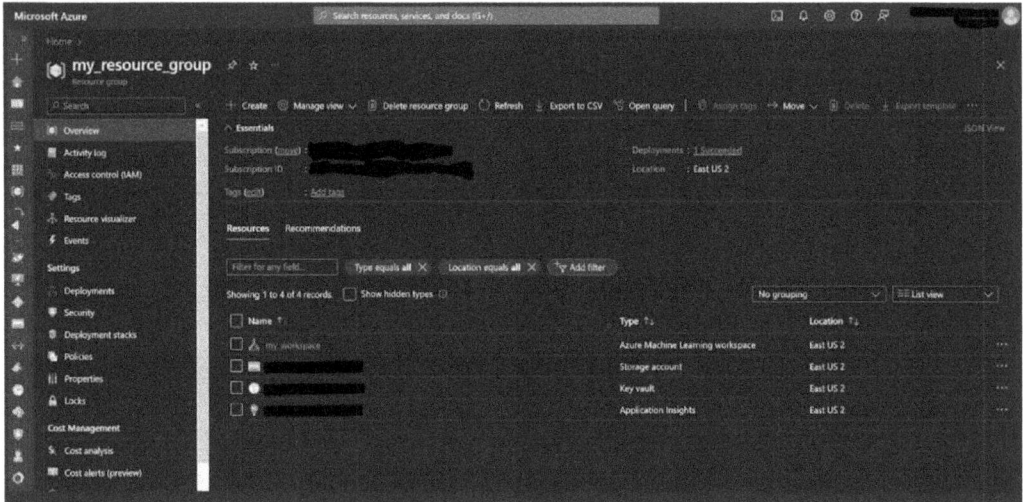

Figure 2.5 – Workspace from the Azure portal

If you run the workspace shown in *Figure 2.5*, it shows the basic resources that are created to support a robust, secure, and scalable ML environment in Azure, each serving a specific purpose to support the end-to-end ML lifecycle. The details of these resources are as follows:

- **Storage account**: Stores datasets, model artifacts, and logs needed for ML operations
- **Azure Container Registry (ACR)**: Manages and stores Docker container images for training and deployment environments
- **Azure Application Insights**: Monitors the performance and health of deployed models, providing actionable insights
- **Key Vault**: Securely stores and manages sensitive information such as API keys and connection strings

These CLI commands and configurations provide a robust framework for creating and managing **AML workspaces**, ensuring that users can efficiently handle their ML resources and settings.

Now we have the workspace set up, let's understand the next concept that makes the workspace useful: the model training process. The two key concepts we will cover here are jobs and experiments.

Jobs and experiments in AML

In AML, the concepts of *jobs* and *experiments* are fundamental to organizing, executing, and tracking ML workflows.

Jobs

A **job** in AML refers to a single execution of a training script or a model deployment script. Jobs are used to perform tasks such as training models, tuning hyperparameters, or deploying models to production. Each job runs in a specific compute environment and can be configured with its own set of parameters and data inputs. Jobs are the building blocks of any ML workflow in Azure, allowing data scientists and developers to automate and scale their ML tasks efficiently.

Experiments

An **experiment** is a grouping mechanism in AML that helps you organize and keep track of multiple runs. A **run**, in this context, is an instance of a job execution. Experiments are useful for comparing the performance of different runs, tracking the progress of model development over time, and systematically managing the lifecycle of ML models. Each experiment can contain multiple runs, and AML provides tools to log, monitor, and compare the metrics and outputs of these runs.

Together, jobs and experiments provide a structured way to manage ML projects, enabling teams to maintain a clear and organized workflow, track the evolution of models, and ensure reproducibility and accountability in ML operations.

In these projects, running training jobs and conducting experiments is a crucial process that bridges the gap between data preparation and model deployment. It involves systematically testing different models, hyperparameters, and datasets to identify the best-performing solution. By experimenting with different configurations, you can understand your models' behavior and make informed decisions about which model to select.

The diagram in *Figure 2.6* provides a high-level overview of the experiment lifecycle in AML:

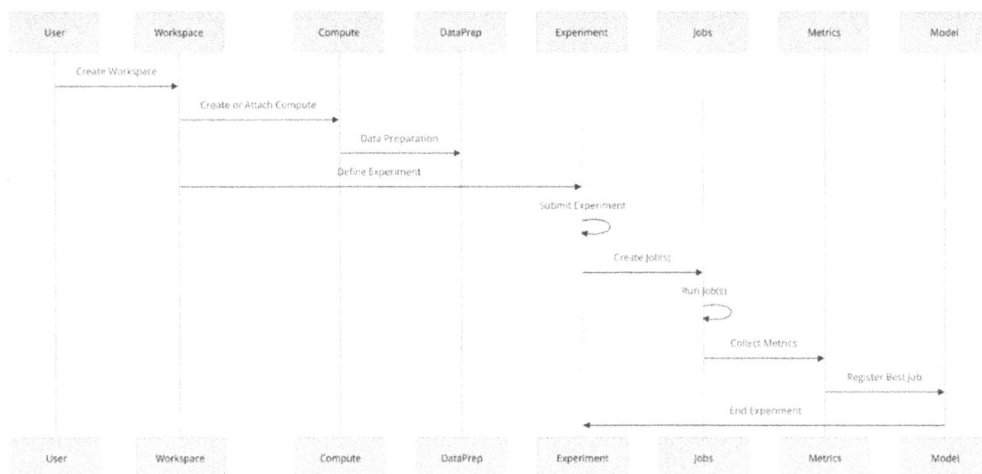

Figure 2.6 – Experiment, a high-level look

This figure shows the sequential steps involved, starting from workspace creation and compute resource setup, through data preparation and experiment definition, to job execution and metrics collection. The process concludes with the registration of the best-performing model, showcasing a structured workflow that ensures systematic management and reproducibility of the ML experiment.

Jobs and experiments: Why they matter

There are a number of advantages that come with using jobs and experiments:

- **Systematic organization**: Jobs and experiments help structure the model development process by allowing you to organize multiple runs, track their performance, and manage resources efficiently.

- **Experimentation and comparison**: By grouping jobs under experiments, you can easily compare different runs, identify trends, and determine which configurations yield the best results. This comparison is essential for selecting the most suitable model for production.

- **Reproducibility**: When managed correctly, jobs and experiments ensure that your training processes are reproducible. You can track the exact configurations used, making it easier to reproduce results and avoid discrepancies.

- **Optimization**: Experimentation is the cornerstone of optimization in ML. By running multiple jobs with varying configurations, you can fine-tune your models and hyperparameters to achieve optimal performance.

Now that we understand these concepts, let's move to the next step: preparing data.

Data preparation

In this section, we will delve into setting up experiments, defining jobs, and using the **AML CLI** to run and monitor training jobs. By mastering this process, you will be equipped to conduct meaningful experiments that help you select the right model for your specific use case. The success of any ML project hinges on the quality of its data. Before diving into model training, data preparation is crucial to ensure your data is clean, consistent, and ready for analysis.

Steps in data preparation

This process typically involves several key actions:

- **Cleaning**: Identifying and correcting errors or inconsistencies in your data. This might involve removing duplicates, fixing missing values, and handling typos.

- **Formatting**: Ensuring data types are consistent and formatted correctly. For example, converting dates to a standard format or transforming categorical variables into numerical representations.

- **Handling missing values**: Deciding how to deal with missing or null values. Options include removing them, imputing them with appropriate values, or using specific techniques depending on the data and modeling approach.

- **Outlier treatment**: Identifying and handling outliers that could skew your results. Outliers are data points that fall far outside the expected range. You might choose to remove them, transform them, or keep them after careful analysis.

The overall process that makes the data ready for experimentation looks like the following figure:

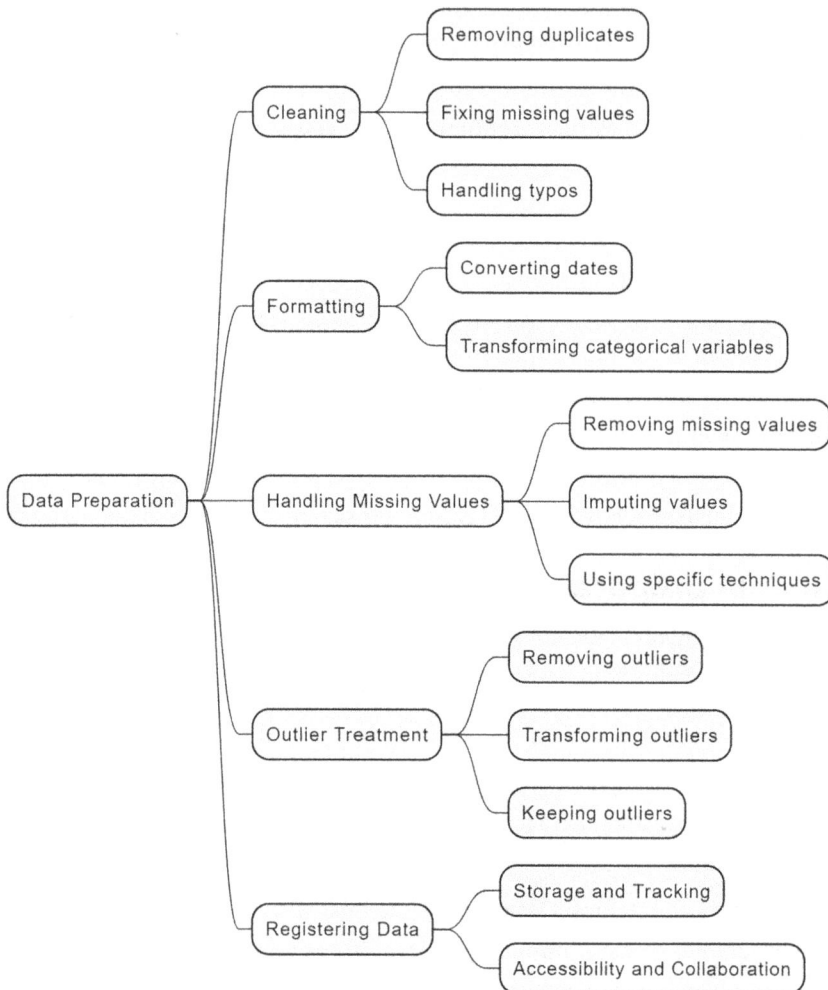

Figure 2.7 – Data preparation in AML

With these key steps completed, your data becomes ready for experimentation and model development. But why is this effort so crucial in your ML workflows?

What are the benefits of proper data preparation?

By meticulously preparing your data, you lay the foundation for creating reliable and accurate ML models. Clean and well-structured data allows your models to learn effectively from patterns and relationships within the data, ultimately leading to better predictions.

Registering data in the AML workspace

Once your data is prepared, the next step is to register it within your **AML workspace**. Registering essentially means creating a record of your data asset within the workspace. This process offers the following advantages:

- **Storage and tracking**: The data is uploaded to a managed location within the workspace, making it readily accessible for various experiments. AML also tracks different versions of your data, allowing you to compare and revert if needed.

- **Accessibility and collaboration**: Registered data becomes easily accessible across different experiments and team members. Everyone working on the project can find and use the same data source, promoting consistency and reproducibility.

How can data be registered?

In AML, registering data involves creating a dataset object. This dataset object holds information about your data, including its name, version, and location within the workspace. This process typically follows data preparation and ensures your datasets are organized, versioned, and accessible for experiments and pipelines. To clarify, here is how this process fits into your workflow:

- **Data preparation**: This is the overarching process of getting your data into a form that can be effectively used by ML algorithms. In AML, data preparation involves several steps, from cleaning to outlier treatment, all of which are necessary for building reliable models:

  - **Cleaning**: Cleaning involves removing duplicates, fixing missing values, and correcting typos in your dataset. In AML, this might involve using data wrangling tools or writing custom scripts to clean data stored in AML data stores, ensuring the data is accurate and consistent.

  - **Formatting**: Formatting is about converting dates and transforming categorical variables into formats suitable for ML. This step ensures that the data is in the correct format for model training. AML provides tools such as the DataPrep SDK to handle these transformations efficiently.

  - **Handling missing values**: This involves either removing missing values or imputing them using specific techniques. AML allows you to handle missing data systematically, ensuring your model can work with the available data without being skewed by gaps.

- **Outlier treatment**: Outliers can skew model results, so they need to be identified and treated. AML offers various tools for detecting and handling outliers, whether by removing, transforming, or deciding to keep them based on their relevance to the problem.

- **Registering data**: In AML, registering data involves organizing, storing, and tracking datasets in AML data stores. This step ensures data accessibility and collaboration across teams, making it easier to share and reuse datasets.

Now that we laid the concepts of data as an asset and registered in the workspace for this to be used in jobs, let's get into how to set up the jobs in an experiment.

Setting up an experiment

As we learned in the previous section, an experiment in AML acts as a container for your training runs. It groups together different iterations of model training, allowing you to track their progress, compare results, and analyze performance.

Here's a breakdown of the key steps involved in setting up an experiment using the **AML CLI**:

1. **Prepare your data**: Ensure your data is clean and registered within the workspace, as discussed earlier.

2. **Feature selection**: Identify the features in your data that are most relevant to your predictions. AML offers tools to help you select features that contribute significantly to your model's performance.

3. **Choose a model/algorithm**: Select an ML model that aligns with the nature of your problem. Common choices include linear regression for continuous predictions or logistic regression for binary classifications. AML also provides ways to define your model configuration.

Creating a simple experiment by running a job

Now, let's explore how to set up and run a simple training job within an experiment using the **AML CLI**. Here's a step-by-step guide:

1. **Define the experiment**: Specify the name for your experiment within the job configuration file (YAML format). This file defines various aspects of your training job. Here's an example YAML configuration snippet:

```
$schema: https://azuremlschemas.azureedge.net/latest/commandJob.
schema.json

command: python train.py --data-folder ${{inputs.training_data}}
```

```
experiment_name: my-first-experiment  # Name of your experiment

environment: azureml:myenv:1  # Replace with your environment name
and version

inputs:
  training_data:
    type: uri_folder
    path: azureml://datastores/workspaceblobstore/paths/my-dataset/
# Replace with your dataset path

outputs:
  model_output:
    type: uri_folder
    path: azureml://datastores/workspaceblobstore/
        paths/model-output/  # Location for model artifacts
```

2. **Prepare training and scoring scripts**: Ensure you have two Python scripts:

   - **Training script**: This script handles data loading, model training, and logging metrics.

   - **Scoring script**: This script defines how to load the trained model and generate predictions on new data. The scoring script typically takes the model path and new data as inputs and returns the predictions.

3. **Create a YAML job configuration file**: The YAML file defines various configurations for running your training job, like the previous example.

   Here's an updated version incorporating the scoring script:

```
YAML
$schema: https://azuremlschemas.azureedge.net/latest/commandJob.
schema.json
experiment_name: my-first-experiment  # Referenced experiment name

# Training Script and Data
command: python train.py --data-folder ${{inputs.my_data}}
environment: azureml:myenv:1  # Replace with your environment name
```

```
inputs:
  my_data:
    type: uri_folder
    path: azureml://datastores/workspaceblobstore/
          paths/my-dataset/  # Path to your registered dataset

# Scoring Script and Outputs
outputs:
  model_output:
    type: uri_folder
    path: azureml://datastores/workspaceblobstore/
          paths/model-output/
post_run_scripts:
  - arguments:
      model_name: ${{outputs.model_output}}
        # Path to the trained model
      data_path: <path/to/new/data.csv>
        # Replace with path to your new data
    command: python score.py --model-path ${{arguments.model_name}}
            --data ${{arguments.data_path}}
```

Let's walk through the different sections of this YAML to understand more:

- The `post_run_scripts` section defines a script to run after the training job completes.

- The scoring script (`score.py`) is executed with arguments specifying the trained model path (`model_name`) and the path to new data (`data_path`) for generating predictions.

Here's a basic example structure for a scoring script (`score.py`):

```
import pickle
import pandas as pd

# Load the trained model
model_path = "<model_path>"  # Replace with argument received
with open(model_path, "rb") as f:
    model = pickle.load(f)
```

```
# load new data
data = pd.read_csv("<data_path>")  # Replace with argument received

# Generate predictions
predictions = model.predict(data)

# You can process or return the predictions here
print(f"Predictions: {predictions}")
```

Let's break down the preceding code block:

- The script loads the trained model using the provided path.
- It loads the new data for prediction using pandas.
- The script uses the loaded model to generate predictions on the new data.

You can modify this script to process or return the predictions in the desired format.

1. **Submit the job**: Use the **AML CLI** to submit the job, providing the path to your YAML configuration file. Here's the corresponding CLI command:

```Bash
az ml job create --file my-job.yml
```

2. **Monitor the job**: Track the progress of your job through the AML Studio or using the following CLI v2 command:

```Bash
az ml job show --name <job_name>
```

3. **Review the outputs**: Once the job is completed, you can review the outputs, logs, and metrics. This information is crucial for evaluating the performance of your model and making any necessary adjustments. The outputs will typically be stored in the location specified in the outputs section of your YAML configuration file.

The previous example shows an end-to-end example of running training and doing some basic scoring of the model. Make sure to do the following:

- Replace the placeholders in the YAML configuration file with your specific information.
- Ensure you have an **AML workspace** set up and the Azure CLI with the ML extension (az ml) installed before running these commands.

By incorporating a scoring script into your job configuration, you can automate the process of generating predictions on new data using your trained model within an AML experiment. This streamlined approach simplifies the model deployment and evaluation workflow, which we will talk about in later chapters.

At this point, we have the experiment set up and the jobs are running; each successful run will produce one or models as artifacts. The next section discusses the process to choose the right model that is suitable for the real business scenario.

Choosing the model/algorithm

Selecting the appropriate ML algorithm is a fundamental step in building an effective model. The choice of algorithm can significantly impact the model's performance and its ability to generalize to new data. This decision is typically based on the problem, the dataset's characteristics, and the evaluation metrics used to gauge performance. By running multiple jobs and evaluating their outcomes, you can determine which algorithm best meets your project's requirements. The following sections will guide you through selecting the right algorithm using the **AML CLI**, ensuring that you start your ML journey on the right foot.

Defining the evaluation criteria

The parameters for defining the evaluation criteria are as follows:

- **Performance metrics**: This involves identifying KPIs that align with your business goals (e.g., accuracy, loss, precision, recall, F1 score, ROC-AUC for classification, and RMSE and MAE for regression).
- **Resource usage**: This entails tracking training time, memory usage, and compute costs to assess model efficiency.
- **Interpretability**: This involves evaluating the interpretability of models, especially if business decisions rely on understanding predictions.

Collecting metrics and artifacts

The parameters for collecting metrics and artifacts are as follows:

- **Metrics logging**: This entails ensuring that the metrics for each model are properly logged during the experiment. AML automatically captures metrics for each job.
- **Output artifacts**: This requires capturing model outputs such as confusion matrices, feature importances, and other relevant artifacts for evaluation.

Comparing models

The parameters for comparing models are as follows:

- **Cross-validation scores**: This involves comparing models based on cross-validation scores to ensure their performance generalizes well.

- **Overfitting check**: This covers evaluating whether any model is overfitting or underfitting by comparing training and validation metrics.

- **Visual analysis**: This entails using visualization tools to compare model performance visually. AML Studio provides a rich interface for visual comparison.

Selecting the best model

The parameters for selecting the best model are as follows:

- **Performance vs. efficiency**: This requires striking a balance between model performance and resource efficiency. A model with slightly lower performance but significantly lower resource usage might be preferable.

- **Business requirements**: This entails ensuring that the selected model aligns with business requirements in terms of accuracy, latency, interpretability, and regulatory compliance.

- **Finalize model**: Once the best model is identified, promote it to the production stage and proceed with deployment.

This structured approach, summarized in *Figure 2.8*, ensures that the selected model not only performs well but also aligns with the ML project's broader objectives.

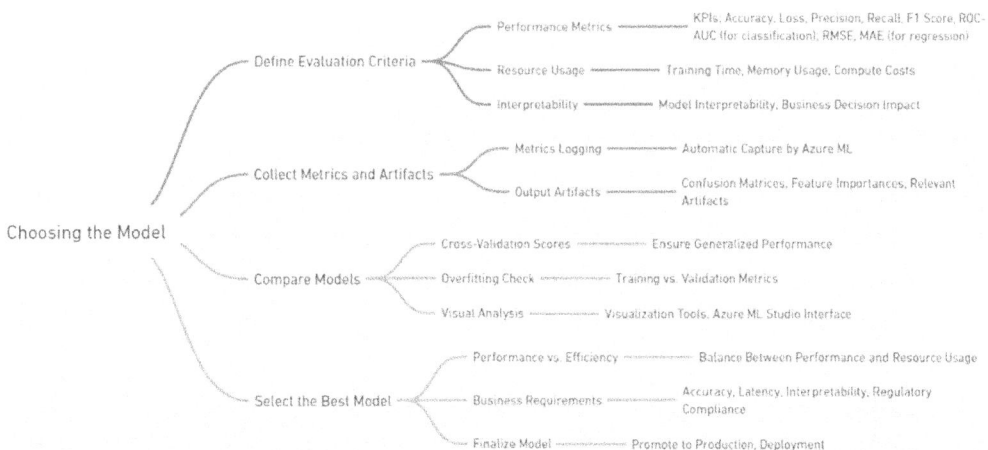

Figure 2.8 – Mapping the model selection process

After defining your evaluation criteria and comparing model performance based on key metrics, the next essential step is to ensure that these metrics are meticulously logged and tracked. Accurate tracking of experiment data not only aids in model comparison but also enhances reproducibility and efficiency in the ML lifecycle.

Tracking and comparing model experiments in ML

In the realm of ML, the ability to track and compare experiments is crucial for developing effective models. This section delves into the methodologies and tools that facilitate the meticulous recording and analysis of model experiments. Utilizing platforms such as MLflow in conjunction with AML enhances the management of the lifecycle of ML experiments. MLflow integrates seamlessly with AML to log metrics and artifacts, providing a robust framework for tracking experiments across various environments, whether they are on local machines, remote compute targets, or cloud-based services such as Azure Databricks and Azure Synapse Analytics.

Tracking involves the detailed logging of experiment metadata, which includes code versions, environmental details, input data, model parameters, and evaluation metrics. This comprehensive data collection is pivotal for experiment reproducibility and analysis. Moreover, comparing these experiments is facilitated through visual tools and APIs that allow researchers to discern performance metrics and make informed decisions about model adjustments or iterations.

The next section will guide you through setting up and utilizing these tracking tools, configuring experiments, and effectively comparing the outcomes to refine your ML models. By mastering these practices, you can ensure systematic progress in your ML projects, leading to more reliable and optimized models.

Tools for tracking

Several tools are available for tracking experiments in ML, each with its own strengths and integration capabilities. Here's a brief overview of popular tools:

- **MLflow**: This is an open source platform primarily for managing the end-to-end ML lifecycle, including experimentation, reproducibility, and deployment.
- **TensorBoard**: Deeply integrated with TensorFlow, this provides visualization and tooling needed for ML experimentation, including tracking metrics, visualizing model graphs, and viewing histograms.
- **Comet.ml**: This is a cloud-based service that allows you to track code, experiments, and results automatically across various ML libraries and frameworks.

While these tools are powerful, AML provides a comprehensive and integrated environment that can leverage these tools while adding unique capabilities, especially when using the **AML CLI** for seamless integration. In the setup that follows, we will learn how to use MLflow for logging and tracking model KPIs.

Setting up MLflow tracking with AzureML CLI v2

To effectively use AML for experiment tracking, let's use MLflow for this example. Follow these steps:

1. Integrate with Mlflow. AML can act as a backend for MLflow, allowing you to store all your logs and metrics in Azure while using MLflow's simple APIs.

2. Configure MLflow to use AML as its tracking URI:

```python
import mlflow

mlflow.set_tracking_uri(
    "azureml://northcentralus.api.azureml.ms/mlflow/v1.0/"
    "subscriptions/your_subscription_id/"
    "resourceGroups/your_resource_group/"
    "providers/Microsoft.MachineLearningServices/"
    "workspaces/your_workspace_name"
)
mlflow.set_experiment("your_experiment_name")
```

3. Run and track experiments. Use the Azure CLI to run your experiments and automatically log metrics, parameters, and artifacts:

```
az ml job create --file experiment.yml
```

4. Monitor and manage these experiments directly from your **AML workspace**.

Comparing jobs in an experiment

After running multiple jobs and evaluating their performance based on KPIs, the best-performing model is identified. This model, which has demonstrated superior metrics in terms of accuracy, precision, recall, or other relevant criteria, is deemed ready for business use and deployment. The next steps involve registering this model with AML to ensure it is available for deployment and can be easily managed and monitored.

To achieve this, you can use **AML CLI** commands to locate the best model from the job outputs and officially register it within the workspace. The following advantages highlight the benefits of comparing jobs within an experiment:

- **Visual comparison**: AML Studio offers powerful visualization tools to help you compare different experiments. By plotting metrics such as loss, accuracy, and other custom indicators against each other, you can easily identify the most promising models. This visual comparison simplifies the process of analyzing multiple jobs and selecting the best model.

- **Statistical analysis**: AML also provides tools for performing statistical analysis and generating reports that compare different experiments. These capabilities enable you to make data-driven decisions by thoroughly evaluating the performance and reliability of each model.

- **Streamlined job comparison**: It is simpler and easier to visually examine the jobs within an experiment, select the most interesting ones, and perform a detailed comparison to identify the best model.

The following example demonstrates how to use the AML Studio and CLI for this purpose. Here are the steps for the visual comparison in AML Studio:

1. Navigate to the AML Studio.

2. Open the experiment you are interested in.

3. Use the built-in visualization tools to compare metrics such as loss, accuracy, precision, recall, and so on.

The following figure is a view of an experiment with multiple job runs:

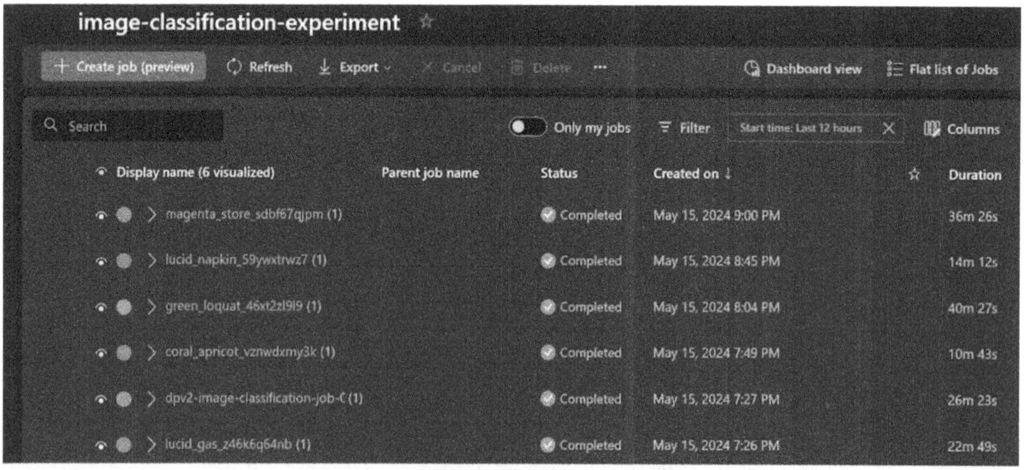

Figure 2.9 – Jobs inside an experiment from the AML Studio portal

The following figure compares the jobs from the preceding figure across some of the metrics:

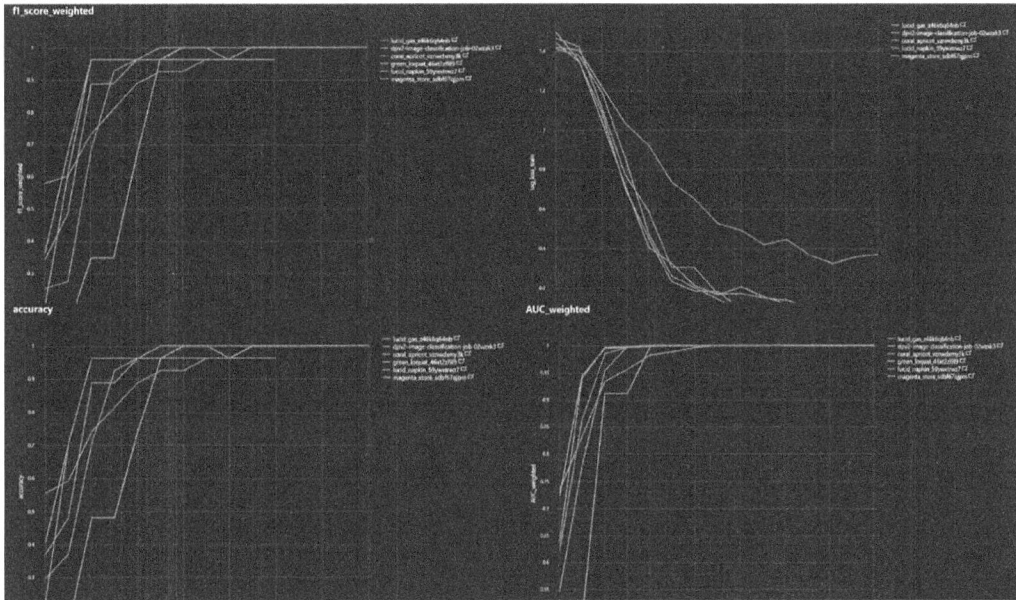

Figure 2.10 – Comparing models by different metrics

The CLI currently does not provide a direct way to achieve a similar approach. However, that does not limit us from creating a simple script to achieve the same using the CLI:

```bash
#!/bin/bash
# Experiment name
EXPERIMENT_NAME="my-first-experiment"

# List all jobs in the experiment
JOB_NAMES=$(az ml job list --experiment-name $EXPERIMENT_NAME --query "[].
name" -o tsv)

# Initialize an empty array to hold job metrics
declare -A job_metrics

# Loop through each job and retrieve metrics
for JOB_NAME in $JOB_NAMES; do
    METRICS=$(az ml job show --name $JOB_NAME --query metrics)
    job_metrics[$JOB_NAME]=$METRICS
done
```

```
# Compare metrics (example: comparing accuracy)
for JOB_NAME in "${!job_metrics[@]}"; do
    ACCURACY=$(echo ${job_metrics[$JOB_NAME]} | jq '.accuracy')
    echo "Job: $JOB_NAME, Accuracy: $ACCURACY"
done


# Add additional comparison logic as needed
```

Here is an explanation of what the preceding code block represents:

- **Listing jobs**: The script first lists all jobs in the specified experiment.
- **Retrieving metrics**: It then loops through each job and retrieves its metrics using the az ml job show command.
- **Comparing metrics**: Finally, it prints out the accuracy for each job. You can modify the script to compare other metrics or implement more complex comparison logic.

Register the best model based on metrics

After running the script and identifying the best model based on the metrics, you can register the model as follows:

```
BEST_JOB_NAME="job-with-highest-accuracy"

az ml model create --name my_best_model --version 1 --path azureml://
jobs/$BEST_JOB_NAME/outputs/artifacts
```

This approach provides a flexible way to compare job metrics across different jobs within an experiment using the **AML CLI** and simple scripting.

Optimizing models

Once you have identified the best-performing model based on your evaluation metrics, the next critical step in your ML pipeline is hyperparameter tuning. While selecting a model is essential for understanding which algorithm works best for your data, optimizing this model's performance requires fine-tuning its hyperparameters. This process, known as **hyperparameter tuning**, can significantly enhance the effectiveness and predictive power of your model. Let's explore various techniques to achieve optimal performance.

Hyperparameter tuning

In ML, the distinction between hyperparameters and model parameters is crucial. Model parameters are learned from data automatically during the training process and are integral to the model's ability to make predictions. In contrast, hyperparameters are the settings predetermined by the ML engineer before training begins. These settings might include the learning rate, the number of hidden layers in a neural network, or the number of trees in a random forest.

Hyperparameter tuning is essential because the right hyperparameter settings can dramatically improve model performance. Conversely, poorly chosen hyperparameters can result in models that fail to learn effectively, regardless of algorithm sophistication or data quality.

Tuning techniques

Several techniques are available for hyperparameter tuning, each with its own advantages:

- **Grid search**: This method involves exhaustively searching through a manually specified subset of the hyperparameter space. It's straightforward but can be computationally expensive.

- **Random search**: This technique samples hyperparameter settings randomly. It is often more efficient than grid search, as it can find good configurations with fewer trials.

- **Bayesian optimization**: This method builds a probabilistic model of the function mapping from hyperparameter values to the target evaluated on a validation set. It then uses this model to select the most promising hyperparameters to evaluate the true objective function.

- **Automated methods such as AutoML**: Tools such as Azure's AutoML automate the selection and tuning of hyperparameters, greatly simplifying the ML pipeline.

Sweep jobs

Sweep jobs in AML are designed to facilitate the hyperparameter tuning process by automating the search for the best-performing hyperparameter configurations. They systematically explore the hyperparameter space using various sampling algorithms and early termination policies to efficiently identify optimal settings. This automated approach not only saves time but also ensures more robust model performance by leveraging advanced techniques such as random sampling, Bayesian optimization, and bandit policies.

Example using the CLI

Let's walk through an example of hyperparameter tuning using the **AML CLI**, focusing on a sample ML model:

1. First, define your environment and dependencies:

    ```yaml
    # conda_dependencies.yml
    dependencies:
      - python=3.11
      - scikit-learn
      - pip:
        - azureml-defaults
    ```

2. Then, prepare the training script. Include a `train.py` Python script that uses scikit-learn to train a logistic regression model on the Iris dataset. The script should be set to accept hyperparameters as arguments.

3. Next, set up the sweep job configuration. AML's sweep job is used to automate hyperparameter tuning. Configure it to use random parameter sampling and a bandit policy for early termination of poorly performing runs:

    ```yaml
    # sweep_job_config.yml
    $schema: https://azuremlschemas.azureedge.net/latest/sweepJob.
    schema.json
    type: sweep
    experiment_name: sweep-test
    trial:
      code:
        local_path:
      command: >
        python train.py --C {search_space.C} --max_iter {search_space.
    max_iter}
      environment: azureml:my-conda-env:1
    search_space:
      C: uniform(0.1, 1.0)
      max_iter: choice(100, 150, 200)
    sampling_algorithm: random
    early_termination:
    ```

```
    type: bandit
    evaluation_interval: 2
    slack_factor: 0.1
  objective:
    primary_metric: accuracy
    goal: maximize
  compute: azureml:cpu-cluster
```

The following figure is a simpler translation of the preceding YAML; think of it as a mechanism that runs multiple jobs with different parameters to find the best-performing combination. Notice the loop component in *Figure 2.11*.

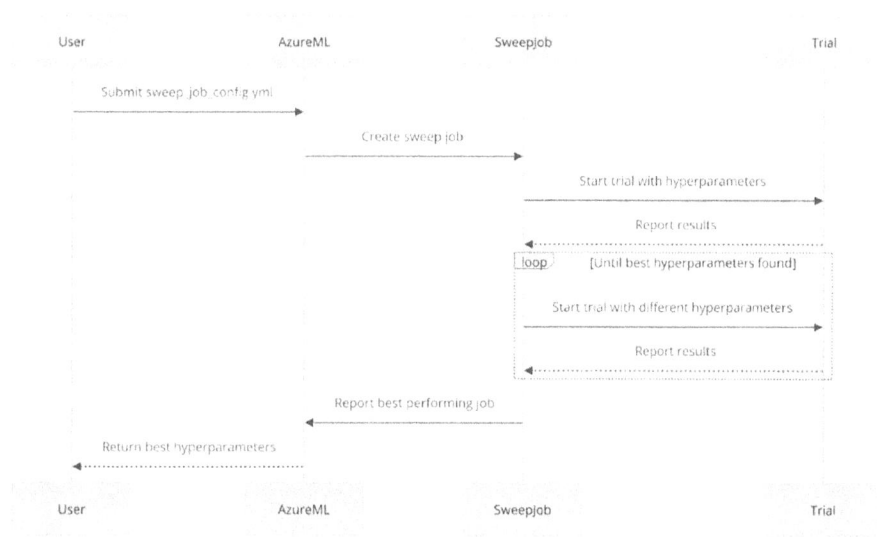

Figure 2.11 – Sweep job with hyperparameter tuning

4. Run the sweep (hyperparameter tuning) job by executing the tuning using the **AML CLI**:

```
az ml job create ……..
```

Once your sweep job has completed and the best-performing hyperparameters have been identified, the next step is to evaluate the model's performance thoroughly and iterate to refine your experiments for production readiness.

Evaluation and iteration

After running hyperparameter tuning, it's crucial to evaluate the effectiveness of different settings to ensure that the model achieves optimal performance and to identify the most promising hyperparameter combinations. AML provides tools to visualize and analyze the results of sweep job experiments, allowing you to compare the performance of different hyperparameter combinations.

This is an iterative process and, based on the results, you might choose to refine the search space or adjust the tuning algorithm to focus on more promising areas of the hyperparameter space. This visualization demonstrates the results of a sweep job with various hyperparameter settings: the performance metrics for each child job.

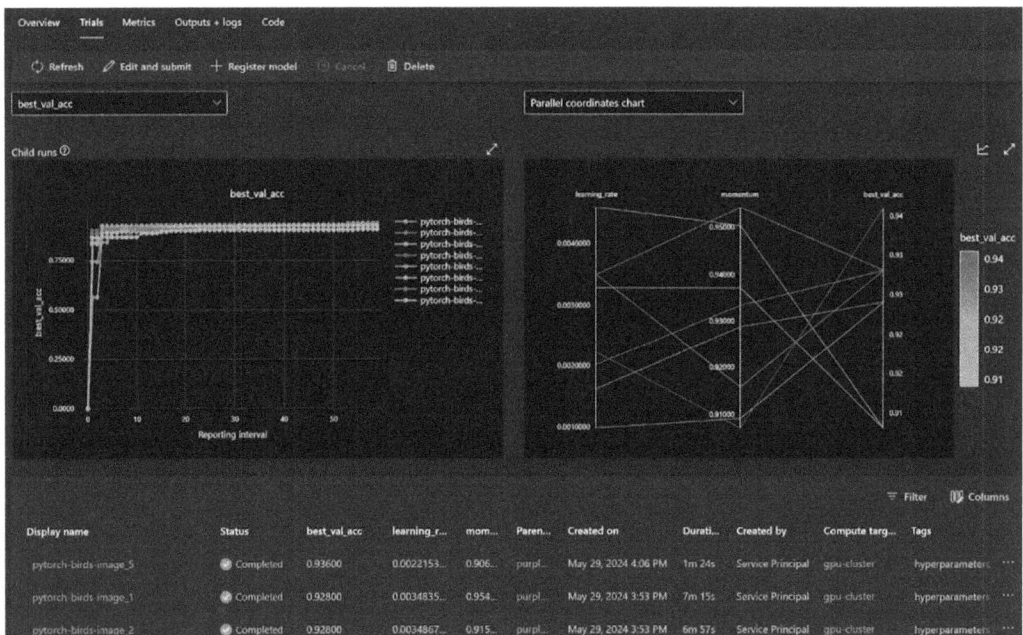

Figure 2.12 – Child jobs of a sweep job with hyperparameters

Note

We understand that the introduction of new concepts such as sweep jobs and YAML schemas may seem overwhelming, especially for those focused on DevOps and cloud engineering. However, think of these configurations as lines of code that will be checked into a code base. Most of the detailed work will be handled by data scientists. The reason these topics are discussed here is to provide you with a high-level understanding, ensuring you are well prepared to collaborate effectively in a cross-functional team.

AML provides a comprehensive suite of tools for managing and optimizing ML experiments, from data preparation and hyperparameter tuning to model evaluation and deployment. By leveraging these capabilities, teams can ensure their models are robust, reproducible, and ready for deployment in real-world applications. For hands-on practice and advanced scenarios, it is recommended to check the GitHub samples here: `https://github.com/Azure/azureml-examples/tree/main/cli/jobs`.

Summary

This chapter has provided a comprehensive overview of the foundational stages of ML model development: creating and managing workspaces, designing and conducting simple experiments, tracking and comparing these experiments, and optimizing models through hyperparameter tuning.

We explored how to set up these workspaces using tools such as the **AML CLI**, emphasizing best practices in environment configuration and version control. We then proceeded to design and implement simple experiments, using AML to streamline the process of model testing and evaluation. This section underscored the importance of systematic experiment management, which facilitates easier scaling and reproducibility.

Finally, we delved into hyperparameter tuning, exploring various techniques and their implementations within the AML framework. This is a critical step in refining model performance and ensuring that the chosen models are the best fit for their intended tasks.

By applying the principles learned in this chapter, you will be well prepared for the challenges of deploying robust, efficient, and effective ML systems. In the next chapter, we will use these as the building blocks for automation and reproducibility (the core principles of DevOps/MLOps) in the next chapter.

Tools documentation

Deepen your practical knowledge by referring to the official documentation of the tools and libraries discussed in this chapter:

- **AML CLI documentation**: `https://docs.microsoft.com/en-us/azure/machine-learning/`
- **MLflow documentation**: `https://mlflow.org/docs/latest/index.html`
- **TensorBoard documentation**: `https://www.tensorflow.org/tensorboard/`
- **Scikit-learn user guide**: `https://scikit-learn.org/stable/user_guide.html`

Part 2

Implementing MLOps

This part takes you beyond experimentation into the systematic operationalization of ML models at scale. It covers critical aspects of MLOps workflows, including model registration, packaging, and deployment, empowering you to confidently deliver models for both batch scoring and real-time services. You will learn how to capture and secure governance data, ensuring compliance and traceability throughout the ML lifecycle, and implement monitoring and alerting systems to maintain performance and reliability in production. By the end of this part, you will be equipped to manage models robustly in live environments, ensuring that they deliver value while maintaining quality, compliance, and operational excellence.

This part has the following chapters:

- *Chapter 3, Reproducible and Reusable ML*
- *Chapter 4, Model Management (Registration and Packaging)*
- *Chapter 5, Model Deployment: Batch Scoring and Real-Time Web Services*
- *Chapter 6, Capturing and Securing Governance Data for MLOps*
- *Chapter 7, Monitoring the ML Model*
- *Chapter 8, Notification and Alerting in MLOps*

3

Reproducible and Reusable ML

This chapter builds upon the concepts introduced in *Chapter 2*, focusing on automating the **machine learning** (**ML**) lifecycle for robust and efficient model development and deployments. Reproducibility and reusability are fundamental principles in ML to ensure the reliability and efficiency of your projects. Reproducibility allows you to recreate the same results consistently, which is essential for verifying experiments and building trust in your models. Reusability enables you to leverage existing components and workflows, saving time and resources while maintaining consistency across different projects.

This chapter delves into strategies for automating a typical ML workflow, with a strong emphasis on enhancing debuggability, reproducibility, and reusability. Key topics include an exploration of the importance of reproducibility and reusability within the ML lifecycle and how they contribute to robust and scalable solutions. The chapter also covers the construction, management, and automation of ML pipelines using **Azure ML** (**AML**), providing insights into defining and reusing pipeline components effectively. It further demonstrates how GitHub Actions can be integrated to automate various ML processes. Additionally, the chapter discusses the significance of managing isolated ML environments within AML and offers best practices and tools for dependency management to ensure consistent and reliable setups across different stages of development.

We will cover the following main topics:

- Defining repeatable and reusable steps for data preparation, training, and scoring
- Learning about components and pipelines in AML
- Tracking and reproducing software dependencies in projects
- Hands-on example – Building an ML pipeline with the AML CLI, Git, and GitHub Actions

By the end of this chapter, you will have a comprehensive understanding of how to create reproducible and reusable ML workflows, ensuring robust and efficient deployments. These practices are essential for managing complexity as ML projects scale, enabling seamless collaboration between data scientists and DevOps engineers. Building on the foundation from *Chapter 2*, you'll see how automation with shared components not only streamlines your development but also makes your ML solutions production-ready and maintainable in real-world environments.

Defining repeatable and reusable steps for data preparation, training, and scoring

In the previous chapter, we introduced a basic ML workflow as shown in *Figure 3.1*. However, it is very common that in enterprises, those different parts are controlled by different **subject matter experts (SMEs)**. So, if we place the SMEs in the respective workflow stages, the transformation would look like this:

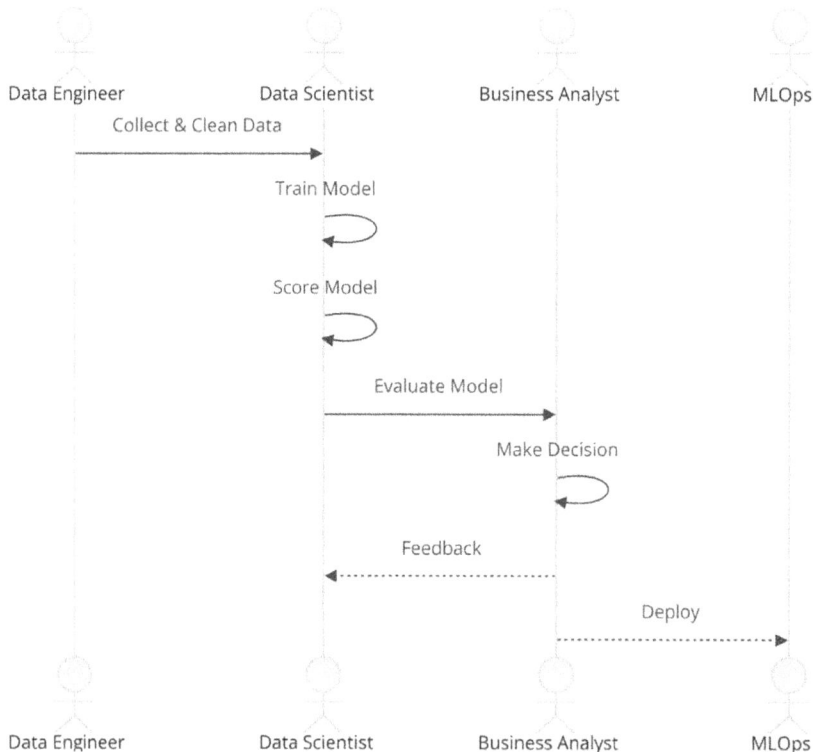

Figure 3.1 – Collaboration and reusability in MLOps

As the complexity grows as more data is added, and across the other steps in the MLOps process (*Figure 3.1*), it becomes essential to have SMEs focus on different parts. So, reusability, sharing, versioning, and a lot of other DevOps concepts are very useful here. In this chapter, we will gradually start building up toward automating the whole workflow.

To decipher the aforementioned stages, let's break them apart and try to understand the high-level substages that can be authored and managed by respective SMEs:

1. **Data acquisition**: This stage automates fetching data from various sources. AML pipelines offer pre-built components for common data sources such as the following:

    *   Azure Blob Storage
    *   **Azure Data Lake Storage (ADLS)**
    *   SQL databases
    *   External cloud storage (for example, **Amazon Web Services Simple Storage Service (AWS S3)**)
    *   Public datasets (UCI Machine Learning Repository)

    Example: You can define a step that reads a specific dataset from your Azure Blob Storage account. The component would take the storage container name and blob file path as inputs and output the loaded data as a DataFrame.

2. **Data preprocessing**: This stage automates cleaning, transforming, and preparing your data for model training. AML pipelines offer components for various preprocessing techniques:

    *   **Cleaning**: Handling missing values, outliers, and inconsistencies
    *   **Normalization**: Scaling numerical features to a common range
    *   **Feature engineering**: Creating new features from existing ones to improve model performance

    Example: You can define a step that removes missing values from specific columns, then normalizes numerical features using a min-max scaling technique. This component would take the DataFrame as input and output the preprocessed DataFrame.

3. **Model training**: This stage automates the training process for your chosen ML model. AML pipelines integrate with various ML frameworks such as scikit-learn, TensorFlow, and PyTorch.

Example: You can define a step that trains a classification model using a pre-built algorithm (for example, Logistic Regression) and hyperparameters you specify (for example, learning rate, regularization). The component would take the preprocessed DataFrame, algorithm choice, and hyperparameters as inputs and output the trained model.

4. **Model evaluation**: This stage automates evaluating the performance of the trained model using various metrics. AML pipelines offer components for calculating metrics such as the following:

    *   Accuracy (classification)
    *   **Mean Squared Error (MSE)** (regression)
    *   F1-score (classification)

    Example: You can define a step that calculates the accuracy score on a held-out test set. The component would take the trained model and test data as inputs and output the accuracy score as a metric. Pipelines can also involve components for comparing multiple models based on their evaluation metrics to choose the best-performing one.

5. **Model deployment**: This stage automates deploying the trained model to a production environment for real-world use. AML offers options for deployment to the following:

    *   AML service endpoints for web service API access
    *   **Azure Kubernetes Service (AKS)** for containerized deployments

    Example: You can define a step that deploys the chosen model to an AML service endpoint. The component would take the trained model as input and configure the endpoint for receiving scoring requests.

By defining these stages as reusable parts in your AML workflow, you gain several benefits:

*   **Consistency**: The same preprocessing steps are applied each time the workflow runs, ensuring consistent data preparation for training.
*   **Efficiency**: You avoid writing repetitive code for common tasks, saving development time.
*   **Maintainability**: Changes to a component can be easily applied across all workflows that use it.

By leveraging these reusable parts, you can build a robust and scalable end-to-end ML workflow that streamlines your development process and ensures reliable model performance.

This is a good point in the chapter to introduce the concept of a pipeline, using *Figure 3.1* to illustrate how each reusable step in the ML workflow maps to a **component** within the **pipeline**.

Learning about components and pipelines in AML

The concepts of reproducibility, reusability, and sharing are achieved by AML pipelines. ML pipelines are workflows built using interconnected components (see the next section) that automate the entire ML lifecycle. These components represent specific stages within the pipeline, allowing you to manage and track each step independently.

Components

Imagine a building with Lego bricks. Each Lego brick is a small, independent component. You can snap these components together in different ways to build all sorts of things – a car, a spaceship, a robot!

Similarly, AML pipelines have pre-built components that act like Lego bricks for your ML project. These components handle specific tasks, such as loading data, cleaning data, training a model, or putting the model to use (scoring).

Just like you wouldn't build a whole spaceship with just one type of Lego, you wouldn't build an entire ML pipeline with just one component. You connect these pre-built components together in the order you need to complete each step of your project.

Some other ways to understand components are as follows:

- **Think of components as tools for specific jobs**: Each component has a specific task within an MLOps pipeline. These steps could be one of the following: collect and clean data, train, score, evaluate a model, deploy a model, and so on. So, essentially, each step could be a component.
- **Reuse components to save time**: You can reuse the same component in multiple pipelines, just like you can reuse the same Lego brick in different builds.
- **Connect components to create a workflow**: You snap the components together, just like Lego bricks, to define the order of steps in your ML project.

AML components themselves aren't directly written in code you might typically see (such as Python or R). However, they are defined using YAML, which is a human-readable way to define configurations, and from the YAML, it references some code/script, which does the heavy lifting.

Here's a simplified example to give you an idea:

```
name: prep_data
version: 1
display_name: Prep Data
```

```
description: Convert data to CSV file, and split to training and test data
inputs:
  input_data:
    type: uri_folder
    optional: false
outputs:
  training_data:
    type: uri_folder
  test_data:
    type: uri_folder


code: ./prep_data.py


environment: azureml:environment_name:environment_version


command: >
  python prep_data.py
  --input_data ${{inputs.input_data}}
  --training_data ${{outputs.training_data}}
  --test_data ${{outputs.test_data}}
```

The code file could be something like this:

```python
import argparse
import os
import pandas as pd
from sklearn.model_selection import train_test_split


def parse_args():
    parser = argparse.ArgumentParser(
        description="Convert data to CSV file, and split to training and
        test data"
    )
    parser.add_argument(
        '--input_data',
        type=str,
        help='Path to the input data',
        required=True
```

```
    )
    parser.add_argument(
        '--training_data',
        type=str,
        help='Path to the output training data',
        required=True
    )
    parser.add_argument(
        '--test_data',
        type=str,
        help='Path to the output test data',
        required=True
    )
    return parser.parse_args()
def main():
    args = parse_args()

    # Read input data
    input_data_path = args.input_data
    input_files = [
        os.path.join(input_data_path, f)
        for f in os.listdir(input_data_path)
        if f.endswith('.csv')]

    # Concatenate all input CSV files
    dataframes = [pd.read_csv(f) for f in input_files]
    data = pd.concat(dataframes, ignore_index=True)

    # Split data into training and test sets
    train_data, test_data = train_test_split(
        data,
        test_size=0.2,
        random_state=42
    )

    # Create output directories if they don't exist
    os.makedirs(args.training_data, exist_ok=True)
```

```
        os.makedirs(args.test_data, exist_ok=True)

        # Save training data
        train_output_path = os.path.join(args.training_data, 'train_data.csv')
        train_data.to_csv(train_output_path, index=False)

        # Save test data
        test_output_path = os.path.join(args.test_data, 'test_data.csv')
        test_data.to_csv(test_output_path, index=False)

        print(f"Training data saved to {train_output_path}")
        print(f"Test data saved to {test_output_path}")

    if __name__ == '__main__':
        main()
```

Then, you can run the CLI command to create this component so that it can be reused:

```
az ml component create --file prep_data_component.yaml --resource-group
my-resource-group --workspace-name my-workspace
```

Once you create this component, this will show up in the Azure Studio portal as depicted in *Figure 3.2*. It shows a component named **Prep Data** that takes one input and splits it into two outputs with their corresponding types.

Figure 3.2 – Component representation

This YAML defines a component named DataReader that takes an input parameter named dataset_name (as a string). The component then runs a script named download_data.py and passes dataset_name as an argument using ${{inputs.dataset_name}}. The output of the component is a dataset named dataframe.

These are the key features of components, as we understand them so far:

- Components are defined in YAML files, not traditional programming languages.
- They specify inputs, outputs, and the script to run for that specific step.
- Inputs and outputs allow components to connect and share data between them.

While you don't directly code the components themselves, understanding this structure is helpful for building and using pipelines in AML. You'll typically be working with pre-built components and configuring them for your specific needs.

Pipelines

You define a pipeline by connecting these components in the desired order to achieve a goal. The whole process shown in *Figure 3.1* could be a pipeline.

By using reusable components, you can build complex ML pipelines without starting from scratch every time. It's like having a toolbox full of handy tools to build and automate your ML projects! Pipelines have the following benefits:

- **Automation**: Once defined, the pipeline can be triggered automatically on various events, such as new data arrival, code updates, or scheduled intervals.
- **Azure integration**: AML pipelines seamlessly integrate with other Azure services such as Data Storage, Compute resources, and Container Registry for streamlined data access, scalable model training, and consistent environment management throughout the ML lifecycle.
- **Reproducibility**: AML pipelines guarantee consistent results by ensuring the same steps are executed every time the pipeline runs. This is crucial for maintaining model performance and avoiding regressions.
- **Reusability**: Components within pipelines can be reused across different projects, saving time and development effort. You can build modular pipelines by combining reusable components for specific tasks.
- **Scalability**: AML pipelines can handle complex workflows and large datasets efficiently. Scaling compute resources becomes easier as pipelines can leverage distributed training capabilities.
- **Interconnectivity**: Components are connected to define the workflow, ensuring that the output of one component serves as the input for the next. This helps SMEs bring in their knowledge of components and stitch them together to achieve a greater goal.

- **Monitoring and tracking**: AML provides comprehensive monitoring and tracking features for pipelines. You can track the execution status of each step, view logs, and analyze metrics to identify potential issues.

By leveraging ML pipelines in AML, you can streamline your ML development process, ensure consistent and reliable results, and achieve efficient model deployment at scale. The following figure shows what a pipeline looks like from the designer view (AML portal).

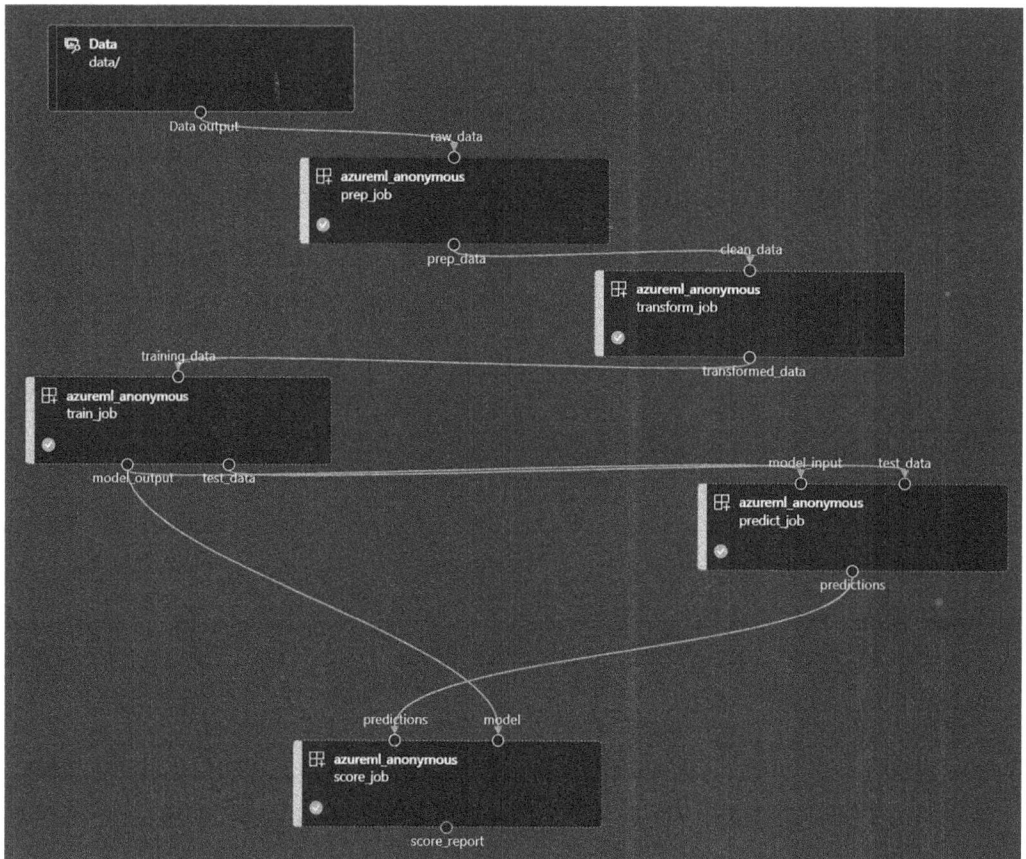

Figure 3.3 – AML pipeline designer view

Let's walk through the pipeline:

- **Data input**: At the top left, there is a component labeled Data that serves as the initial input source. This component holds the raw dataset that will be used for the ML pipeline.

- **Data preparation**: The raw data from the Data component flows into the prep_job component.

The prep_job component is responsible for preparing the data. This could involve cleaning the data, handling missing values, or performing initial preprocessing steps. The output from this step is labeled prep_data.

- **Data transformation**: The prepared data (prep_data) is then passed to the transform_job component.

  The transform_job component further processes the data, possibly including feature engineering, normalization, or other transformations to make it suitable for model training. The output from this step is labeled transformed_data.

- **Model training**: The transformed data is then passed to the train_job component.

  The train_job component is responsible for training the ML model using the prepared dataset. This component outputs the trained model (model_output) and test data (test_data).

- **Model prediction**: The trained model (model_output) and the test data are fed into the predict_job component.

  The predict_job component uses the trained model to make predictions on the test data. The output from this step is the predictions (predictions).

- **Model scoring**: Finally, the predictions and model are passed to the score_job component.

  The score_job component evaluates the model's performance by comparing the predictions with the actual values in the test data. The result of this step is a score report (score_report), which provides metrics on the model's accuracy, precision, recall, and so on.

By utilizing AML pipelines, you can streamline and automate your ML workflows, ensuring reproducibility, scalability, and efficient collaboration across different stages of your ML project. This visual representation in the designer view helps in understanding the flow of data and the sequence of operations, making it easier to manage and optimize the ML pipeline.

For automation, ensuring consistent and reproducible results is paramount. This is where **isolated reproducible environments** come into play. They act as controlled sandboxes where software dependencies and configurations are explicitly defined, guaranteeing a predictable execution environment for your ML projects.

Understanding ML environments

Here are some of the benefits of isolated environments:

- **Reproducibility – consistent software dependencies**: Imagine training a fantastic model, but when you deploy it to production, something goes wrong! Often, the culprit is inconsistent software dependencies. Different environments (development machine, training cluster, production server) might have different versions of libraries or packages. This inconsistency can lead to unexpected behavior and hinder reproducibility.

  Isolated environments to the rescue: By using isolated environments, you define the exact versions of all software dependencies (libraries, frameworks) needed for your project. This ensures that the same environment is used for training, testing, and deployment, leading to consistent and reproducible results.

  Example: Let's say your model relies on a specific version of scikit-learn (for example, `scikit-learn==1.1.2`). An isolated environment would ensure that this exact version is used in all stages of your pipeline, from development to deployment.

- **Experimentation – isolating different model versions**: During ML development, you often experiment with different model architectures or hyperparameter configurations. Isolated environments are instrumental in managing these experiments effectively.

  Isolating experiments: Each experiment can have its own isolated environment, ensuring that different model versions don't interfere with each other or corrupt dependencies. This allows for clean comparisons and facilitates the selection of the best-performing model.

  Example: You might be trying two different **neural network** (**NN**) architectures for your image classification task. Each architecture can have its own isolated environment with the specific libraries and configurations needed for training and evaluation.

- **AML environments**: AML offers a robust environment management system that simplifies defining and utilizing isolated environments for your ML projects. It works by specifying environments with YAML. AML environments are defined using YAML files. These files specify the exact versions of all software dependencies needed for your project and become a blueprint for creating consistent environments across your development and deployment stages.

The following is an example YAML for an environment:

```
name: my_aml_environment
channels:
  - conda-forge
dependencies:
  - python=3.8
  - scikit-learn==1.1.2
  - pandas==1.4.2
```

- **Creating isolated compute clusters**: AML allows you to create isolated compute clusters with preconfigured environments. This ensures that all compute resources within the cluster have the same software dependencies, guaranteeing consistent training and deployment across machines.

By leveraging isolated environments with AML, you gain several advantages:

- **Reproducible results**: Consistent software dependencies across your ML lifecycle
- **Efficient experimentation**: Easy isolation and comparison of different model versions
- **Streamlined development**: Simplified environment management with YAML configurations

Overall, isolated environments are a cornerstone of robust ML development. By ensuring consistent software dependencies and facilitating experimentation, they empower you to build reliable and reproducible models.

To further enhance your understanding of managing dependencies, it's important to delve into techniques for tracking and reproducing software dependencies in projects.

Tracking and reproducing software dependencies in projects

Dependency management in ML involves specifying and controlling external libraries and packages that your code relies on to ensure consistency, reproducibility, and smooth collaboration across different environments. This process helps avoid conflicts and unexpected behavior caused by mismatched or missing dependencies.

Next, we will delve into tools for managing these dependencies and the importance of building reproducible environments.

Python offers two primary tools for managing dependencies:

- `conda`: Often used for scientific computing, `conda` manages environments and packages within a virtual environment. This allows you to isolate project dependencies from your system-wide Python installation.
- `pip`: The default package installer for Python, `pip` works best for installing individual packages within an existing environment.

Imagine building a complex ML model, but when a colleague tries to run it, they encounter errors due to missing or outdated dependencies. This is where the following files come in handy; they contain a list of the exact Python packages to be installed for running the code:

- `requirements.txt` (`pip`): This file lists all the necessary packages and their specific versions required for your project. Anyone with Python and `pip` can install these dependencies and replicate your environment.
- `conda.yaml` (`conda`): Similar to `requirements.txt`, this file specifies the packages and their versions needed for your `conda` environment. This allows for recreating the entire environment with all its dependencies.

By leveraging dependency management tools and defining your dependencies in a requirements file, you gain several advantages:

- **Reproducible results**: Specifying exact versions ensures everyone uses the same code and libraries, leading to consistent and reproducible model behavior.
- **Simplified collaboration**: Sharing your code along with a requirements file allows colleagues to easily set up their environment and run your code without encountering dependency issues.
- **Project sharing**: Sharing projects with requirements files makes it easier for others to understand the dependencies needed and replicate your environment.
- **Version control**: You can version control your requirements file alongside your code, ensuring everyone uses the same set of dependencies throughout the project lifecycle.
- **Reduced errors**: By explicitly managing dependencies, you minimize the risk of errors caused by missing or incompatible libraries.

Dependency management is crucial for building robust ML projects. Tools such as `conda` and `pip`, along with defining dependencies in a requirements file, help create consistent environments, streamline collaboration, and ensure reproducible results. Just as code, configurations, pipelines, and components discussed earlier in this chapter are tracked in a Git repository, environments are also considered part of the code and configuration.

In the following section, we will explore how this Git-centric approach supports automating MLOps steps using Git and GitHub Actions. A basic example of this is shown in *Figure 3.4*, which demonstrates how GitHub Actions can be used to automate key stages of your AML pipeline:

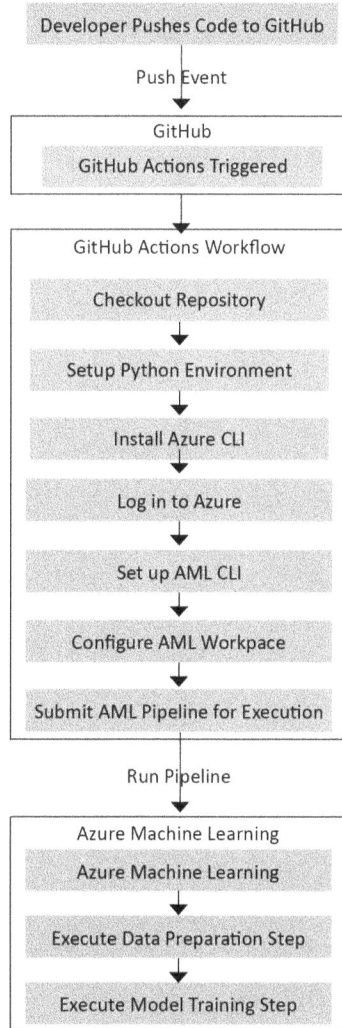

Figure 3.4 – Triggering ML pipeline using GitHub

You can customize these workflows to fit your specific needs and integrate them seamlessly with your code version control using Git. By leveraging Git and GitHub Actions, you can streamline your ML development process, ensure consistent and reproducible workflows, and maintain control over your code base throughout the deployment lifecycle. In the following section, let's run through a hands-on exercise to explore this process to have a good working grasp.

Hands-on example — Building an ML pipeline with AML CLI, Git, and GitHub Actions

This example demonstrates building a simple ML pipeline for data download and training a basic classification model using the AML CLI, Git, and GitHub Actions.

Here are the prerequisites:

- Azure subscription with an AML workspace
- Azure CLI installed and configured
- Basic understanding of Python and Git
- A GitHub account

Here is the scenario:

We'll create a pipeline that downloads a public dataset (Iris flower classification) and trains a simple Logistic Regression model. The pipeline will be triggered automatically upon code changes in a Git repository hosted on GitHub.

Here are the steps:

1. **Create an AML component (YAML):** Create a file named download_data.yaml with the following content:

```
name: DownloadData
inputs:
    url: string
    output_path: string
outputs:
    dataframe: Dataset
run_step:
    script_name: download_data.py
    arguments:
        --url: ${{inputs.url}}
        --output_path: ${{inputs.output_path}}
```

This YAML file defines a component named DownloadData that takes a URL (dataset location) and output path as inputs and outputs a loaded dataset (DataFrame).

2. **Write the download script (Python)**: Create a file named download_data.py with the following content:

```python
import pandas as pd

def main():
    url = "https://archive.ics.uci.edu/ml/machine-learning-
databases/iris/iris.data"
    output_path = "data/iris.csv"

    data = pd.read_csv(url)
    data.to_csv(output_path, index=False)

    print(f"Data downloaded and saved to: {output_path}")

if __name__ == "__main__":
    main()
```

This Python script downloads the Iris dataset from the specified URL and saves it as a CSV file.

3. **Define a pipeline (YAML)**: Create a file named train_pipeline.yaml with the following content:

```yaml
description: Train a Logistic Regression model on Iris dataset

steps:
    - name: Download data
      reference: downloads/download_data.yaml
      arguments:
          url: "https://archive.ics.uci.edu/ml/machine-
learning-          databases/iris/iris.data"
          output_path: "data/iris.csv"
    - name: Train model
      script_mode: PythonScript
      source_directory: train_script
      script_arguments: ["data/iris.csv"]
```

This defines a pipeline with two steps:

- The first step references the `DownloadData` component we created
- The second step trains the model using a Python script located in the `train_script` directory (we'll create this script next)

4. **Create a training script (Python)**: Create a directory named `train_script` and a file named `train_model.py` within it, with the following content:

```python
import pandas as pd
from sklearn.model_selection import train_test_split
from sklearn.linear_model import LogisticRegression

def main(data_path):
    data = pd.read_csv(data_path)

    X = data.drop("target", axis=1)
    y = data["target"]

    X_train, X_test, y_train, y_test = train_test_split(
        X, y, test_size=0.2
    )

    model = LogisticRegression()
    model.fit(X_train, y_train)

    # Save the model
    # (you can implement model registration with Azure ML here)
    # ...

    print("Model training complete!")

if __name__ == "__main__":
    import sys
    data_path = sys.argv[1]
    main(data_path)
```

This script loads the downloaded data, splits it into training and testing sets, trains a Logistic Regression model, and saves it (model registration with AML can be integrated here).

5. **Initialize a Git repository**:

    1. Open a terminal and navigate to your project directory.

    2. Initialize a Git repository using git init.

    3. Add all your files (download_data.yaml, download_data.py, train_pipeline.
        yaml, train_script/train_model.py).

6. **Create a GitHub repository**: Go to GitHub and create a new repository for your project.

7. **Push code to GitHub**: Add the initialized Git repository as a remote to your local repository:

```
git remote add origin
git@github.com:<username>/<repository_name>.git
```

8. Replace <username> with your GitHub username and <repository_name> with the name
    you chose for your repository.

9. Commit your changes and push them to the remote repository:

```
git add .
git commit -m "Initial commit"
git push origin main
```

10. Create a GitHub Actions workflow:

    1. Go to your GitHub repository settings and navigate to the **Actions** tab.

    2. Click on **New workflow** and choose **Set up a workflow yourself**.

    3. Create a new YAML file named github/workflows/aml_pipeline.yml with the
        following content:

```yaml
name: Train ML Pipeline

on:
  push:  # Trigger on code push to any branch

jobs:
  train_and_deploy:
    runs-on: ubuntu-latest
    steps:
      -name:  Checkout repo
      - uses: actions/checkout@
v2  # Checkout code from repository
```

```
  # Login to Azure (replace with your credentials)
- name: Login to Azure
  uses: Azure/login@v2
  with:
    clientId: ${{ secrets.AZURE_CLIENT_ID }}
    clientSecret: ${{ secrets.AZURE_CLIENT_SECRET }}
    tenantId: ${{ secrets.AZURE_TENANT_ID }}
- name: Install Azure CLI
  uses: Azure/setup-cli@v2
- name: Install Azure ML  CLI
  run: |
    az extension add -n ml
- name: Run Azure ML  pipeline
  run: |
    az ml workspace list
    # Assuming your workspace name is "myamlworkspace"
    # and resource group is "myresourcegroup"
    az ml job create -n train_pipeline \
        -f train_pipeline.yaml \
        -w myamlworkspace \
        -g myresourcegroup

  # Additional steps for model registration with
Azure ML        # can be added here
```

Let's now look at an explanation of the workflow:

- This workflow is triggered whenever there's a push to any branch in your repository
- The workflow uses pre-built actions for the following:

  - Checking out code from the repository
  - Logging in to Azure using secrets stored in GitHub (replace placeholders with your credentials)
  - Optionally installing Azure CLI if not pre-installed

- The workflow runs Azure CLI commands to do the following:

  - List available AML workspaces (for verification)

- Create an ML pipeline using the `train_pipeline.yaml` file you defined earlier (replace placeholders with your actual workspace name and resource group name)

To execute this GitHub pipeline action, we will first configure Azure credentials as secrets. Here's how:

1. Go to your GitHub repository settings | **Secrets** | **Actions**.
2. Create three new secrets:

   - `AZURE_CLIENT_ID`: Your Azure service principal client ID
   - `AZURE_CLIENT_SECRET`: Your Azure service principal client secret
   - `AZURE_TENANT_ID`: Your Azure tenant ID

Next, we will push changes and observe the pipeline run by following these steps:

1. Push your changes to the GitHub repository using `git push origin main`.
2. Navigate to the **Actions** tab in your GitHub repository. You should see a new workflow run triggered by your recent push.
3. If successful, the workflow log will show the pipeline creation process using Azure CLI commands.

> Note
>
> This is a basic example to showcase the integration between Git, GitHub Actions, and the AML CLI for triggering pipeline execution. You might need to adjust the workflow depending on your specific environment and desired functionalities. More examples of MLOps pipelines can be found in the AML sample notebook repository (`https://github.com/Azure/MachineLearningNotebooks/tree/master/how-to-use-azureml/machine-learning-pipelines/intro-to-pipelines`).

By implementing this workflow, you've automated the pipeline execution process. Whenever you make changes to your code (data download script, training script, or pipeline definition), the pipeline will automatically be recreated and will potentially retrain the model based on the latest code. This setup promotes a more streamlined and automated development workflow for your ML projects.

Summary

This chapter emphasized the significance of automation and environment management for building robust and reusable ML workflows. By leveraging ML pipelines, Git, GitHub Actions, and AML environments, you can effectively streamline ML development and ensure consistent, repeatable results across your projects. We learned how to define repeatable and reusable steps for data preparation and training, ensuring consistency and efficiency. We also delved into the importance of managing ML environments to maintain reproducibility and track dependencies. Now, as we move forward, it's time to focus on another crucial aspect of MLOps: model management. Just as a well-built house requires a strong foundation, a successful ML project needs a robust model management strategy. In *Chapter 4*, we will explore the core practices of model management, including registration and packaging.

Join the CloudPro Newsletter with 44000+ Subscribers

Want to know what's happening in cloud computing, DevOps, IT administration, networking, and more? Scan the QR code to subscribe to **CloudPro**, our weekly newsletter for 44,000+ tech professionals who want to stay informed and ahead of the curve.

https://packt.link/cloudpro

4

Model Management (Registration and Packaging)

In the previous chapter, we explored techniques for automating machine learning pipelines using the AML CLI. These pipelines often generate a final artifact: the trained machine learning model. This model represents the culmination of your project's efforts, encapsulating the knowledge and insights gleaned from your data. As such, it's critical to effectively manage the model throughout its lifecycle to ensure its reliability, maintainability, and successful deployment.

This chapter digs into the world of model management within Azure Machine Learning, focusing on the core concept of model registration. We'll explore how to leverage the AML CLI (v2) to seamlessly integrate model registration into your automated MLOps workflows.

By the end of this chapter, you will understand how to effectively manage machine learning models in AML, including how to register models with appropriate metadata, choose the right model formats, and utilize datastores for storage. You'll also gain hands-on experience integrating model registration into automated pipelines using the AML CLI v2—an essential step toward building robust and reproducible MLOps workflows.

This chapter will cover the following topics:

- Model metadata
- Model registration
- Model format
- Datastores
- Registering models in action

Model metadata

Metadata refers to the data that provides information about other data. In the context of machine learning, metadata includes details about datasets, models, experiments, and the environment in which the model was trained and deployed.

Machine learning models are not static entities. They evolve and change over time, often requiring retraining, versioning, and careful tracking. Effective metadata management practices are essential for several reasons:

- **Reproducibility:** The ability to recreate a specific model version at any point in time is crucial for debugging issues, comparing performance across different training runs, or retraining with new data. Metadata management ensures that all aspects of the model's lifecycle are documented and can be reproduced.

- **Governance and control:** Metadata management allows you to associate tags, descriptions, and other relevant information with your models. This facilitates easy identification and control, ensuring responsible model usage and regulatory compliance.

- **Scalability and efficiency:** By managing metadata in a central repository, you can streamline deployment processes. Metadata helps in tracking all versions of your model, making them readily available for deployment to various environments, thus simplifying scaling and managing multiple deployments.

- **Version control and rollback:** Robust metadata management allows for tracking different iterations of your model. If a deployed model encounters issues, you can quickly revert to a previous, well-performing version, minimizing downtime and maintaining service continuity.

Metadata management using Azure Machine Learning (AML)

Effective machine learning demands meticulous record-keeping of the metadata. AML provides robust tools to manage and leverage metadata, ensuring transparency, reproducibility, and efficiency in your ML lifecycle. Here's how AML empowers you to capture, track, and utilize essential metadata for informed decision-making:

- **Capture lineage:** AML tracks various aspects of your ML projects using metadata. This includes data used for training, the code that trained the model, and the compute resources used. This lineage information helps us understand how a model arrived at its predictions.

- **Version control integration:** AML integrates with Git, allowing you to track which code repository, branch, and commit were used to train a specific model version.

- **Data tracking**: AML datasets help you manage, profile, and version your data. This ensures data quality and traceability throughout the ML lifecycle.

- **Model interpretability**: AML allows you to understand how models make predictions. This can aid in debugging, improving fairness, and meeting regulatory requirements.

- **Model registry**: This is the core of metadata management. The model registry acts as a central repository to store and track registered models. It captures metadata associated with each model version, including the following:

    - Training experiment details

    - Deployment information (where it's deployed)

    - Model performance metrics

    - User-defined tags for searchability

With a comprehensive understanding of your ML project's metadata in place, the next critical step is to effectively manage and version your trained models. Model registration serves as the cornerstone of this process, providing a structured approach to store, track, and deploy your models.

Model registration

Model registration refers to the process of uploading your trained model and its associated metadata to the Azure Machine Learning workspace. This creates a managed copy of your model within the service, allowing for centralized storage, version control, and simplified access to deployment tools.

The Azure Machine Learning CLI (v2) provides a powerful tool for registering models with a single, user-friendly command: `az ml model create`. This command streamlines the registration process, allowing you to specify the following:

- **Model name:** This is a unique identifier for your model within the workspace.

- **Model path:** This is the location of your trained model files (local storage, Azure Blob Storage, etc.).

- **Model version:** Explicitly define the version of your model for better tracking. This is optional because, in the absence of it, the next available version will be created automatically.

- **Model format:** This is optional because the default is *custom*.

- **Metadata:** Attach additional information such as descriptions, tags, or custom properties to enrich your model record. This is optional because this is for information only, not directly impacting any operation.

While model registration within the workspace offers a convenient way to manage models associated with specific projects, Azure Machine Learning also offers a dedicated model registry service. This service acts as a central hub for storing and managing models across your entire Azure Machine Learning environment, offering additional benefits over workspace-based registration, such as the following:

- **Global accessibility**: Models registered in the central registry are readily available for deployment across all your projects and workspaces within the same Azure subscription.

- **Enhanced governance**: The model registry provides more granular access control options, allowing you to define permissions for model usage and deployment at a global level.

- **Integration with deployment tools**: The model registry seamlessly integrates with various Azure Machine Learning deployment tools, simplifying the process of deploying registered models to production environments.

While this section focuses on workspace-based model registration using the AML CLI v2, the concepts translate directly to the model registry service. We will explore the model registry and its advanced functionalities in the following section.

AML registry

Let's learn about the **AML registry**. In *Chapter 2*, we discussed the concept of a workspace, which is a central hub that contains all compute resources and configurations needed for ML projects. A registry, however, is a specialized container specifically designed to store and manage assets.

Workspaces in Azure Machine Learning are usually scoped to specific teams or projects within an organization. They provide a dedicated environment where data scientists can experiment, train models, and deploy applications. These workspaces are mainly for internal collaboration and are not typically designed for sharing assets beyond the team.

To facilitate sharing across teams and workspaces, Azure Machine Learning offers the AML registry. This registry serves as a central repository for organization-wide asset management, storing models, datasets, environments, and endpoints. It provides a centralized location ideal for sharing reusable components across different teams and projects.

Let's understand the role of the AML registry using a simple example workflow as follows: A data science team develops a sophisticated image classification model. After rigorous testing and validation, they decide to share the model with other teams within the organization. To achieve this, they register the model in the Azure Machine Learning registry. Other teams can then access and utilize the registered model for their own applications, without the need to replicate the development process.

By leveraging the registry, organizations can foster knowledge sharing, promote code reuse, and accelerate ML development across different teams.

Here's an example of how to create a registry using the CLI:

1. First, we will create a .yml file (`registry.yml`) to contain the details of the registry (e.g., which region it will be in):

   ```
   name: mygreat_registry
   location: eastus
   description: "My Azure ML Registry"
   tags:
   "Awesome : Great"
   "ML is" : "Fun"
   ```

2. To create the registry using the CLI, run the following command:

   ```
   az ml registry create --resource-group my-resource-group --file registry.yml
   ```

   Once this registry is created, it can hold different assets (models, environments, components, data). This is what a registry would look like from the AML portal:

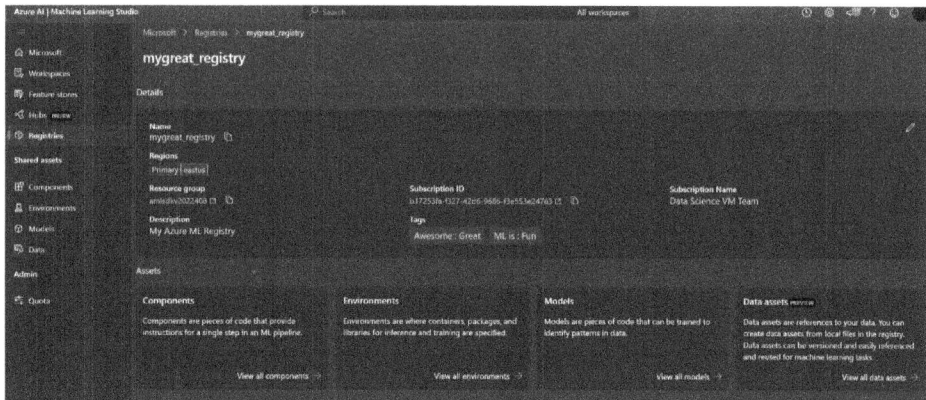

Figure 4.1 – AML registry

With the understanding of an AML registry, we now have the option to register this model to a workspace or to a registry. But before showing how to register a model, we need to clarify a couple of related concepts – **model format** and **datastore**.

Let's go through each one of them before showing some examples of how to register a model with different options.

Model format

Think of a model format as a standardized blueprint for packaging and preserving a machine learning model. Just as different products require specific packaging for transportation and storage, models need a consistent format for efficient management and deployment.

Standardizing the model format (MLflow)

MLflow is an open source platform that aims to standardize the packaging of machine learning models. Here's what makes it so valuable:

- **Framework agnostic**: MLflow defines a universal format for packaging models, regardless of the framework used for training (e.g., scikit-learn, TensorFlow, PyTorch). This ensures consistency and interoperability when registering models in tools such as Azure Machine Learning.
- **Comprehensive packaging**: The MLflow format goes beyond just the model itself. It also encapsulates the model's dependencies (required libraries and environments) and additional artifacts such as input data schemas or example data. This comprehensive packaging approach ensures your model can be readily reproduced and deployed across different environments without worrying about missing components.
- **Benefits for MLflow**: By leveraging MLflow, you establish a standardized way to store, track, and deploy your machine learning models. This simplifies tasks such as version control, model lineage tracking, and integration with deployment tools within your MLOps workflows.

Here's an analogy: Imagine building a house (your model). MLflow provides a standardized blueprint (packaging format) that captures not just the house structure (model itself) but also the materials used (dependencies) and the blueprints for any additional features (artifacts). This comprehensive approach makes it easier to rebuild the house (reproduce the model) or move it to a different location (deploy the model) with minimal effort.

Many popular ML frameworks have built-in functionalities to save models in the MLflow format. By leveraging these functionalities within your training scripts, you can seamlessly integrate your models with Azure Machine Learning for registration and deployment.

Custom model formats

While MLflow offers a powerful standardized approach for model packaging, there might be scenarios where your project demands a custom model format. Here's why custom formats might be necessary:

- **Unique frameworks**: If you're venturing beyond popular frameworks and utilizing a less common machine learning framework for training, that framework might not have built-in support for saving models in the MLflow format. In such cases, you might need to define a custom format specific to the framework you're using.

- **Specialized requirements**: Certain models might have intricate dependencies or additional artifacts that go beyond what MLflow typically captures. For example, your model might require custom hardware accelerators or specific software libraries that aren't commonly used. A custom format allows you to tailor the packaging to encompass these unique needs.

Here's an analogy: Imagine you're building a one-of-a-kind robot (your model) with specialized components. MLflow provides a standardized blueprint for robots with common functionalities. However, your robot might require unique parts or functionalities that aren't captured in the standard blueprint. A custom format allows you to define a specific blueprint that accommodates the unique aspects of your robot (model).

Challenges and considerations

While custom formats offer flexibility, they come with additional considerations:

- **Increased complexity**: Registering custom models requires additional configuration in Azure Machine Learning to define how the model should be handled (loading, scoring, deployment). This can add complexity to the registration process compared to using the standardized MLflow format.

- **Limited interoperability**: Custom formats might not be readily compatible with other tools or platforms outside of Azure Machine Learning. This can hinder the reusability and sharing of your models.

Given these challenges, it becomes important to carefully evaluate which model format best fits your workflow and long-term operational goals.

Choosing the right format

In most cases, leveraging the MLflow format is the recommended approach due to its standardization and ease of use. However, if you have specific requirements that necessitate a custom format, Azure Machine Learning offers the flexibility to accommodate those needs. In the *Registering models in action* section, we will look into the practicalities of model registration using the Azure Machine Learning CLI v2, considering both MLflow and custom formats.

Now let's assume we got a model from a job output, and we want to register it to the workspace so that it can be shared and used in later stages.

Before registering a model, let's quickly understand the storage that holds all the model files and other artifacts for MLOps.

Datastores

Datastores play a critical role in managing the various artifacts associated with your machine learning projects. Think of them as well-organized libraries where you store all the building blocks for your projects. Datastores provide a centralized location to house essential assets such as the following:

- **Training scripts**: This is the code used to train your models.
- **Datasets**: This is the data used to train and evaluate your models.
- **Model outputs**: These are the trained models themselves, often consisting of multiple files (weights, configurations, etc.).
- **Other artifacts**: Depending on your project needs, datastores can also accommodate additional artifacts such as experiment logs, output data from intermediate pipeline steps, or even pre-processed datasets.

AML datastores provide a secure way to link your Azure Storage services to your workspace, allowing you to access storage without embedding connection details directly in your scripts. The connection secrets, such as authentication credentials for the storage service, are securely stored in your workspace's key vault.

Upon creating a workspace, an Azure Storage account is automatically generated as an associated resource. Within this account, a blob container is created, and its connection details are saved as a datastore named `workspaceblobstore`. This datastore acts as the default storage for the workspace, housing workspace artifacts, machine learning job logs, and outputs.

To put theory into practice, let's explore how to register a model obtained from a completed job output.

Registering models in action

By registering a model, you make it a managed entity within your workspace, enabling sharing and utilization in subsequent stages of your MLOps workflow. The AML CLI empowers you to seamlessly register models stored in various locations and formats, such as the following:

- **Local storage**: If your model files reside on your local machine, you can register them using the `az ml model create` command, specifying the path to the model directory.

- **Job output (datastore)**: Many Azure Machine Learning pipelines generate models as outputs and store them within a designated datastore (e.g., Azure Blob Storage). The `az ml model create` command can directly reference the model **Uniform Resource Identifier (URI)** within the datastore for registration.

When registering a model from a job output, you need to know the datastore name and the relative path to the model files within that datastore. This information is typically available in the job output logs or within the pipeline configuration itself.

Examples of model registration with the AML CLI

Let us look at a couple of examples:

- **Registering a model from local storage**: If the model is already available in your local storage, it can be directly uploaded during model registration by specifying the path.

- **Registering a model from job output**: If your model data originates from a job output, you have two options for specifying the model path, accommodating a wide range of locations. If you didn't register your model directly within the training script using MLflow, you can use this method to establish a lineage between the registered model and the job it was trained from. Some of the recognized formats can be seen in the following figure:

Location	Syntax
Local computer	`` `<model-folder>/<model-filename>` ``
Azure Machine Learning datastore	`` `azureml://datastores/<datastore-name>/paths/<path_on_datastore>` ``
Azure Machine Learning job	`` `azureml://jobs/<job-name>/outputs/<output-name>/paths/<path-to-model-relative-to-output>` ``
MLflow job	`` `runs:/<run-id>/<path-to-model-relative-to-root-of-artifact-location>` ``
Model asset in a Machine Learning workspace	`` `azureml:<model-name>:<version>` ``
Model asset in a Machine Learning registry	`` `azureml://registries/<registry-name>/models/<model-name>/versions/<version>` ``

Figure 4.2 – Model registration path support

(source: https://learn.microsoft.com/en-us/azure/machine-learning/how-to-manage-models?view=azureml-api-2&tabs=cli#supported-paths)

You can run this CLI command to register the model (e.g., from an MLflow job):

```
az ml model create --name my-registered-model --version 1 --path runs:/
my_run_0000000000/model/ --type mlflow_model
```

Once a model is registered, it will have all the metadata. The following is an example of model metadata as shown in the AML portal:

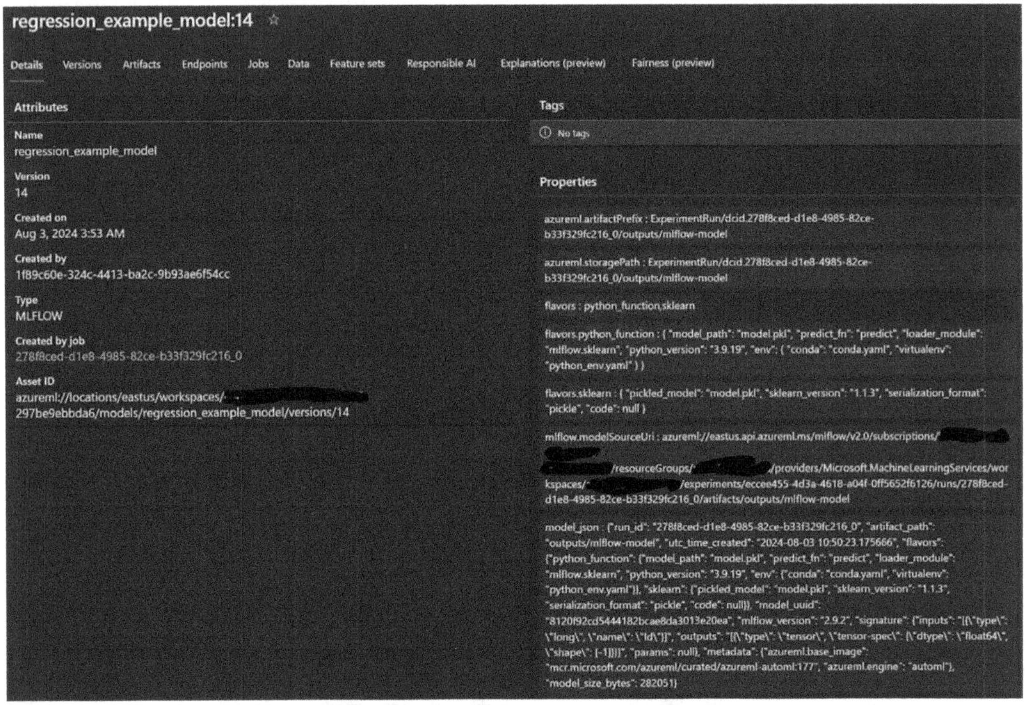

Figure 4.3 – Registered model with metadata

Notice the rich metadata in *Figure 4.3*, along with the **Created by job** section. You can go back to the training job that was responsible for the registration of this model and see all the related information. Along with that, it has the version information, which shows the different versions that are registered (the screenshot shows version **14**).

The primary goal of registering a model is to prepare it for the next stage of the MLOps lifecycle: using the model for a business use case. To achieve this, the model must be deployed within a serving mechanism. This mechanism accepts input, performs necessary transformations, feeds the data to the model, obtains the output (prediction/inferencing), and returns it to the requester.

We'll discuss these concepts and their various implementations in detail in *Chapter 5*. For now, let's maintain a high-level overview of this serving process.

The serving process can be complex and highly dynamic. For instance, during deployment, a model may require hundreds of packages to be installed on the serving platform. These packages could originate from private feeds or highly secure environments, each with unique network requirements. Such constraints can cause installation failures. To mitigate these issues, model packaging becomes a crucial step.

Model packaging

Model packaging involves preparing a model along with all its dependencies, configurations, and necessary artifacts so that it can be easily deployed to the target serving infrastructure. This includes the following:

- **Serialization**: This entails converting the model into a format that can be easily stored and transferred (e.g., saving a TensorFlow model as an .h5 file).

- **Dependency management**: This refers to including all libraries and packages the model depends on, ensuring they are available and compatible with the deployment environment.

- **Configuration files**: This entails providing configuration files (e.g., YAML, JSON) that specify how the model should be loaded and run.

- **Containerization**: This refers to using container technologies such as Docker to encapsulate the model and its dependencies, ensuring consistency across different environments.

- **Versioning**: This involves keeping track of different versions of the model to manage updates and rollbacks effectively.

By addressing these aspects, model packaging aims to reduce deployment failures, streamline private networking configurations, and manage packages in secure environments, ultimately making the deployment process more reliable and efficient.

Commands for model packaging

In the AML CLI, there is a separate command group for the model package – it is az ml model package.

As an example, let's consider that the following is a .yml file that will be used by the CLI to create a package for a model:

```
package.yml

target_environment: model-packaged-environment
base_environment:
    type: environment_asset
```

```
    source: azureml:AzureML-ACPT-pytorch-1.11-py38-cuda11.3-gpu:1
inferencing_server:
    type: azureml_online
    code_configuration:
        code: src
        scoring_script: score.py
model_configuration:
    mode: download
inputs:
    labels:
        path: azureml:labels-data:1
        type: uri_folder
        mode: copy
```

The following CLI command can be used to create a model package named `model-packaged-environment`:

```
az ml model package --name my-model --version my-version  --file package.
yml
```

Properties of a package operation

The base environment, inferencing server, model, and other inputs are the important properties of a package operation that determine the output environment that gets generated. Let's learn more about these:

- **Base environment**: This is the base image used to construct the package. Any required dependency that cannot be provided as input should be part of the environment resource. This mainly includes pip and conda packages, or any serving software if this is a custom package.

  Purpose: Its purpose includes any required dependencies that cannot be provided as inputs, such as pip and conda packages or custom serving software.

  Example: In the YAML file, the base environment is defined as `azureml:AzureML-ACPT-pytorch-1.11-py38-cuda11.3-gpu:1`.

- **Inferencing server**: This is the server used for serving the model.

  Purpose: It specifies the inferencing server type, which can be AzureMLOnline (AML's standard inferencing solution), AzureMLBatch, Triton, or Custom. For custom servers, the server is assumed to already be present in the provided environment.

Example: The inferencing server is defined as `azureml_online`, with the code and scoring script specified.

- **Model:** This is the reference to the model that needs to be included in the package.

  Purpose: It ensures that the model is available in the resulting environment, either by copying or downloading.

  Example: The model configuration is set to `download`.

- **Inputs:** These are any additional data that needs to be included in the package.

  Purpose: It allows for the inclusion of custom data, such as labels, that might be required during inferencing.

  Example: Inputs include `labels-data` specified as a URI folder to be copied.

Creating a package

To create a package, use the following CLI command:

```
az ml model package --name regression_example_model --version 14 -f
package.yml
```

Once the packaging service gets this request it does quite a bit of heavy lifting behind the scenes. The details are as follows:

1. **Get the model name:** Retrieve the model named `my_model`.
2. **Base environment setup:** Start with the initial base environment specified in the `base_environment` section.
3. **Install packages:** Install all necessary Python packages in the base environment. These Python packages are typically part of the `conda.yml` file.
4. **Download the model:** Ensure the model is downloaded in the current path and available in the environment.
5. **Copy scoring script:** Copy the required scoring script from the specified path.
6. **Include additional data:** Copy any other requirements, such as custom data, that might be needed during inferencing.
7. **Prepare the environment:** Combine all components to create a ready-to-use environment, saved as `model-packaged-environment`.

At the end of this process, the resulting package (which is an environment) is fully prepared and ready for deployment, ensuring all dependencies and configurations are correctly set up, as shown in *Figure 4.4*.

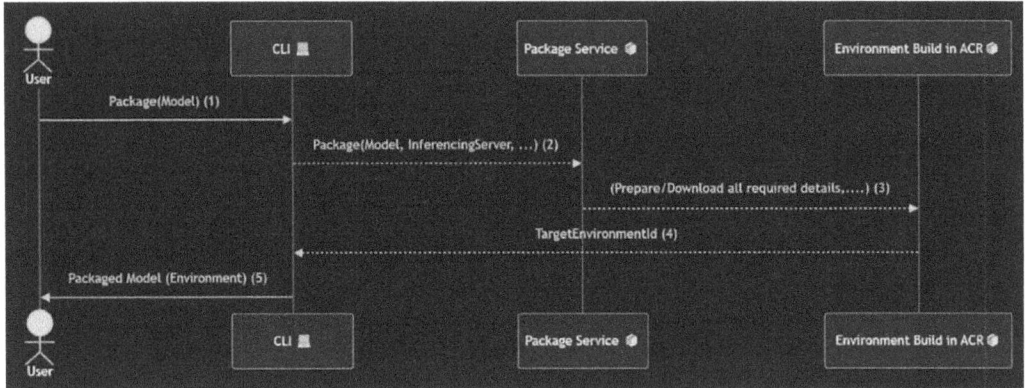

Figure 4.4 – Package operation overview

Once a model package operation is in progress, you can see the status in the AML portal – **Running** is shown in *Figure 4.5*:

Figure 4.5 – Model package look and feel

Once the operation ends, the package (environment) is ready.

Ensuring that your model, which is the cornerstone of machine learning, is properly registered and stored is crucial for seamless integration into later stages of ML pipelines. This section has demonstrated how to achieve this foundational process, setting the stage for efficient and reliable MLOps workflows.

Summary

This chapter introduced the critical concept of model management within AML. We explored how effective management practices ensure the reliability, reproducibility, governance, maintainability, and successful deployment of your machine learning models.

With these commands and concepts, you should now be able to build your own pipeline step/component that will take a model from your pipeline job and register/package it. This is a nice addition to the E2E pipeline you already have from *Chapter 3*, where it generated a model, and now, we have added to it.

The chapter then explained how uploading your trained model and its metadata to the Azure Machine Learning workspace or the dedicated model registry is the cornerstone of model management. Next, we saw how standardized model formats such as MLflow ensure interoperability and simplify deployment. Custom formats, while offering flexibility, introduce complexity.

We explored the `az ml model create` command for registering models from local storage or job outputs, along with the different format options (MLflow and custom).

The chapter also provided a high-level introduction to model packaging, a crucial step for preparing models for deployment. We discussed the role of serialization, dependency management, configuration files, containerization, and versioning in this process.

In the next chapter, we'll delve deeper into model deployment strategies within Azure Machine Learning, exploring various deployment options and best practices for serving your models in production environments.

5

Model Deployment: Batch Scoring and Real-Time Web Services

In *Chapter 4*, we explored the crucial steps of model registration and packaging, ensuring that your trained models are well-documented, versioned, and ready for deployment. With your models securely registered and their metadata meticulously tracked, the next logical step in the MLOps lifecycle is to serve these models in a production environment. This chapter will guide you through the process of model serving or deployment, enabling your models to deliver real-time predictions and drive business value.

Having successfully registered and packaged your ML models, you now possess well-managed and version-controlled artifacts ready for deployment. The journey from model creation to deployment is akin to preparing a product for market release; all the meticulous preparations culminate in a model that is ready to be served to end users or integrated into applications. This chapter delves into the intricacies of model serving within **Azure Machine Learning** (AML), exploring various deployment strategies and best practices to ensure your models are robust, scalable, and reliable in production environments.

Before diving into deployment strategies, it's important to distinguish between model **packaging** and **deployment**. Model packaging, covered in *Chapter 4*, involves preparing your model with its environment dependencies and scoring logic into a deployable artifact. Deployment (also referred to as **serving** throughout this chapter) is the actual process of making that packaged model available to receive and respond to prediction requests in a production environment.

This session will explore key aspects of deploying ML models using AML. We will begin by examining the various model deployment options available, such as real-time inference and batch scoring, to help you choose the most suitable approach for your use case.

Next, we'll delve into setting up and optimizing the underlying infrastructure to ensure your models perform efficiently and scale as needed. Finally, we will discuss how to integrate deployment into your automation pipelines, enabling a smooth and reliable transition from development to production environments.

We will be covering the following main topics:

- Model deployment options
- Online inferencing
- Batch inferencing

By the end of this chapter, you will have a comprehensive understanding of how to effectively serve your ML models, enabling them to deliver actionable insights and drive decision-making in real-world applications. Let's embark on this next phase of the MLOps journey, transforming your registered models into powerful, deployed solutions.

Model deployment options

There are a variety of deployment options tailored to different use cases and performance requirements. The two primary methods for deploying models are **real-time inference** and **batch scoring**. Understanding these methods and their appropriate applications will enable you to choose the best deployment strategy for your specific needs.

Real-time inference

Real-time inference, also known as **online inference**, involves deploying models in a manner that allows them to respond to prediction requests immediately. This method is ideal for scenarios where timely predictions are crucial, such as fraud detection, recommendation systems, or real-time decision-making applications.

Some key characteristics of this method are as follows:

- **Low latency**: Real-time inference is designed to provide predictions with minimal delay, often within milliseconds.
- **Scalability**: It's capable of handling fluctuating loads, ensuring consistent performance even during peak times.

- **Availability**: It's typically deployed in high-availability configurations to ensure continuous service.

With a solid understanding of real-time inference and its critical characteristics, you're now ready to explore how to implement this deployment strategy using AML. In the following section, we'll walk through how AML supports real-time endpoints, enabling you to serve predictions reliably and at scale.

Implementation in AML

Real-time inference can be implemented in AML in the following ways:

- **Kubernetes service (K8s)**: It's a good practice to deploy models on an open source Kubernetes cluster for high scalability and availability. The Kubernetes service allows you to handle large numbers of concurrent requests and scale out as needed. It is ideal for teams needing fine-grained control over deployment infrastructure.

- **Managed online endpoints**: AML offers managed endpoints that abstract away the complexity of infrastructure management, providing an easy way to deploy and scale models with built-in monitoring and logging. It is well-suited for teams that prioritize ease of use and faster deployment cycles without compromising on reliability.

With these deployment options in mind, the next step is to understand the underlying infrastructure that supports them, ensuring your real-time inference services are reliable, scalable, and production-ready. Let's take a closer look at the deployment infrastructure behind these approaches.

Deployment infrastructure

This section will cover a high-level overview of a typical ML model serving architecture. The details of the inference infrastructure are as follows:

- **Serving framework**: A model serving framework handles the actual serving of the model. This could be a specialized ML serving system, such as TensorFlow Serving, TorchServe, or Seldon Core, or a general API serving framework, such as FastAPI or Flask.

- **Inference server**: The inference server is a scalable, often containerized, environment where the model is hosted. It listens for incoming inference requests, processes them using the model, and returns predictions. This server can be deployed on cloud platforms (e.g., AWS SageMaker, Google AI Platform, AML) or on-premises.

Once deployed, it's typically exposed through an API gateway and load balancer, which handle traffic management and ensure high availability. The API gateway and load balancer work in the following manner:

- **API gateway:** It acts as an entry point for client applications, routing requests to the appropriate inference servers. It provides features such as authentication, rate limiting, and request validation.

- **Load balancer:** It distributes incoming inference requests across multiple instances of the inference server to ensure high availability and scalability.

Next, let's get an understanding of how monitoring and logging function:

- **Monitoring:** This entails tools and frameworks for monitoring the health and performance of the model serving infrastructure. Metrics such as latency, throughput, error rates, and resource utilization are tracked.

- **Logging:** It entails logging of inference requests and responses for auditing, debugging, and performance analysis. This includes capturing inputs, outputs, and any errors or exceptions.

Lastly, autoscaling and resource management work in the following way:

- **Autoscaling:** This includes mechanisms to automatically scale the inference infrastructure based on demand. This ensures that the system can handle varying loads efficiently.

- **Resource management:** This entails efficient allocation of computational resources (CPU, GPU, memory) to balance cost and performance.

To illustrate this setup visually, refer to *Figure 5.1*, which represents a **typical online inference architecture**. This diagram provides a high-level overview of the key components and interactions between them, ensuring efficient deployment and serving of ML models:

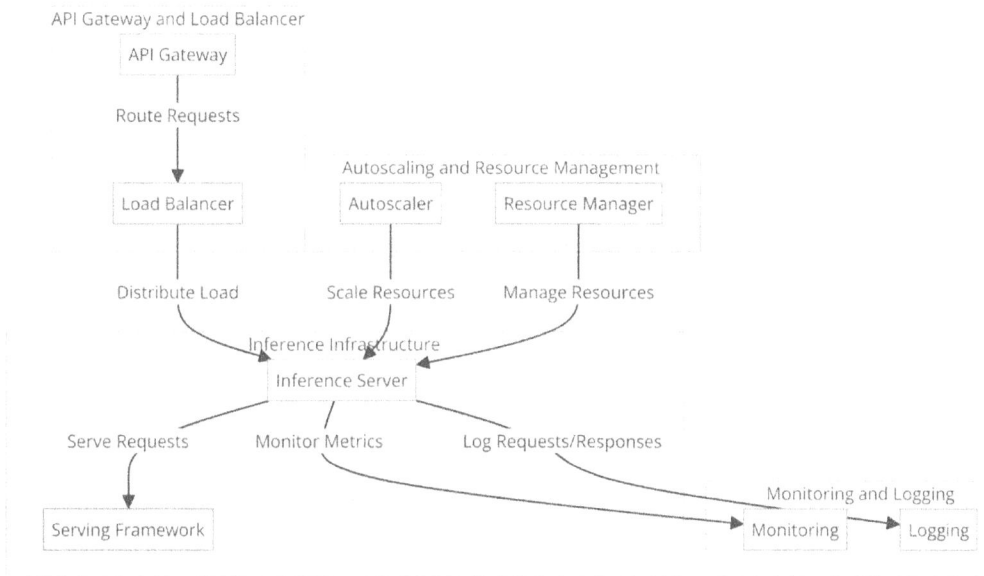

Figure 5.1 – Typical online inference architecture

Next, let's move on to batch inference.

Batch inference/scoring

Batch scoring, also known as **offline inference**, is suited for scenarios where predictions are generated on large datasets at scheduled intervals. This method is ideal for use cases such as generating nightly recommendations, processing large volumes of data for analytics, or scoring entire databases.

Some key characteristics of batch inference are as follows:

- **High throughput**: It's designed to process large volumes of data efficiently.
- **Scheduled execution**: It often runs at predefined intervals (e.g., hourly, daily) rather than on demand.

- **Resource optimization:** It utilizes compute resources efficiently by processing data in bulk.

- **Input/output:** Data is provided in files or blobs, and the predictions are also output to files or blobs.

- **Response time:** Batch inferencing is asynchronous and typically has higher latency since it processes large volumes of data.

With these characteristics in mind, let's now explore how batch inference is implemented in AML and how its tooling supports large-scale, scheduled prediction workflows with efficient resource management.

Implementation in AML

Batch inference is implemented in AML in the following ways:

- **Azure Batch:** One can leverage Azure Batch for large-scale parallel processing. Azure Batch can distribute the workload across many nodes, ensuring efficient processing of large datasets.

- **Databricks:** Integration with Azure Databricks can be done for a seamless experience in running batch inference jobs on big data.

- **Pipeline steps:** AML pipelines can be used to create batch scoring jobs that can be scheduled and managed efficiently, allowing for automated and repeatable batch inference processes.

With these implementation options available in AML, it's important to understand the underlying infrastructure that supports batch inference at scale. In the next section, we'll look at how the deployment architecture is structured to ensure efficient, reliable, and scalable processing of large datasets.

Deployment infrastructure

Figure 5.2 illustrates a high-level overview of a batch inference infrastructure using Azure services:

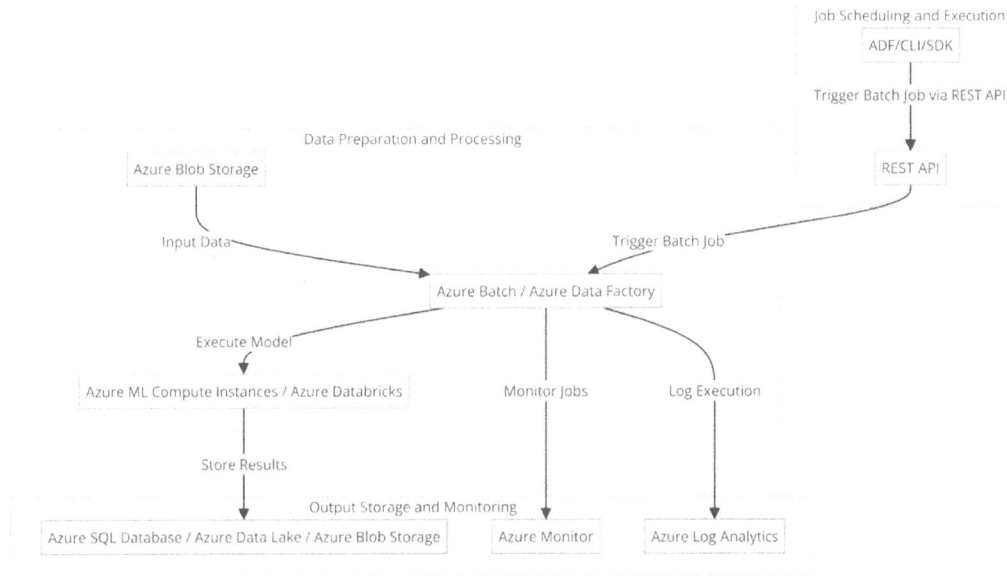

Figure 5.2 – Typical batch inferencing in a nutshell

Figure 5.2 represents a **typical batch inference architecture** and provides a high-level overview of the key components and interactions between them. Let's break it down into three main components:

- **Data Preparation and Processing component**:

    - **Azure Blob Storage**: This is where the input data for the batch inferencing is stored. It acts as a centralized storage solution for unstructured data.

    - **Azure Batch / Azure Data Factory (ADF)**: These services are responsible for orchestrating the data processing workflow. They fetch the input data from Azure Blob Storage and manage the execution of batch jobs.

- **AML Compute Instances / Azure Databricks:** Once the input data is prepared, these compute resources are used to execute the ML models for inferencing. The choice between AML compute instances and Azure Databricks depends on the specific use case and requirements, such as the need for big data processing capabilities or specialized ML compute environments.

- **Job Scheduling and Execution component:**

  - **ADF/CLI/SDK:** Jobs can be scheduled and managed using Azure Data Factory, **Command Line Interface (CLI)**, or **Software Development Kits (SDKs)**. These tools provide flexibility in how batch jobs are triggered and managed.

  - **REST API:** Batch jobs can also be triggered programmatically via a REST API, allowing for integration with other applications or automation scripts.

- **Output Storage and Monitoring component:**

  - **Output Storage:** After the inferencing is completed, the results are stored in various storage solutions such as Azure SQL Database, Azure Data Lake, or Azure Blob Storage. These options provide scalability and flexibility in storing structured and unstructured data.

  - **Monitoring and Logging:** Azure Monitor and Azure Log Analytics are used to monitor the performance and execution of the batch jobs. They provide insights into job status, resource utilization, and logs for debugging and auditing purposes.

A key workflow in the context of AML looks as follows:

1. Input data is stored in Azure Blob Storage.
2. Azure Batch or ADF is used to orchestrate the inferencing workflow.
3. An ML model is executed on AML compute instances or Azure Databricks.
4. The results are stored in a suitable output storage solution.
5. Monitoring and logging are handled by Azure Monitor and Azure Log Analytics to ensure smooth operations and quick troubleshooting.
6. These steps allow for scalable, efficient batch inferencing, suitable for processing large volumes of data and generating predictions in bulk.

We have now explored the two primary model deployment approaches available in AML: real-time inference for immediate predictions with low latency, and batch inference for processing large datasets efficiently at scheduled intervals. With this foundational understanding of deployment architectures and their respective use cases, we can now move on to implementing these deployment strategies using AML CLI tools.

Now we have a high-level idea of how models can be served in two different ways. Let's use the CLI to execute these two types.

Online inferencing

In this section, we will start with a model, then deploy it as an online endpoint and show how to use inferencing.

Preparing the model

We'll start with a simple model created using the Iris dataset (`https://archive.ics.uci.edu/dataset/53/iris`), which has different measurements of flowers and their classifications. The following Python code creates this model and saves it as `model.pkl`:

```python
from sklearn.datasets import load_iris
from sklearn.model_selection import train_test_split
from sklearn.ensemble import RandomForestClassifier
import joblib

#Load the iris dataset
iris = load_iris()
X, y = iris.data, iris.target

Split into train and test sets
X_train, X_test, y_train, y_test = train_test_split(
    X, y, test_size=0.2, random_state=42
)

#Train a simple Random Forest model
model = RandomForestClassifier(n_estimators=100, random_state=42)
model.fit(X_train, y_train)

Save the model as a pickle file
joblib.dump(model, 'model.pkl')
```

To generate the model so that it could be registered in the next step, execute this command:

```
python model.py
```

This will create a file named `model.pkl`

Registering the model

Once the model is created, it needs to be registered in your AML workspace so it can be used within it for other parts of the MLOps stages. Assume the model has been registered as iris-model with version 1.

```
az ml model create --name iris-model --version 1 --path ./model.pkl--
resource-group <your-resource-group> --workspace-name <your-workspace-
name>
```

The registered model can be referenced in other AML commands using the azureml:iris_model:1 path. This is CLI syntactic sugar, where it's expanded to the real URI where the model lives. The same is true for compute and environments, as you will notice through this chapter in the YAML files.

Scoring script

Since the registered model will be hosted in a virtual machine within a container, there needs to be a handler that will take the input to the model and run the necessary steps before sending the input to the model, get the output from the model, and then send it out. This handler is commonly called the **scoring script** – distinct from scoring scripts used during model evaluation, this deployment scoring script specifically handles the interface between incoming requests and your trained model in production. Let's use the following code and save it as online_score.py:

```python
```python
import json
import joblib
import numpy as np

def init():
    global model
    model_path = os.path.join(os.getenv("AZUREML_MODEL_DIR"),('model.pkl')
    model = joblib.load(model_path)

def run(raw_data):
    try:
        data = np.array(json.loads(raw_data)['data'])
        result = model.predict(data)
        return json.dumps({"result": result.tolist()})
    except Exception as e:
        return json.dumps({"error": str(e)})
```
```

Configuring the environment

The scoring script and model need to run inside a Docker container with specific dependencies.

Let's use this environment configuration and save it in a file named `environment.yml`.

```yaml
$schema: https://azuremlschemas.azureedge.net/latest/environment.schema.
json
name: iris-env
 version: 1
image: mcr.microsoft.com/azureml/minimal-ubuntu22.04-py39-cpu-inference
 conda_file: conda_file.yml
```

This environment creation installs the necessary python packages, which will be used to setup the execution environment inside Docker mentioned in `conda_file.yml` as shown:

```yaml
channels:
  - conda-forge
dependencies:
  - python=3.10
  - numpy
  - pip
  - scikit-learn
  - scipy
  - pip:
      - joblib
      - azureml-inference-server-http
      - inference-schema
name: iris-env
```

Let's register this environment with the name `iris-env` with version 1:

```bash
az ml environment create --file environment.yml --resource-group <your-
resource-group> --workspace-name <your-workspace-name>
```

The registered environment can be referenced in other AML commands using the `azureml:/environments/iris-env/versions/1` path.

Deployment

Next, we'll create an endpoint and deploy the model using a managed online endpoint. This involves defining the deployment configuration in a YAML file.

Creating an endpoint means getting the network endpoint setup with a name, so a URI is created for users to call into.

Let's define the `online-endpoint.yml` which describes the online endpoint name and auth type:

```yaml
name: iris-online-endpoint
auth_mode: key
```

To create, execute the following command:

```bash
az ml online-endpoint create --file online-endpoint.yml  --resource-group
<your-resource-group> --workspace-name <your-workspace-name>
```

This will create a managed online endpoint.

Once the endpoint is created, we have a router to send our requests. Now, let's create a deployment inside the endpoint that will do the real serving of the request. This deployment will need the model, scoring script, and the environment.

Let's save the following file as `iris-online-deployment.yaml`:

```yaml
$schema: https://azuremlschemas.azureedge.net/deployment-1.1.0.schema.json

name: iris-online-deployment # Name of the online deployment

endpoint_name: iris-endpoint # Name of the endpoint where the deployment
                             # will be exposed

model: azureml:iris-model:1  # Reference to the model version to be
                             # deployed
```

```
code_configuration:
  code: .   # Path where your code files (including online_score.py) are
            # stored
  scoring_script: online_score.py   # The script used for online
                                    # inferencing

environment: azureml:iris-env:1   # Reference to the environment version
                                  # that defines dependencies

instance_type: Standard_F2s_v2   # Specifies the VM SKU type to be used for
                                 # the deployment

Instance_count: 1 # Number of vm instances to be created

...
```

To create the deployment, we will use the following command.

```bash
az ml online-deployment create --file iris-online-deployment.yaml
--resource-group <your-resource-group> --workspace-name <your-workspace-
name>
```

For more in-depth setting and configuration options, please refer to https://learn.microsoft.com/en-us/azure/machine-learning/reference-yaml-deployment-managed-online?view=azureml-api-2.

Inference on deployment

Now that the model is deployed, you can send a request to the endpoint for prediction. The request should be in JSON format, matching the input expected by the model. For example, in this scenario, we deployed an iris model that takes a collection of arrays, where each array has four real numbers separated by commas. This would be input to the model, and the output would be the following:

```
`sample_request.json`:
```json
{
  "data": [
```
```

```
    [5.1, 3.5, 1.4, 0.2],
    [6.2, 3.4, 5.4, 2.3]
  ]
}
```

Invoke the endpoint passing the content of this file as our input:

```bash
az ml online-endpoint invoke --name iris-online-endpoint --deployment-name
iris-online-deployment  --request-file sample_request.json --resource-
group <your-resource-group> --workspace-name <your-workspace-name>
```

A typical output of this command will look like this:

```
"\"{\\\"result\\\": [0, 2]}\""
```

With this understanding of how basic online inferencing works, let's use this knowledge to achieve a similar goal with batch inferencing.

Batch inferencing

Before using the iris model for batch inferencing, let's understand the accommodations that are required for batch inferencing.

For batch inferencing, we need to modify the scoring script and the deployment `configuration`. `yaml` file, as the operational details and handling of data are different from the line counterpart. Let's investigate these more closely.

Scoring script

These are the different aspects of a scoring script. The first of these is data handling, which includes the following:

- **Online inferencing**: The scoring script (`online_score.py`) is designed to handle a single request at a time. It receives data in real time, processes it, and immediately returns predictions. This works well for scenarios where low latency and quick responses are critical.

- **Batch inferencing**: The scoring script (`batch_score.py`) is optimized for handling data in bulk. Instead of dealing with individual requests, it processes entire files or blobs of data at once. The script reads from input files, processes them in batches, and writes the predictions to output files. This approach is better suited for situations where latency isn't a concern, but processing large datasets efficiently is essential.

Next is asynchronous processing, the details of which are as follows:

- **Online inferencing**: The script operates synchronously, handling one request at a time, making it ideal for use cases that require immediate results. For example, in an airport security system, you show a person's face, and it quickly checks and says whether the security background is clear or not.

- **Batch inferencing**: The batch script is designed for asynchronous processing. It allows for parallel or distributed execution across large datasets, where predictions can be computed in chunks (mini-batches), and the final output is saved after processing all the input data. For example, I have hundreds of credit card applications and I want to run a job that will process all the applications and store the results in files indicating which applications are approved for the card.

The aspects of I/O operations include the following:

- **Online inferencing**: Input data is typically passed directly in the request body (e.g., JSON format), and the predictions are returned in the HTTP response.

- **Batch inferencing**: Input and output are managed via files or blobs. The script reads data from files or blob storage, processes it, and then writes the results back to output files or blobs. This file-based I/O is a crucial distinction for handling large datasets that can't be efficiently processed through real-time HTTP requests.

Error handling works in the following manner:

- **Online inferencing**: Since the script is synchronous and deals with real-time requests, errors are captured and immediately returned as part of the response, which is critical for monitoring and retry mechanisms.

- **Batch inferencing**: Errors are handled across batches, and logs or error files may be generated instead of immediate responses. This allows for more comprehensive error reporting and retry mechanisms for specific batches rather than the entire job.

So, now let's modify the scoring script and make it a file named `batch_score.py`:

```python

import json
import joblib
import numpy as np

import os
```

```python
def init():
    global model
    model_path = os.path.join(os.getenv("AZUREML_MODEL_
DIR"),('model.pkl'))

  model = joblib.load(model_path)

 def run(mini_batch):
    try:
        results = []
        for file_path in mini_batch:
            with open(file_path, 'r') as f:
                data = np.array(json.load(f)['data'])
                result = model.predict(data)
                results.append({"input": file_path, "prediction":
result.tolist()})
        output_file_path = os.path.join(os.getenv("AZUREML_BI_
OUTPUT_PATH", ""), "predictions.json")
        with open(output_file_path, 'w') as out_f:
            json.dump(results, out_f)
        return output_file_path
    except Exception as e:
        return str(e)
 try:
    results = []
    for file_path in mini_batch:
        with open(file_path, 'r') as f:
            data = np.array(json.load(f)['data'])
            result = model.predict(data)
            results.append({
                "input": file_path,
                "prediction": result.tolist()
            })
    output_file_path = os.path.join(
        os.getenv("AZUREML_BI_OUTPUT_PATH", ""),
        "predictions.json"
    )
    with open(output_file_path, 'w') as out_f:
        json.dump(results, out_f)
```

```
            return output_file_path
      except Exception as e:
            return str(e)
   ```
```

By tailoring the scoring script to the nature of batch processing, it can be used for efficient execution of large-scale inferencing workloads, making it ideal for scenarios where data needs to be processed in bulk without real-time constraints.

## Configuring the environment for online deployment

Let's use this environment configuration and save it in a file name environment_batch.yml file:

```yaml
$schema: https://azuremlschemas.azureedge.net/latest/environment.schema.
json
name: iris-env-batch
 version: 1
image:  mcr.microsoft.com/azureml/openmpi4.1.0-ubuntu20.04:latest
 conda_file: conda_file_batch.yml
   ```
```

This environment creation installs the necessary Python packages, which will be used to setup the execution environment inside Docker mentioned in conda_file_batch.yml as below:

```yaml
channels:
  - conda-forge
dependencies:
  - python=3.8.5
  - pip<22.0
  - pip:
      - joblib
      - scikit-learn
      - scipy
      - pandas
      - azureml-core
      - 'azureml-dataset-runtime[fuse]'

name: iris-env-batch
   ```
```
```

Deployment configuration

The deployment YAML will also adjust to support batch deployment. Let's assume we create a batch endpoint, with the name `iris-batch-endpoint`, to invoke the batch job request. Let's create a deployment inside the endpoint. This deployment will need the model, scoring script, and the environment, and some extra settings that are required for batch inferencing, when compared with the settings of the online one.

Configuring the environment for batch deployment

Let's use this environment configuration and save it in a file name environment_batch.yml file.

```yaml
$schema: https://azuremlschemas.azureedge.net/latest/environment.schema.
json
name: iris-env-batch
 version: 1
image:  mcr.microsoft.com/azureml/openmpi4.1.0-ubuntu20.04:latest
 conda_file: conda_file_batch.yml
```

This environment creation installs the necessary Python packages, which will be used to setup the execution environment inside Docker mentioned in `conda_file_batch.yml` as below:

```yaml
channels:
  - conda-forge
dependencies:
  - python=3.8.5
  - pip<22.0
  - pip:
      - joblib
      - scikit-learn
      - scipy
      - pandas
      - azureml-core
      - 'azureml-dataset-runtime[fuse]'

name: iris-env-batch
```

Let's save the following file as `iris_online_deployment.yaml`:

```yaml
```yaml
$schema: https://azuremlschemas.azureedge.net/deployment-1.1.0.schema.json

name: iris-batch-deployment   # Name of the batch deployment

endpoint_name: iris-batch-endpoint   # Name of the endpoint to which this
                                     # deployment belongs

type: model   # Specifies that this deployment is a model deployment

model: azureml:iris-model:1   # Reference to the model version to be used in
                              # the deployment

code_configuration:
  code: .   # Path where your code files (including batch_score.py) are
            # stored
  scoring_script: batch_score.py   # The script used for batch scoring

environment: azureml:iris-env-batch:1
                                   # Reference to the environment version
                                   # that defines dependencies

compute: azureml:batch-
cluster   # Name of the compute target (cluster) to run the batch job

resources:
  instance_count: 2   # Number of compute instances to be used for the
                      # batch job
settings:
  max_concurrency_per_instance: 2   # Maximum number of parallel tasks to
                                    # run on each compute instance
  mini_batch_size: 2   # Number of records to process in one mini-batch
  output_action: append_row   # Specifies how the output should be
                              # combined; 'append_row' adds results to a
                              # single file
  output_file_name: predictions.csv   # Name of the output file where
```
```

```
                                        # predictions will be stored
  retry_settings:
    max_retries: 3  # Maximum number of times to retry a failed task
    timeout: 300  # Maximum time (in seconds) a single task is allowed to
                  # run before timing out
  error_threshold: -1  # Specifies the number of failed records allowed
                       # before the job is
  # terminated (-1 means no limit)
  logging_level: info  # Sets the logging verbosity level; 'info' provides
                       # informational messages
  ```
```

This YAML file defines a batch deployment for AML, using `iris-batch-deployment` on `iris-batch-endpoint`. It specifies the model, code, environment, compute target, resources, settings, and traffic distribution for efficient batch processing with error handling and logging. Each entry has a comment followed by # for easy explanation.

To create the deployment, we will use the following command.

```bash
az ml batch-deployment create --file iris-batch-deployment.yaml
--resource-group <your-resource-group> --workspace-name <your-workspace-
name>
```

Additional concepts related to batch deployment

Before wrapping up the chapter, let's look at the additional concepts only applicable to batch deployment and not to online deployment:

- **Compute target**: A compute cluster (batch cluster) is typically used instead of the instance types specified for online endpoints. This allows for parallel processing across multiple nodes. To create a compute cluster, the CLI can be used: `az ml compute create --name batch-cluster --size Standard_NC6 --min-instances 0 --max-instances 5 --type AmlCompute --resource-group my-resource-group --workspace-name my-workspace`.

- **Mini-batch size**: The `mini_batch_size` parameter controls how much data is processed at once. This is essential for batch jobs to handle large datasets efficiently by breaking them into smaller chunks.

- **Input and output**: The input and output paths point to the locations in Azure Blob Storage (or other storage services) where the input data files reside and where the output predictions will be saved.
```

- **Retry settings**: The `retry_settings` section allows specifying the number of retries and timeouts for each mini-batch.

- **Error threshold**: You might want to tolerate a certain number of errors without failing the entire job. The `error_threshold` parameter allows you to set this tolerance level.

AML batch deployment supports various settings. To know more about them, please refer to `https://learn.microsoft.com/en-us/azure/machine-learning/reference-yaml-deployment-batch?view=azureml-api-2`.

Now, to invoke this batch endpoint, the following would be a sample CLI command:

```
az ml batch-endpoint invoke --name iris-batch-endpoint  --deployment-
name  iris-batch-deployment  --input ./input_data_ folder --output-path
azureml://datastores/workspaceblobstore/paths/tests/ output --resource-
group my-resource-group --workspace-name my-workspace
```

One difference here, compared to an online endpoint, is that this will schedule a job that will run in the background. Once the job is complete, the result will be stored in the output path. The input is also provided by the folder path. Note that batch endpoints can be invoked on-demand as shown previously, or integrated into scheduling systems. For automated scheduling, you would typically use Azure Data Factory pipelines, Azure Logic Apps, or external orchestration tools such as Apache Airflow to trigger batch jobs at regular intervals (daily, weekly, etc.) rather than requiring manual cron jobs.

Once the job is successfully completed, the results file can be downloaded locally:

```
az ml job download --name <job_name_from_theoutput_of_the_batch_invoke_
command>  --output-name <job_output_path> --download-path  ./
```

In earlier chapters, we discussed GitHub automation, demonstrating how data processing, training, and evaluation can be integrated into a GitHub workflow. In this chapter, we have learned how to use the model for inferencing. These inferencing steps can be encapsulated in a script that handles tasks such as creating endpoints, deployments, and so on.

This script can then be integrated into the GitHub pipeline, which will trigger the entire workflow upon any Git commit. This trigger could be related to changes in the dataset, updates to the training script, modifications to the model evaluation script, alterations to the inferencing/scoring script, environment definition changes, and more. As a result, the model will be automatically deployed and ready for your business to use.

This is a natural extension to the earlier automation, advancing toward a full end-to-end MLOps process, as shown in *Figure 5.3*:

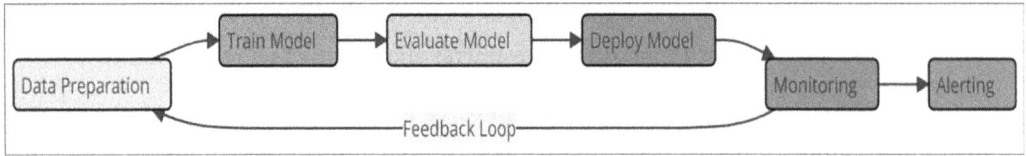

Figure 5.3 – MLOps full cycle

Summary

This chapter focused on the crucial step of deploying your trained ML models, transforming them from well-managed artifacts into real-world assets that deliver value. We explored various deployment strategies and best practices within AML.

By effectively deploying your models, you bridge the gap between development and production, ensuring your models reach their full potential and drive impactful business decisions.

Having successfully completed the core aspects of MLOps, it's essential to shift our focus toward quality and governance. The next chapter will delve into the critical process of capturing governance data throughout the ML lifecycle.

By meticulously logging lineage information, including model publication details, reasons for changes, and deployment timelines, we can ensure accountability, compliance, and security in our AI systems. The next chapter will guide you on how to leverage AML's capabilities to register, package, deploy, and monitor models, thereby maintaining a comprehensive audit trail of all ML assets.

6

Capturing and Securing Governance Data for MLOps

Governance in MLOps is a critical aspect of **machine learning operations** (**MLOps**), ensuring the ethical, legal, and secure use of models throughout their lifecycle. It involves establishing policies, procedures, and standards to manage risks, comply with regulations, and maintain the integrity of ML solutions. Governance provides a structured framework for all stakeholders, from data scientists to business leaders, to work collaboratively and responsibly.

In this chapter, we will delve into the essential components of governance in MLOps, beginning with the foundational focus areas that set the stage for responsible MLOps. These include accountability, compliance, security, and quality assurance—core principles that guide how ML systems should be developed and maintained within organizations.

A key aspect of governance is ensuring model integrity. This involves maintaining high data quality, implementing robust version control, validating models throughout their lifecycle, and addressing ethical considerations to avoid bias or unintended consequences. Closely tied to this is understanding and meeting governance requirements such as regulatory compliance, proper documentation, and maintaining audit trails to ensure transparency and accountability.

Lineage tracking is another critical topic covered in this chapter. We'll explore its importance in tracing the origins and evolution of datasets and models, and how this can be effectively implemented within AML. To support traceability, we'll discuss best practices around logging and documentation, which are fundamental for both debugging and governance audits.

We'll also examine how governance practices can be implemented across the entire ML lifecycle—from data ingestion and preprocessing to model training, evaluation, and deployment. Security and compliance are highlighted as ongoing concerns, with strategies for protecting sensitive data and adhering to regulatory standards.

To bridge governance with operational efficiency, we'll look at how these practices can be integrated into CI/CD pipelines and embedded within an organization's broader DevOps culture. Finally, we'll bring theory into practice with a hands-on example that demonstrates how MLOps governance can be applied using AML.

This chapter will have the following main headings:

- Key governance focus areas
- Implementing governance across the AML lifecycle
- Governance strategies for compliance and quality assurance
- Ethical considerations
- Comprehensive governance in action

By the end of this chapter, you'll have a solid understanding of MLOps governance principles and how to implement them effectively using AML tools and workflows.

Key governance focus areas

Governance in MLOps provides a structured framework to address several foundational focus areas that are critical for ensuring the ethical, legal, and secure use of ML models throughout their lifecycle. These key focus areas include the following:

- **Accountability and compliance**: Governance assigns clear roles and responsibilities, ensuring accountability for actions taken during the ML lifecycle. It also ensures compliance with regulations such as GDPR and HIPAA, which mandate strict data privacy and security controls. Non-compliance can lead to legal repercussions and financial penalties, making governance a critical aspect of risk management.

- **Security and transparency**: Effective governance includes measures to secure data and models from unauthorized access and cyber threats, implementing robust security protocols and access controls. Governance also promotes transparency by documenting decisions, changes, and outcomes, enabling clear explanations for model behavior and facilitating audits.

- **Quality assurance**: Governance frameworks include quality control measures to ensure model reliability, accuracy, and performance. This continuous improvement process helps maintain high standards and build trust in ML solutions.

Building on the key focus areas, governance plays a pivotal role in upholding model integrity throughout the entire ML lifecycle. This involves not only implementing robust technical controls but also addressing ethical considerations to ensure models perform as expected and adhere to organizational values. The following subsections will delve deeper into specific mechanisms for maintaining data quality, validating model performance, and addressing ethical concerns.

Ensuring model integrity

This involves a range of practices, from managing data quality and implementing rigorous validation processes to addressing ethical considerations and ensuring continuous monitoring. The following key areas explore these aspects in detail, highlighting strategies for upholding model integrity throughout its lifecycle:

- **Data quality management and version control**: Governance enforces strict data quality standards, ensuring accurate, complete, and representative data for model training and testing. It also involves meticulous version control and lineage tracking, documenting changes and updates to models, and ensuring that modifications are justified and traceable.

- **Validation, testing, and monitoring**: Governance includes rigorous validation and testing protocols to evaluate model performance against predefined criteria. Post-deployment governance involves continuous monitoring to detect performance degradation or drift, ensuring that models remain reliable and effective.

- **Ethics**: Governance frameworks enforce ethical guidelines to prevent harmful or discriminatory model development and deployment. This includes bias detection and mitigation strategies to ensure fair treatment of all user groups. There will be more on this in the section named *Ethical considerations*.

These integrity measures form the foundation for establishing comprehensive governance requirements that guide ML development and deployment practices.

Compliance requirements in ML

Effective ML governance relies on clear requirements that ensure responsible development and consistent standards across projects. The following key requirements form the foundation of MLOps governance:

- **Regulatory compliance and data governance**: Adhering to regulations such as GDPR and HIPAA is crucial for data privacy, security, and ethical AI use. Data governance establishes policies for data collection, storage, usage, and disposal, ensuring data quality, access control, and anonymization.

- **Model documentation and audit trails:** Comprehensive documentation of model development processes, including data sources, algorithms, and performance metrics, is essential for transparency and reproducibility. Audit trails maintain detailed logs of actions and changes, ensuring accountability and compliance.

Lineage

Lineage information is the detailed documentation of the history and provenance of data and models throughout the ML lifecycle. It includes metadata about data sources, transformations, model training, versions, and deployment. This is crucial as it helps with the following:

- **Transparency and trust:** Provides insights into data and model journeys, building trust among stakeholders

- **Accountability:** Tracks changes to data and models, identifying who made modifications and when

- **Reproducibility:** Facilitates the reproduction of experiments and results, essential for verification and building upon previous work

- **Compliance:** Meets regulatory requirements for data and model handling, avoiding legal and financial penalties

- **Debugging and troubleshooting:** Allows efficient issue resolution by tracing back through data and model history

- **Operational efficiency:** Provides a clear overview of dependencies and workflows, optimizing resource management

After establishing the fundamental governance requirements in ML, understanding lineage becomes crucial for ensuring the integrity and transparency of your processes. Lineage information offers a comprehensive view of the data and model histories, which supports transparency, accountability, and operational efficiency. The following section delves into the importance of maintaining detailed lineage documentation and its impact on various aspects of ML governance.

Tools and techniques for lineage tracking in AML

AML offers a range of tools and techniques for tracking data and model lineage. These capabilities enable teams to trace the entire lifecycle of datasets, experiments, and models, ensuring that every change is documented and auditable. The following list highlights the key features that support lineage tracking in AML:

- **Datasets and datastores:** Register and version datasets, providing metadata on data sources, formats, and transformations.

- **Experiment tracking**: Track experiments, including parameters, metrics, and outputs, using the AML SDK and Studio.

- **Model registry**: Store, version, and annotate models, linking each version to the datasets and experiments that produced it.

- **Pipelines**: Orchestrate complex workflows, tracking lineage information at each stage of data processing, model training, and deployment.

- **Audit logs**: Capture detailed information on access and changes to data and models, maintaining a comprehensive audit trail.

- **Data drift and monitoring**: Monitor data drift and model performance over time, tracking changes in data distributions and model behavior. This will be covered in more detail in the following chapter, titled *Monitoring the ML Model*.

Best practices for logging and documenting lineage

With Azure ML's tools for lineage tracking in place, it's important to follow best practices to ensure that this information is logged and documented effectively. Adopting these practices helps maintain accuracy, consistency, and traceability across the entire ML lifecycle, making it easier to manage and audit the lineage data. The following recommendations outline key strategies for effective lineage logging and documentation:

- **Automate logging**: Use automated tools (e.g., **MLflow**) to capture lineage consistently and accurately, reducing errors.

- **Comprehensive metadata**: Capture all relevant metadata, including data sources, preprocessing, model hyperparameters, and evaluation metrics.

- **Version control**: Implement robust version control for datasets, code, and models using tools such as Git and AML versioning.

- **Consistent naming**: Adopt naming conventions for datasets, models, and experiments to facilitate lineage tracing.

- **Documentation**: Maintain thorough documentation of processes, decisions, and changes, including model update rationales and data selection criteria.

- **Access controls**: Implement strict access controls to ensure that only authorized personnel can make changes.

With a clear understanding of the foundational governance areas, ranging from accountability, compliance, and model integrity to lineage tracking and documentation, you now have the essential building blocks for responsible ML operations.

The next step is to see how these principles are applied in practice. In the following section, we'll explore how to implement governance across the entire AML lifecycle, ensuring that these controls are embedded from data ingestion through to model deployment and beyond.

Implementing governance across the AML lifecycle

Ensuring governance during data ingestion, preprocessing, and model training involves data quality management, version control, and ethical considerations. IT governance during model evaluation and validation includes rigorous testing protocols, bias detection, and performance monitoring to ensure compliance and model integrity.

Governance in model deployment and monitoring involves continuous monitoring for performance drifts, ensuring that models remain reliable and compliant with regulations. There will be more details in the next chapter.

AML provides a range of tools and features to support governance across the ML lifecycle, including experiment tracking, model registry, pipelines, and audit logs.

After establishing governance across the AML lifecycle, securing the data and lineage information becomes paramount. Effective governance isn't just about tracking and documenting processes but also about ensuring the security of this data. The following section will dive into the security measures necessary to protect data and lineage information throughout the ML workflow.

Securing data and lineage information

To safeguard both data and lineage information in MLOps, it is essential to implement robust security measures throughout the ML lifecycle. The following points outline key practices for securing this critical information:

- **Security principles in MLOps**: Security is a critical aspect of governance, involving principles such as data encryption, access controls, and regular security audits to protect data and models from unauthorized access and cyber threats.

- **Securing data in AML**: Techniques for securing data in AML include encryption at rest and in transit, access control policies, and data protection features such as differential privacy.

- **Protecting lineage information**: Lineage information should be protected using encryption, access controls, and regular backups. Ensuring the integrity of lineage data is crucial for maintaining an accurate record of model development and deployment.

- **Mitigating risks and ensuring data integrity**: Regular security audits, vulnerability assessments, and incident response planning are essential to mitigate risks and ensure data integrity.

Securing data and lineage information lays the foundation for a robust governance framework, but ensuring compliance and quality assurance is equally critical in maintaining model integrity. The next section focuses on governance strategies that help achieve regulatory compliance and uphold high standards of quality in MLOps.

Governance strategies for compliance and quality assurance

The following strategies highlight essential practices for ensuring regulatory compliance and maintaining quality assurance throughout the ML lifecycle:

- **Regulatory compliance in ML**: Compliance with regulations such as GDPR, HIPAA, and industry-specific standards is essential. AML provides features such as data protection controls and audit logs to support compliance.

- **Quality assurance frameworks**: Quality assurance frameworks ensure model reliability and performance. This is a set of smaller frameworks:

    - **MLflow's model registry framework** manages model versions and transitions, tracks model metadata and artifacts, and supports automated quality gates.

        Note

        While an AML registry (covered in *Chapter 5*) provides native Azure integration, MLflow offers cross-platform compatibility and is useful for hybrid or multi-cloud environments.

    - **Azure ML's testing framework** enables A/B testing through AML endpoints and supports shadow deployment for risk-free testing. Additionally, it facilitates the champion-challenger model evaluation.

    - The **continuous validation framework** includes data quality validation using tools such as Great Expectations, model performance monitoring through AML metrics, and automated retraining triggers based on performance thresholds.

- **Compliance tools in AML**: AML offers tools such as data protection controls, audit logs, and model validation features to support compliance with regulations and quality assurance standards. These are a few examples:

  - **Azure Policy for ML** enforces compliance requirements and organizational standards.

  - **Azure Key Vault** manages secrets and encryption keys securely.

  - **Azure Monitor Application Insights** tracks model performance and usage metrics.

  - **AML MLflow integration** captures experiment metrics and model artifacts.

  - **Azure Role-Based Access Control (RBAC)** manages fine-grained access permissions.

  - **Azure ML's model validation features** ensure model quality through automated validation pipelines.

- **Continuous monitoring and auditing**: Continuous monitoring and auditing are essential to detect and address compliance issues promptly. This includes regular reviews of data usage, model performance, and security measures.

After establishing strategies for compliance and quality assurance, the next step is to operationalize governance within the ML workflow. By embedding governance practices into the day-to-day processes, teams can ensure that compliance, security, and ethical standards are consistently met. The following section outlines how to integrate governance into operational workflows and explores future trends in MLOps governance.

Operationalizing governance in ML

The following key areas outline the framework for integrating governance into the operational aspects of ML, ensuring it becomes an integral part of the ML lifecycle:

- **Integrating governance into CI/CD pipelines**: Governance practices should be integrated into CI/CD pipelines to ensure they are part of the everyday ML workflow. This includes automated governance checks and balances.

- **Automated governance checks**: Automated governance checks can validate data quality, model performance, and compliance with regulations and ethical guidelines.

- **Building a culture of governance**: Building a culture of governance within data science teams involves training and education on governance principles, regular governance reviews, and fostering a collaborative environment where governance is a shared responsibility.

- **Future trends in MLOps governance**: Future trends in MLOps governance include the increasing importance of explainable AI, bias detection and mitigation, and the development of ethical guidelines for ML development and deployment.

As governance continues to evolve, addressing ethical considerations becomes increasingly critical. Ensuring fairness, transparency, and accountability in ML systems is not only a matter of compliance but also of fostering trust and social responsibility. The following section delves into the ethical challenges, particularly around bias detection and mitigation, that must be addressed to uphold these principles.

Ethical considerations

Ethical considerations in ML are paramount to ensure that ML systems are developed and deployed fairly, transparently, and accountably. This involves addressing several key aspects, including bias detection and mitigation.

Bias detection and mitigation

One of the most significant ethical challenges in ML is the potential for bias in ML models. Bias can arise from various sources, including biased training data, biased algorithms, and biased human decisions. To address this, it is essential to implement strategies for detecting and mitigating bias.

Bias detection

Here are some techniques commonly used to help with detection:

- **Data auditing**: Regularly audit datasets to identify and address any biases. This involves examining the data for imbalances and ensuring that it represents diverse populations.

- **Fairness metrics**: Use fairness metrics to evaluate the performance of models across different demographic groups. Metrics such as demographic parity, equalized odds, and disparate impact can help identify biases in model predictions.

- **Transparency**: Maintain transparency in the data collection and model development processes. Documenting the sources of data, the methods used for data preprocessing, and the rationale behind model decisions can help identify potential biases.

Bias mitigation

Mitigation can sometimes be equally challenging. However, the following techniques are considered a good starting point:

- **Preprocessing techniques**: Implement preprocessing techniques to balance the training data. This can include oversampling underrepresented groups, undersampling overrepresented groups, or generating synthetic data to achieve a balanced dataset.

- **Algorithmic fairness**: Use algorithms designed to promote fairness. Techniques such as adversarial debiasing, reweighting, and fairness constraints can help reduce bias in model predictions.

- **Post-processing adjustments**: Apply post-processing adjustments to model outputs to ensure fairness. This can involve modifying the decision thresholds or recalibrating the model to achieve fair outcomes across different groups.

Having explored the ethical challenges and the importance of addressing bias, it is now crucial to translate these principles into actionable practices. This section will guide you through the hands-on implementation of governance in AML, focusing on practical steps to integrate audit logging and ensure comprehensive governance. We will cover setting up the environment, managing datasets and models, securing data, and providing a practical framework to support and operationalize the governance strategies discussed.

Comprehensive governance in action

This section will help you seamlessly integrate the audit logging aspect into the overall governance framework discussed in the chapter. Here, we will walk through the practical steps of setting up an AML environment, registering and versioning datasets, tracking experiments, registering and versioning models, building and tracking pipelines, and securing data and lineage information.

These steps will provide you with a comprehensive understanding of how to capture and secure governance data in AML, ensuring that your MLOps processes are well governed and secure:

1. **Registering and versioning datasets**: Create a datastore to store your data and register your datasets in your workspace. Versioning your datasets is crucial for governance as it allows you to track changes and maintain a history of your data:

    1. Create a datastore:

       ```
       az ml datastore create --name mydatastore --workspace-name
       myMLWorkspace --resource-group myResourceGroup --account-name
       <your-account-name> --container-name <your-container-name>
       ```

2. Register a dataset:

```
az ml data create --name mydataset --path <your-dataset-path>
--type uri_file --workspace-name myMLWorkspace --resource-
group myResourceGroup
```

3. Version the dataset:

```
az ml data create-version --name mydataset --path <your-
dataset-path> --workspace-name myMLWorkspace --resource-group
myResourceGroup
```

2. **Experiment tracking**: Creating experiments and tracking jobs is vital for reproducibility and governance. By logging metrics and keeping track of your experiments, you can ensure that your models are built on reliable and consistent data:

1. Create an experiment and a job:

```
az ml experiment create --name myexperiment --workspace-name
myMLWorkspace --resource-group myResourceGroup
az ml job create --file myscript.yml --experiment-name
myexperiment --workspace-name myMLWorkspace --resource-group
myResourceGroup
```

2. Track metrics and logs (this is SDK code, which needs the Python SDK to be installed; please refer to https://learn.microsoft.com/en-us/azure/machine-learning/concept-v2?view=azureml-api-2#azure-machine-learning-python-sdk-v2):

```python
import mlflow
from azure.ai.ml import MLClient
from azure.identity import DefaultAzureCredential
from azure.ai.ml.entities import Job

ml_client = MLClient(DefaultAzureCredential(), subscription_
id, resource_group, workspace_name)
job = Job(name="myexperiment", experiment_name="myexperiment",
code="myscript.py")
run = ml_client.jobs.create_or_update(job)

# Start an MLflow run
mlflow.start_run(run_id=run.id)
```

```python
# Assuming you have your true labels and predicted labels
true_labels = <true_labels>
predicted_labels = <predicted_labels>

# Calculate the accuracy
accuracy = accuracy_score(true_labels, predicted_labels)

# End the MLflow run
mlflow.end_run()
```

3. **Model registration and versioning**: Registering and versioning your models helps in managing different versions of your models. This is important for governance as it allows you to keep track of model updates and ensure that you are using the correct version in production:

   1. Register a model:

   ```
   az ml model create --name mymodel --path outputs/
   mymodel.pkl --workspace-name myMLWorkspace
   --resource-group myResourceGroup
   ```

   2. Version the model (a similar model from the same experiment with some variation):

   ```
   az ml model create --name mymodel --version 2
   --path outputs/new_mymodel.pkl --workspace-name
   myMLWorkspace --resource-group myResourceGroup
   ```

4. **Building and tracking pipelines**: Creating and running pipelines helps in automating your ML workflows. This step ensures that each component of the workflow is executed in a consistent and reproducible manner, which is crucial for maintaining governance and traceability in MLOps:

   1. Create a YAML file for your pipeline component (e.g., train_step.yml):

   ```yaml
   ```yaml
   $schema: https://azuremlschemas.azureedge.net/latest/
   commandJob.schema.json
   command: >
   ```
   ```

```
  python train.py
environment: azureml:<your-environment>
inputs:
  input_data: <your-input-data>
outputs:
  output_data: <your-output-data>
```

2. Create a YAML file for your pipeline job (e.g., `pipeline_job.yml`):

```yaml
$schema: https://azuremlschemas.azureedge.net/latest/
pipelineJob.schema.json
jobs:
  train_step:
    type: command
    component: train_step.yml
```

3. Submit the pipeline job using the CLI:

```bash
az ml job create --file pipeline_job.yml --workspace-name
myMLWorkspace --resource-group myResourceGroup
```

5. **Securing data and lineage information**: Finally, securing your data and configuring access controls is crucial for governance. Enabling encryption and setting up RBAC ensures that your data is protected and only accessible to authorized users:

```
az storage account update --name <your-storage-account-name>
--resource-group myResourceGroup --encryption-services blob
```

Configure access controls:

```
az role assignment create --assignee <your-assignee> --role "Storage
Blob Data Contributor" --scope <your-scope>
```

6. **Enabling diagnostic settings for the AML workspace**: To explicitly capture audit logs and maintain a comprehensive audit trail, you can enable diagnostic settings in AML. This allows you to capture detailed information on access and changes to data and models. Although this is not part of the AML CLI explicitly, but in the Azure CLI, which is more generic. Here's how you can do it:

```
az monitor diagnostic-settings create --name
myDiagnosticSetting --resource /subscriptions/<subscription-
id>/resourceGroups/myResourceGroup/providers/Microsoft.
MachineLearningServices/workspaces/myMLWorkspace --workspace-id /
subscriptions/<subscription-id>/resourceGroups/myResourceGroup/
providers/Microsoft.OperationalInsights/workspaces/
myLogAnalyticsWorkspace --logs '[{"category": "AuditLogs",
"enabled": true}]'
```

This command enables diagnostic settings for your AML workspace, capturing audit logs and sending them to a Log Analytics workspace. This ensures that all access and changes to data and models are logged, providing a comprehensive audit trail.

Now that we've walked through the hands-on steps of capturing and securing governance data in AML, let's take a moment to visualize the entire process. The following illustration provides a comprehensive overview of the end-to-end workflow, highlighting each critical step from data ingestion to securing data and lineage information.

Putting the practice together

This visual representation in *Figure 6.1* will help you understand how the comprehensive governance example fits into the overall governance framework, ensuring that your MLOps processes are well governed and secure.

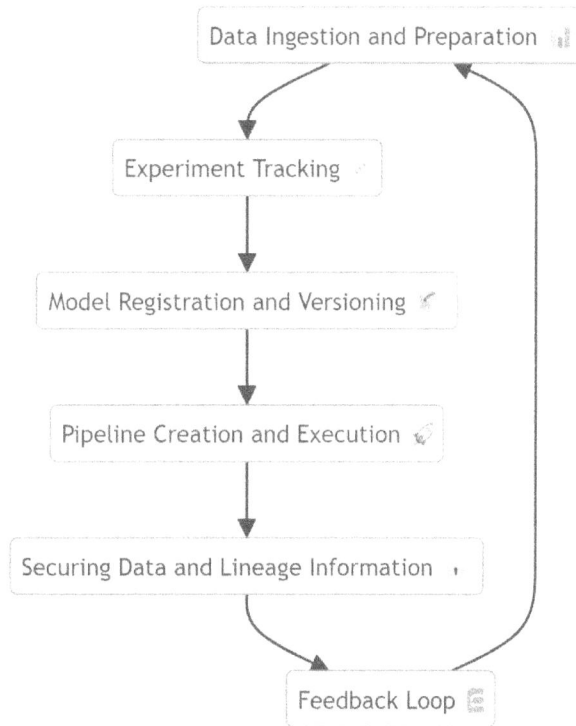

Figure 6.1 – Comprehensive governance process

By following these steps, you can maintain a clear lineage of your data and models, protect sensitive information, and ensure that only authorized personnel have access to critical resources.

The comprehensive governance process illustrated previously demonstrates how different aspects of MLOps governance come together in practice. From data ingestion to model deployment, each step builds upon established governance principles while leveraging Azure ML's robust tooling. This integrated approach ensures the following:

- Complete traceability through automated logging and versioning
- Secure handling of sensitive data and model artifacts
- Compliance with regulatory requirements through proper documentation and access controls
- Quality assurance through systematic validation and testing
- Ethical consideration through bias detection and mitigation measures

Successfully implementing these governance practices not only protects your organization from risks but also builds trust in your ML systems and streamlines the overall MLOps workflow. Also, you can maintain a clear lineage of your data and models, protect sensitive information, and ensure that only authorized personnel have access to critical resources.

Summary

The chapter highlighted the tools and techniques available in AML to support governance, such as experiment tracking, model registry, and audit logs. We also emphasized the importance of securing data and lineage information, ensuring compliance with regulations, and maintaining high-quality standards in ML operations.

In the next chapter, we will build upon these governance principles and delve into the specifics of monitoring deployed models. This will include both functional and non-functional aspects such as operational metrics, data drift, concept drift, and alerting mechanisms.

7

Monitoring the ML Model

In this chapter, we will go through the critical aspects of monitoring **Machine Learning (ML)** models and their supporting infrastructure in AML. We begin by exploring the purpose and importance of monitoring in MLOps, highlighting its role in ensuring the continued reliability, performance, and efficiency of deployed ML solutions.

This chapter provides a comprehensive exploration of monitoring strategies essential for maintaining robust ML operations in AML. We'll examine the critical distinction between model performance monitoring and infrastructure usage monitoring, introduce you to the DataCollector tool and its central role in tracking model behavior, and guide you through setting up data collection for your deployed models. You'll learn how to configure monitoring processes using collected data and understand the key monitoring signals available in AML, including infrastructure metric monitoring at both the endpoint and deployment level. Mastering these monitoring concepts will enable you to proactively identify potential issues, maintain model reliability, optimize resource utilization, and ensure your ML solutions continue to deliver value in production environments. This knowledge forms the foundation for building trustworthy, scalable ML systems that can adapt and respond to changing conditions over time.

By the end of this chapter, you will have a comprehensive understanding of how to implement robust monitoring strategies for your ML models and infrastructure in AML, enabling you to maintain high-quality ML operations and quickly identify and address potential issues.

We will be covering the following main topics:

- The purpose of monitoring
- Monitoring: Model performance versus infrastructure
- Learning about DataCollector
- Setting up data collection
- Infrastructure metric monitoring

The purpose of monitoring

The primary goal of monitoring ML models and the associated infrastructure is to ensure the continued reliability, performance, and efficiency of the deployed solution. In production environments, various factors can impact model effectiveness, making it necessary to monitor several key areas. These include resource consumption, availability, security, and cost management. Each of these elements plays a role in keeping the system scalable, secure, and cost-effective:

- **Monitor resource utilization**: By continuously tracking CPU, memory, and storage usage, teams can ensure efficient resource allocation, avoid performance degradation, and identify potential bottlenecks that might affect the model's responsiveness.
- **Ensure high availability**: Uptime is crucial for ML services, particularly those used in real-time applications. Monitoring the infrastructure ensures that systems remain highly available, with minimal downtime that could disrupt services or lead to missed opportunities.
- **Security and access control**: In a production environment, it is critical to monitor who has access to the infrastructure and the models. By tracking access controls, organizations can prevent unauthorized users from interacting with sensitive data or models, maintaining the security and integrity of the system.
- **Cost optimization**: Monitoring resource usage helps not only with performance but also with cost control. By analyzing usage patterns, teams can optimize their cloud resources, ensuring they are not over-provisioned, thereby reducing unnecessary spending.

Monitoring the performance and health of ML models and their supporting infrastructure is a critical aspect of MLOps. By understanding the distinction between these two monitoring categories, organizations can ensure their deployed ML solutions remain reliable, efficient, and aligned with business goals.

With this foundation in place, let's dive deeper into the specifics of model performance monitoring and infrastructure usage monitoring in the context of AML.

Monitoring: Model performance versus infrastructure

In the context of AML, effective monitoring falls into two main categories: model performance monitoring and infrastructure usage monitoring. Both are essential to ensure that ML solutions remain reliable, cost-effective, and aligned with business goals.

Model performance monitoring evaluates how well a deployed ML model performs its intended task over time. The primary goal is to ensure the model consistently delivers accurate predictions as it processes new data in production. This type of monitoring is crucial because ML models can face two common challenges in production:

- **Data drift**: This occurs when the statistical properties of the input data change over time. For example, if a model was trained on customer transaction data from 2020, but customer spending patterns significantly changed in 2024, the model may become less effective.

- **Concept drift**: This happens when the fundamental relationships between input features and target variables evolve. For instance, in a fraud detection model, fraudsters might develop new techniques that change the relationship between transaction patterns and fraudulent behavior.

By continuously monitoring model performance, organizations can detect these issues early and take corrective actions before they significantly impact business operations.

Central to this process in AML is **DataCollector** (covered in the following section), which is a versatile tool that captures data on model inputs, outputs, and predictions. By systematically gathering this data, it becomes possible to track drifts and detect performance degradation early. DataCollector allows data scientists to define monitoring signals such as accuracy, F1 score, precision, and recall, which act as **Key Performance Indicators** (**KPIs**) for evaluating the model's real-time performance. Through continuous monitoring, organizations can swiftly identify anomalies or changes that might compromise the model's effectiveness.

While model performance monitoring focuses on the accuracy and reliability of predictions, ensuring optimal system performance requires equal attention to the underlying computational resources that support these models.

Infrastructure usage monitoring

While model performance is essential, the infrastructure supporting the model must also be closely monitored. Infrastructure usage monitoring focuses on keeping track of computational resources—CPU, memory, storage, and network throughput—to ensure efficient utilization.

This type of monitoring ensures the model can scale as required, provides insights into optimizing resource allocation, and supports cost management efforts. It also helps maintain system availability by detecting bottlenecks and preventing potential downtime due to resource exhaustion.

In addition, effective infrastructure monitoring in AML often involves integrating with Azure Monitor and Log Analytics, which provide detailed metrics and logs on resource utilization, enabling alignment with broader cloud observability practices. Monitoring infrastructure also supports autoscaling decisions, ensuring model endpoints can dynamically handle variable loads while optimizing costs. To proactively manage system health, thresholds and alerting mechanisms are typically configured, allowing teams to detect and address resource exhaustion issues before they lead to downtime or degraded performance.

To implement effective model performance monitoring in AML, you need the right tools and processes in place. At the core of Azure ML's monitoring capabilities is DataCollector, a powerful tool designed specifically for tracking and analyzing model behavior in production. Let's explore how this essential component enables comprehensive model monitoring.

Learning about DataCollector

At the heart of Azure ML's model performance monitoring is DataCollector, a powerful tool that enables comprehensive logging and tracking of both model inputs and outputs in real time. By centralizing data collection, DataCollector facilitates effective monitoring of model performance, enabling organizations to continuously evaluate key metrics and detect potential issues early.

With DataCollector as the core component, AML offers several tools that support effective model performance monitoring:

- **Model monitoring setup**: AML provides an intuitive interface for configuring model monitoring. Data scientists can define which performance metrics to track, such as accuracy, F1 score, precision, and recall, and set performance thresholds. The system can also be set up to trigger alerts whenever the monitored signals indicate deviations from expected behavior.

- **Monitoring signals**: These are predefined KPIs such as accuracy, F1 score, precision, and recall. AML also supports custom metrics to capture model-specific performance indicators, giving the flexibility to monitor what matters most for each deployment.

- **Model-specific metrics and anomalies**: AML enables deep exploration of model-specific metrics, making it easier to spot anomalies or identify performance degradation. This detailed insight ensures data scientists can take corrective actions when the model begins to underperform or drift.

DataCollector itself offers several critical features that enhance its utility in model monitoring:

- **Centralized data logging**: DataCollector automatically logs and stores inference data (both inputs and outputs) in Azure Blob Storage, creating a central repository for performance analysis and governance.

- **Flexible endpoint support**: Whether using managed online endpoints or Kubernetes online endpoints, DataCollector works seamlessly, making it adaptable to various deployment environments.

- **Deployment-level configuration**: Users have granular control over what data is collected, with the ability to define and adjust data collection settings at the deployment level, ensuring that the system collects the most relevant information for each deployment.

- **Comprehensive logging options**: DataCollector supports both payload logging (which captures raw input and output data) and custom logging (allowing users to log specific data points of interest), giving flexibility in the depth of monitoring required for each model.

With these powerful features and capabilities, DataCollector provides a solid foundation for comprehensive model monitoring in AML. Now, let's see how to implement these concepts in practice through a concrete example.

Setting up data collection

Now that we've covered the concept and features of DataCollector, let's dive into a practical example to see how it works in a real-world scenario. In this section, we'll walk through how to enable data collection while deploying a model to a managed online endpoint (MIR endpoint) in AML.

For this example, we'll revisit the model deployment scenario from *Chapter 5*. The following is the deployment YAML used to create the deployment on an endpoint named `iris-endpoint`, with data collection enabled for both model inputs and outputs:

```yaml
$schema: https://azuremlschemas.azureedge.net/deployment-1.1.0.schema.json

name: iris-online-deployment
endpoint_name: iris-endpoint
model: azureml:iris_model:1
code_configuration:
  code: .
scoring_script: online_score.py
environment:  azureml:iris_env:1
```

```
instance_type: Standard_F2s_v2
traffic:
  - deployment_name: iris-online-deployment
    percentage: 100

data_collector:
  collections:
    model_inputs:
      enabled: 'True'
    model_outputs:
      enabled: 'True'

...
```

Let's break down the data_collector section in the configuration file. Under collections, two types of data are being collected:

- model_inputs: This is set to collect the input data sent to the model.

- model_outputs: This is set to collect the output data (predictions) from the model.

Both model_inputs and model_outputs have their enabled flag set to True, which means DataCollector will log both the input data sent to the model and the output predictions from the model.

This configuration enables comprehensive logging of the model's inference data. When deployed, this setup will do the following:

- Capture all input data sent to the model for inference

- Capture all output predictions generated by the model

- Automatically store this logged data in Azure Blob Storage

By collecting this data, organizations can maintain better control over their deployed models, ensure their continued effectiveness and reliability, and quickly respond to any issues or changes in the production environment. This proactive approach to model monitoring and governance is crucial for maintaining trust in ML systems and ensuring their long-term success and compliance in real-world applications.

Now that we have set up data collection during model deployment, the next step is to utilize this collected data effectively for monitoring and performance analysis. In the following section, we'll explore how to set up monitoring using the data captured by DataCollector to track model health and behavior in production.

Setting up monitoring with collected data

With DataCollector capturing both input and output data from your deployed model, the next step is to implement a monitoring system that leverages this collected data to track KPIs over time. Monitoring allows you to detect data drift, prediction drift, and other model-specific anomalies by comparing live production data with historical or training data.

In the following example, we will use `credit_model`, which predicts credit approval outcomes using features such as credit limit, age, bill amounts, payment history, gender, education, marital status, and past payment statuses. We will set up a monitoring process that feeds on the inference data collected by DataCollector and evaluates it on a daily basis. This process helps ensure that the model continues to perform effectively in production, providing early warning signals for any potential issues, such as data drift. The collected data is stored in the default workspace Blob Storage, and the monitoring setup is configured as follows.

Let's break down this monitoring configuration step by step to understand each component:

1. **Step 1 – basic job configuration**: We begin by defining the monitoring job's basic properties, setting a clear name, display name, and description, and specifying a daily schedule to automate monitoring at a consistent time each day:

   ```
   name: model_performance_monitoring

   display_name: Model performance monitoring

   description: Monitor model prediction performance

   trigger:
     # perform model monitoring activity daily at 5:00am
     type: recurrence
     frequency: day
     interval: 1
     schedule:
       hours: 5
       minutes: 0
   ```

   This section defines the monitoring job's basic properties and sets up a daily schedule to run at 5:00 A.M.

2. **Step 2 – compute and target configuration**: Next, we configure the compute resources that will execute the monitoring job and specify the deployment target for monitoring, ensuring the job runs with the appropriate resources and knows which model to track:

```
create_monitor:
  compute:
    instance_type: Standard_F2s_v2
    runtime_version: "3.3"
  monitoring_target:
    ml_task: classification
    endpoint_deployment_id: azureml:credit-default-ut:main
```

Here, we specify the compute resources for running the monitoring job and identify the target deployment to monitor.

3. **Step 3 – data drift monitoring**: In this step, we set up data drift monitoring by comparing the production data collected by DataCollector with the baseline training data, enabling us to detect changes in input data distributions over time:

```
monitoring_signals:
  data_drift: # monitoring data drift
    type: data_drift
    production_data:
      input_data:
        path: azureml:credit_model_inputs:1  # the production data
# collected by
                                             # data_collector
        type: uri_folder
      data_context: model_inputs
      pre_processing_component: azureml:credit_data_preprocessing:
1 # Optional, if preprocessing steps are applied
    reference_data:
      input_data:
        path: azureml:credit_training_data:1 # use training data
                                             # as a baseline for
                                             # drift
        type: mltable
      data_context: training
      features:
```

```
        top_n_feature_importance: 23 # monitor drift for all
                                      # features in the training data
  # set
      metric_thresholds:
        numerical:
          jensen_shannon_distance: 0.01 # threshold for numerical
                                        # feature drift detection
```

This configures data drift monitoring by comparing production data (collected by DataCollector) against training data as a baseline.

4. **Step 4 – prediction drift monitoring**: Following data drift, we configure prediction drift monitoring to track changes in the model's output predictions by comparing current outputs against validation data, providing visibility into shifts in prediction behavior:

```
      prediction_drift: # monitoring prediction drift
        type: prediction_drift
        production_data:
          input_data:
            path: azureml:iris_model_outputs:1  # the production
                                                # outputs collected by
                                                # data_collector
            type: uri_folder
          data_context: model_outputs
          pre_processing_component: azureml:iris_output_
    preprocessing:1 # Optional
        reference_data:
          input_data:
            path: azureml:iris_validation_data:1 # use validation data
                                                 # as a baseline for
                                                 # output drift
            type: mltable
          data_context: validation
        metric_thresholds:
          categorical:
            pearsons_chi_squared_test: 0.02 # threshold for
                                            # categorical output drift
                                            # detection
```

This section monitors changes in model predictions by comparing current outputs with validation data.

5. **Step 5 – data quality monitoring**: We then set up data quality monitoring to detect issues such as missing values and outliers in the input data, ensuring the data feeding the model remains reliable for inference:

```
data_quality: # monitoring data quality
  type: data_quality
  production_data:
    input_data:
      path: azureml:credit_model_inputs:1  # the production data
                                           # collected by
                                           # data_collector
      type: uri_folder
    data_context: model_inputs
  reference_data:
    input_data:
      path: azureml:credit_training_data:1 # use training data
                                           # as a baseline for
                                           # quality
      type: mltable
    data_context: training
  features:
    top_n_feature_importance: 23 # monitor quality for all
                                 # features in the training
                                 # dataset
  metric_thresholds:
    numerical:
      missing_values: 0.05 # threshold for missing values
                           # detection
      outliers: 0.05 # threshold for outliers detection
```

This monitors data quality issues such as missing values and outliers in the production data.

6. **Step 6 – alert configuration**: Finally, we configure alert notifications to ensure the relevant stakeholders are informed promptly if monitoring thresholds are breached, enabling the proactive remediation of detected issues:

```
alert_notification: # this will be used to send job execution
                    # information
    emails:
      - example@example.com
```

This sets up email notifications when monitoring thresholds are breached.

In simple terms, this setup creates a monitoring job schedule that runs every day at 5:00 A.M. The job checks whether the data being used by the model and the model's predictions have changed compared to the original data. It uses built-in tools in AML to do the calculations and then saves the results so you can review them or get alerted if something unusual happens. We will discuss more on alerting in the next chapter, *Chapter 8, Notification and Alerting in MLOps. Figure 7.1* summarizes the whole process in a simplified manner.

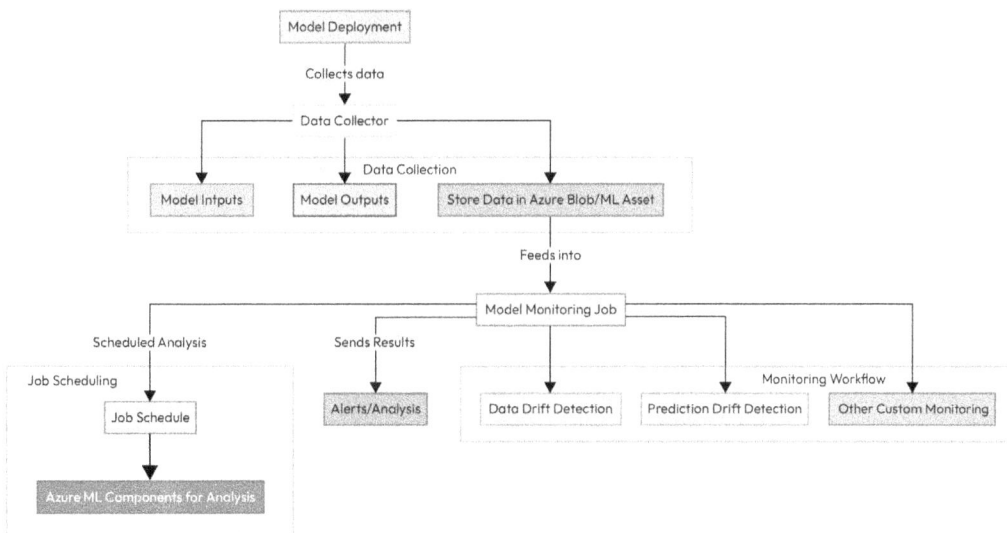

Figure 7.1 – DataCollector and monitoring go hand in hand

After the monitoring jobs are scheduled and run, the signals can be viewed in the AML portal by navigating to the workspace and selecting **Monitoring** from the left-hand menu.

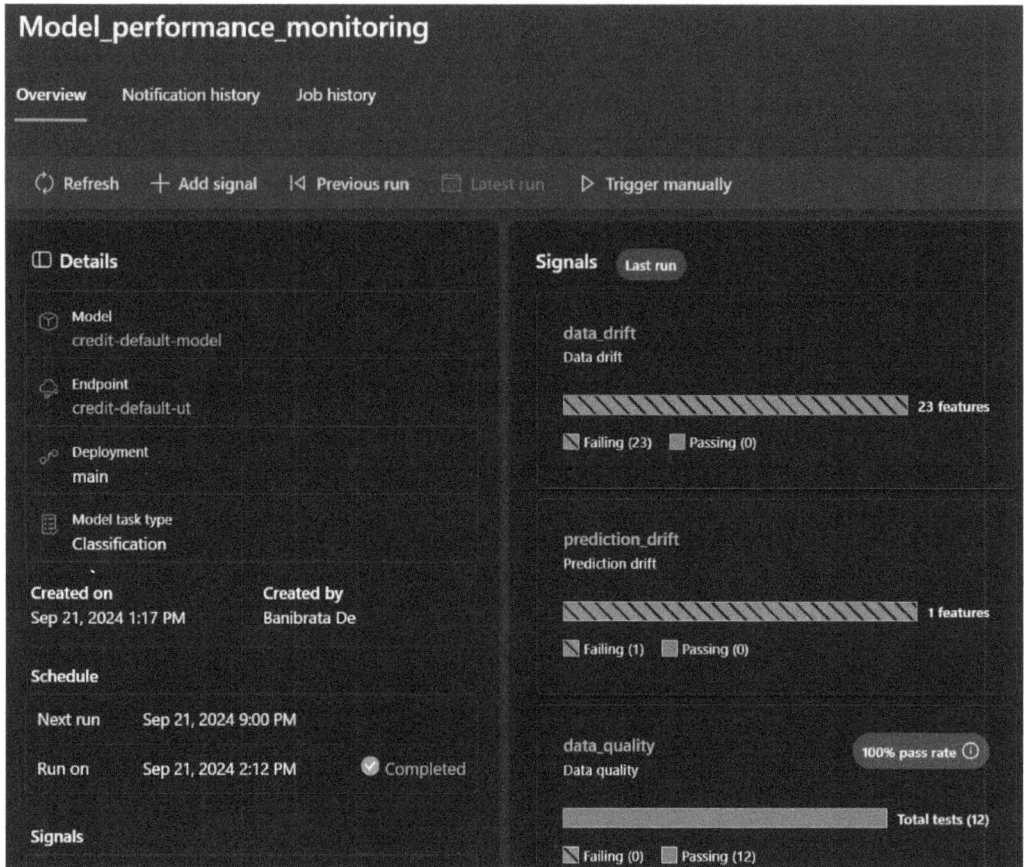

Figure 7.2 – Signal overview in the AML portal

If we select one signal, say, **data_drift**, it shows more detail on which features are showing signs of drift. For example, in the next screenshot, we can see that we drilled inside **data_drift** and selected a feature named **PAY_AMT4**, and it shows significant drift in data when compared with training data and production.

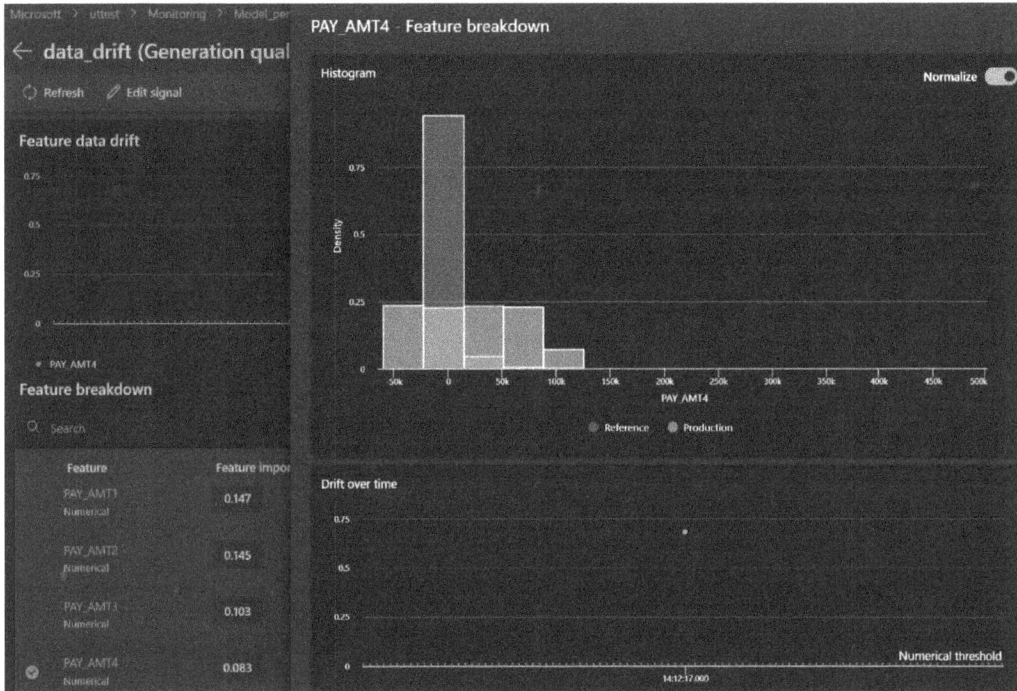

Figure 7.3 – data_drift signal detail

In the setup example, we demonstrated how to configure basic monitoring for a credit model using DataCollector's captured data. This configuration enables daily monitoring of data drift, prediction drift, and data quality, with automated alerts when issues are detected. The monitoring dashboard (*Figure 7.3*) provides a clear visualization of these metrics, allowing teams to quickly identify and respond to potential problems.

Key monitoring signals in AML

Although the previous example is a simple one, it can be expanded to handle more complex and advanced monitoring needs. It is beneficial to understand the full range of monitoring signals available in AML. For instance, it can include other monitoring types, as shown in *Figure 7.2*, or even incorporate custom monitoring setups. For more details, refer to `https://learn. microsoft.com/en-us/azure/machine-learning/concept-model-monitoring?view=azureml- api-2&viewFallbackFrom=azureml-api-1`.

AML provides several key monitoring categories that help ensure comprehensive oversight of your ML models:

- Data quality monitoring:

  - Helps detect issues in input data quality, such as missing values, outliers, or unexpected data patterns
  - Essential for maintaining the reliability of model predictions

- Data drift detection:

  - Tracks changes in the statistical properties of input features
  - Helps identify when model retraining might be necessary due to evolving data patterns

- Prediction drift analysis:

  - Monitors changes in model output distributions
  - Useful for detecting unexpected shifts in model behavior

- Feature attribution drift:

  - Feature attribution refers to how much each input feature contributes to a model's prediction
  - Examines changes in feature importance over time
  - Helps understand whether the relationship between features and predictions is changing

- Custom metric monitoring:

  - Allows teams to define and track metrics specific to their use case
  - Provides flexibility in monitoring business-specific KPIs

- Model bias monitoring:

  - Tracks fairness metrics across different demographic groups or data segments
  - Helps ensure equitable model performance and compliance with fairness requirements

For detailed implementation guidance and advanced configuration options, we recommend referring to the official AML documentation on model monitoring (https://learn.microsoft.com/en-us/azure/machine-learning/concept-model-monitoring?view=azureml-api-2).

This section focused on model performance monitoring, which primarily validates business logic. While it's possible to collect custom infrastructure performance data using custom collectors, Azure provides built-in support for monitoring basic infrastructure metrics, which we'll explore in the next section.

Infrastructure metric monitoring

While the previous section focused on monitoring aspects crucial to data scientists and ML engineers—such as model performance, data drift, and concept drift—this section delves into the operational side of monitoring. Specifically, we will explore infrastructure metrics that are critical for MLOps engineers to ensure smooth deployment and efficient resource utilization. These metrics provide visibility into how the model deployments are performing in terms of infrastructure health, scaling, and request handling.

In AML, monitoring infrastructure is typically done at two key levels.

Endpoint metrics

The endpoint is the entry point for sending inference requests. Multiple deployments can exist behind a single endpoint, and traffic can be managed between them based on specific configurations. Key metrics here focus on inference traffic and performance:

- **Requests per second (RPS)**: Measures the volume of incoming requests to the endpoint
- **Request latency**: Tracks the time it takes for a request to be processed and responded to
- **Success/error rate**: Indicates the success or failure rate of the requests made to the endpoint
- **Traffic distribution**: If the endpoint is routing traffic to multiple deployments, this tracks how traffic is being split among them

These metrics give MLOps engineers insights into the health and performance of the endpoint handling inference requests. *Figure 7.4* shows an example of how key infrastructure metrics—such as request rates and latency—are displayed in the Azure portal for monitoring endpoint performance.

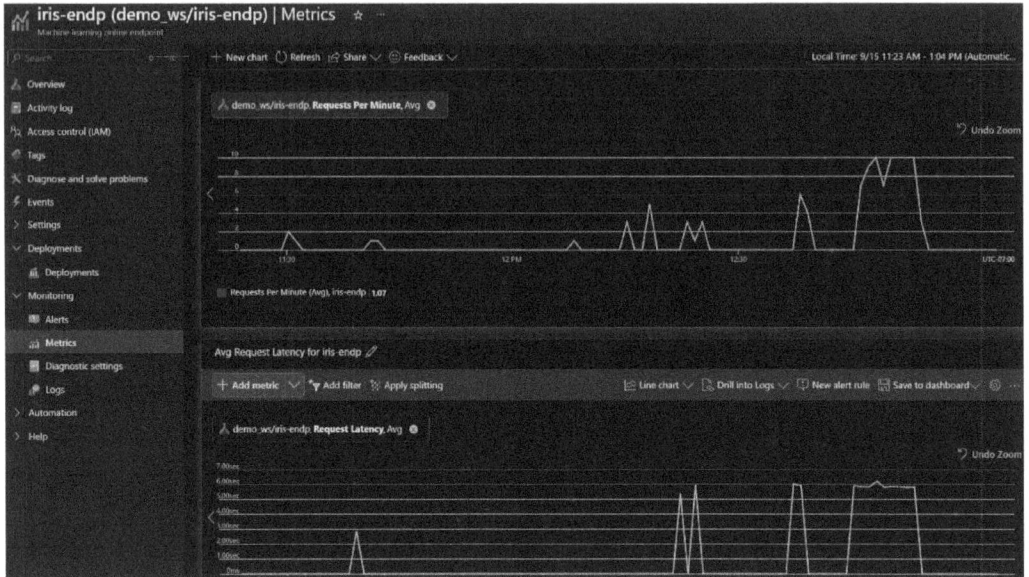

Figure 7.4 – Monitoring endpoint metrics in the Azure portal

Just as endpoint metrics provide insights into how inference requests are handled at the entry point, deployment metrics focus on the performance of the underlying infrastructure that powers the model inference.

Deployment metrics

Deployments are responsible for performing the actual model inference and involve the underlying infrastructure. These metrics are tied to resource usage and system health:

- **CPU utilization:** Monitors the amount of CPU resources consumed by the deployment during inference
- **GPU utilization:** Relevant for deployments using GPU-based models, this tracks GPU resource usage
- **Memory utilization:** Measures the amount of RAM consumed by the deployment
- **Disk utilization:** Tracks disk I/O and storage usage, which is especially useful for deployments requiring large amounts of temporary storage
- **Request-specific metrics:** Like endpoint metrics, but specific to each deployment (RPS, latency, and error rates)

These metrics are crucial for understanding resource utilization, such as CPU, GPU, memory, and disk usage, as well as deployment-specific request metrics. *Figure 7.5* illustrates how these deployment metrics are displayed in the Azure portal, providing visibility into the health and efficiency of each deployment:

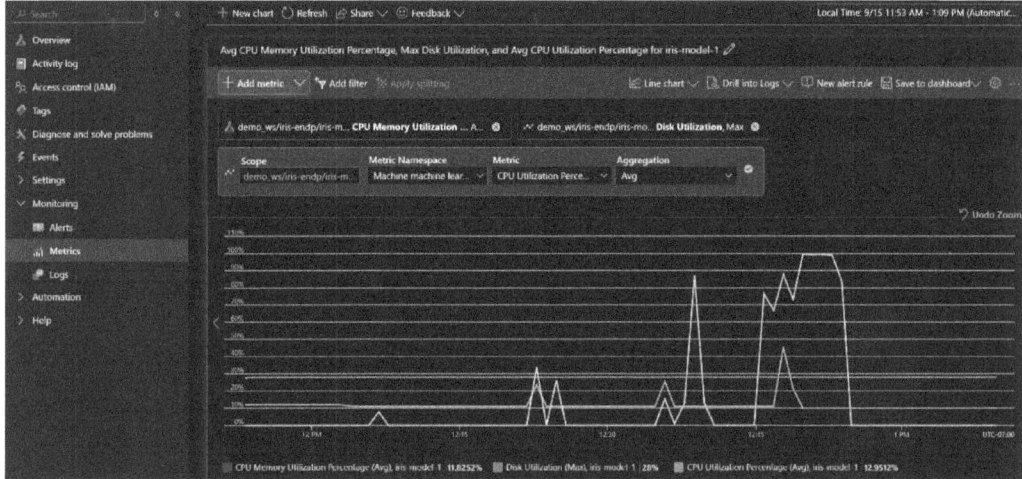

Figure 7.5 – Monitoring deployment metrics in the Azure portal

These infrastructure metrics, at both the endpoint and deployment levels, provide MLOps engineers with comprehensive visibility into their model's operational health. By monitoring these metrics continuously, teams can do the following:

- Proactively identify and address performance bottlenecks
- Optimize resource allocation and costs
- Ensure high availability and reliability of deployed models
- Make data-driven decisions about scaling and infrastructure improvements

When combined with the model performance monitoring that we discussed earlier, these infrastructure metrics complete the monitoring picture, enabling organizations to maintain robust and efficient ML operations in production.

Summary

This chapter explored the critical role of monitoring in maintaining effective and reliable ML models in production environments. We examined two main categories of monitoring in AML: model performance monitoring and infrastructure usage monitoring.

We discussed the DataCollector tool, central to Azure ML's model performance monitoring, and provided practical examples of setting up data collection and monitoring processes. The chapter covered key monitoring signals in AML and explored infrastructure metric monitoring at both the endpoint and deployment levels.

Best practices for implementing effective monitoring strategies in MLOps were outlined, emphasizing clear objectives, regular review, collaboration, and robust alerting systems.

In the next chapter, we will build upon these concepts by exploring notification and alerting in MLOps, covering how to set up effective alert mechanisms that leverage monitoring data to ensure timely responses to issues or threshold breaches.

Join the CloudPro Newsletter with 44000+ Subscribers

Want to know what's happening in cloud computing, DevOps, IT administration, networking, and more? Scan the QR code to subscribe to **CloudPro**, our weekly newsletter for 44,000+ tech professionals who want to stay informed and ahead of the curve.

https://packt.link/cloudpro

8

Notification and Alerting in MLOps

In the dynamic world of **machine learning operations** (**MLOps**), staying informed about critical events and changes is paramount to maintaining efficient and reliable systems. This chapter delves into the crucial aspect of notification and alerting within the MLOps framework, building upon the monitoring concepts discussed in the previous chapter. As ML models become increasingly integral to business operations, the ability to respond promptly to various events throughout the ML lifecycle becomes a key differentiator in operational excellence.

This chapter will guide you through the process of setting up comprehensive notification and alerting systems tailored for MLOps. We'll explore the available AML lifecycle events and demonstrate how to leverage basic alerting capabilities within individual workspaces. From there, we'll advance to implementing cross-workspace alerting for enterprise-scale monitoring, followed by advanced notification techniques using email and webhooks. Finally, we'll cover best practices for alert management to ensure your system remains effective without overwhelming your team.

Through practical examples and in-depth explanations, this chapter will equip you with the skills to create a responsive and efficient MLOps ecosystem, ensuring timely interventions and streamlined workflow management.

In this chapter, we'll identify key events relevant to our ML processes and map them to our operational requirements. From there, we will demonstrate how to set up alerts for specific events within a single workspace.

We will be covering the following main headings in this chapter:

- Understanding alerts and notifications in the MLOps context
- Exploring AML platform logs
- Creating an alert
- Extending alerts to multiple workspaces
- Advanced alerting
- Best practices for alert management

Understanding alerts and notifications in the MLOps context

Before diving into implementation, let's establish some key concepts:

- **Alerts** are automated triggers that fire when specific conditions or thresholds are met in your ML systems, such as model performance degradation or deployment failures.
- **Notifications** are the delivery mechanisms that inform relevant stakeholders about these alerts through channels such as email, SMS, or integration tools.

In MLOps, effective alerting serves as an early warning system that enables proactive intervention before minor issues escalate into critical operational problems.

Throughout the ML lifecycle—from training to inferencing—various events are continuously generated and stored within the AML platform. These events are primarily logged by Azure's built-in platform capabilities and can be accessed by querying the event store.

To effectively set up alerts, it is essential to understand where these signals originate and how to access them within AML. In the next section, we will explore the platform logs that capture these critical events throughout your ML workflows.

Exploring AML platform logs

To start, navigate to your AML workspace in the portal and go to the **Monitoring** section, and select **Logs**. From here, you can choose **Tables** and select **AzureActivity Logs**. These logs capture all activities occurring on the Azure resources, including the ML workspace. You can quickly run a KQL query to view any failed operations in the past 24 hours, as illustrated in *Figure 8.1*:

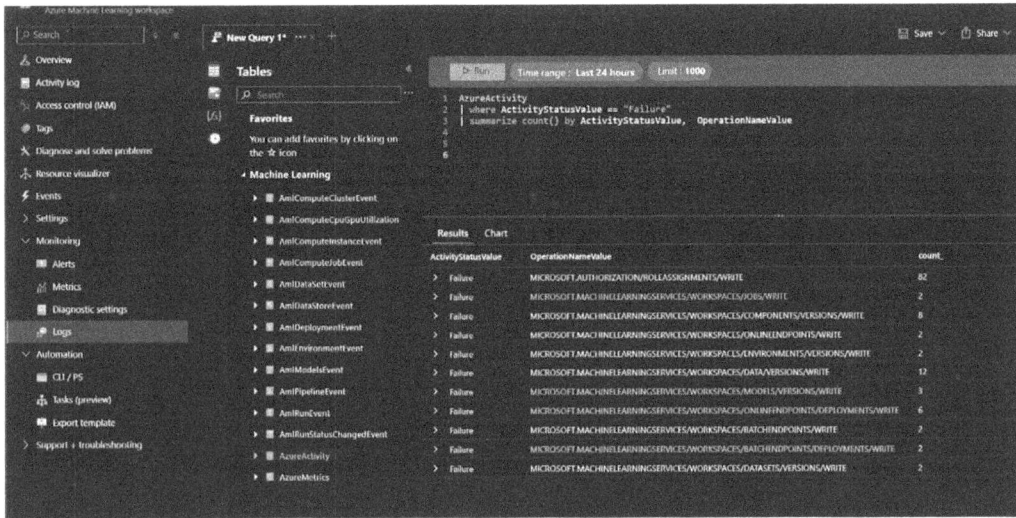

Figure 8.1 – Exploring MLOps events using a KQL query

The role of MLOps engineers focuses on understanding the nature of failures throughout the ML lifecycle and tracking critical events to ensure smooth operations. Monitoring trends and setting up alerts for these key events allows teams to keep the operational metrics healthy and address any issues promptly.

The following table highlights some typical AML events that are essential to track from a monitoring and alerting perspective:

Operation name	Purpose
MICROSOFT.MACHINELEARNINGSERVICES/WORKSPACES/JOBS/WRITE	Experiment run
MICROSOFT.MACHINELEARNINGSERVICES/WORKSPACES/MODELS/VERSIONS/WRITE	Register the model
MICROSOFT.MACHINELEARNINGSERVICES/WORKSPACES/ONLINEENDPOINTS/DEPLOYMENTS/WRITE	Deploy the model for online inference
MICROSOFT.MACHINELEARNINGSERVICES/WORKSPACES/BATCHENDPOINTS/DEPLOYMENTS/WRITE	Deploy the model for batch inference

Table 8.1 – Key AML operations for MLOps monitoring and alerting

By tracking and analyzing these events, organizations can stay on top of any failures or anomalies. For example, examining a model deployment failure for online inference provides valuable insights. *Figure 8.2* shows a failure and details the errors. This information is crucial in helping teams understand why the failure occurred and take corrective action promptly.

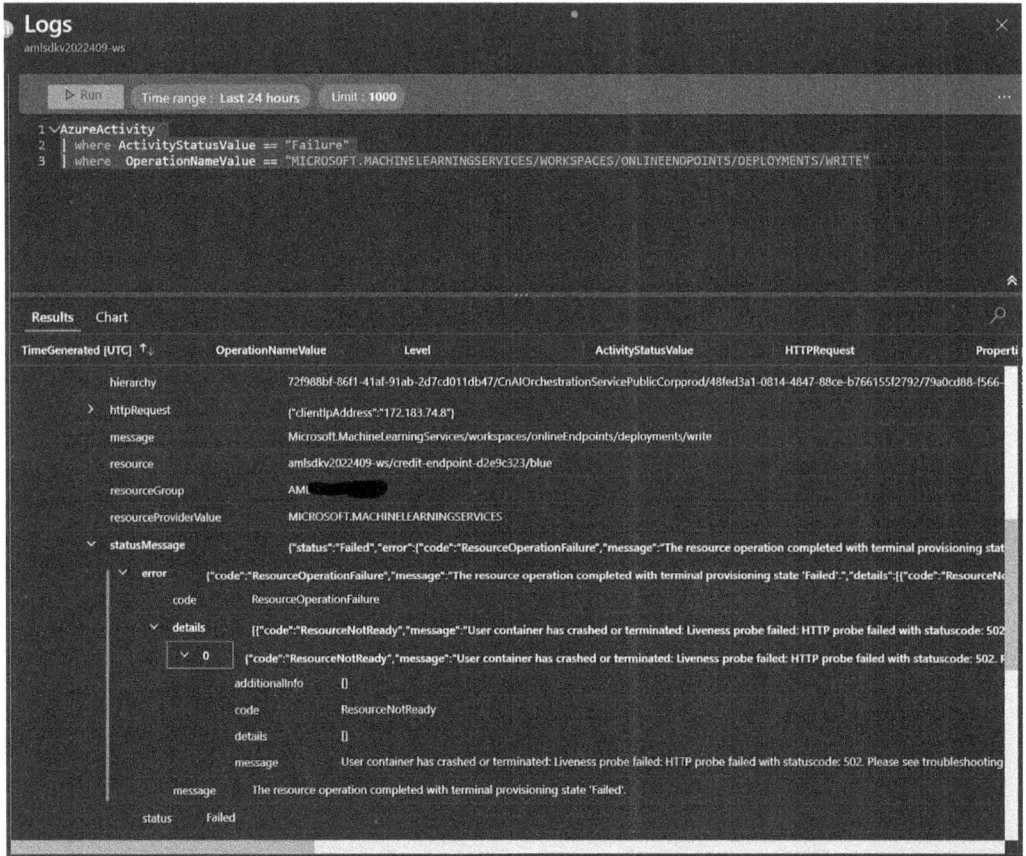

Figure 8.2 – Example details of a deployment failure operation

Now that we have a clearer understanding of failure events and their importance in maintaining healthy operations, let's move forward with setting up an alert on this particular type of failure to notify us when such failures occur.

Creating an alert

To ensure the timely detection of issues, we can create a rule to trigger an alert when a specific failure threshold is met. For further details on Azure Monitor alerts, you can refer to the following link: https://learn.microsoft.com/en-us/azure/azure-monitor/alerts/alerts-overview.

Navigate to your AML workspace in the portal, go to the **Monitoring** section, and select the **Alerts** option. This will allow you to define your alerting logic. Using the query from *Figure 8.2*, let's assume that if 10 model deployments for an online endpoint fail in a single day, an Ops engineer should be notified to act.

Create a custom alert with the name `MonitorOnlineDeploymentFailures`, which will send a notification (via email or SMS) when this threshold is reached. These notification preferences, along with other details, can be configured during the alert setup, as shown in the following figure:

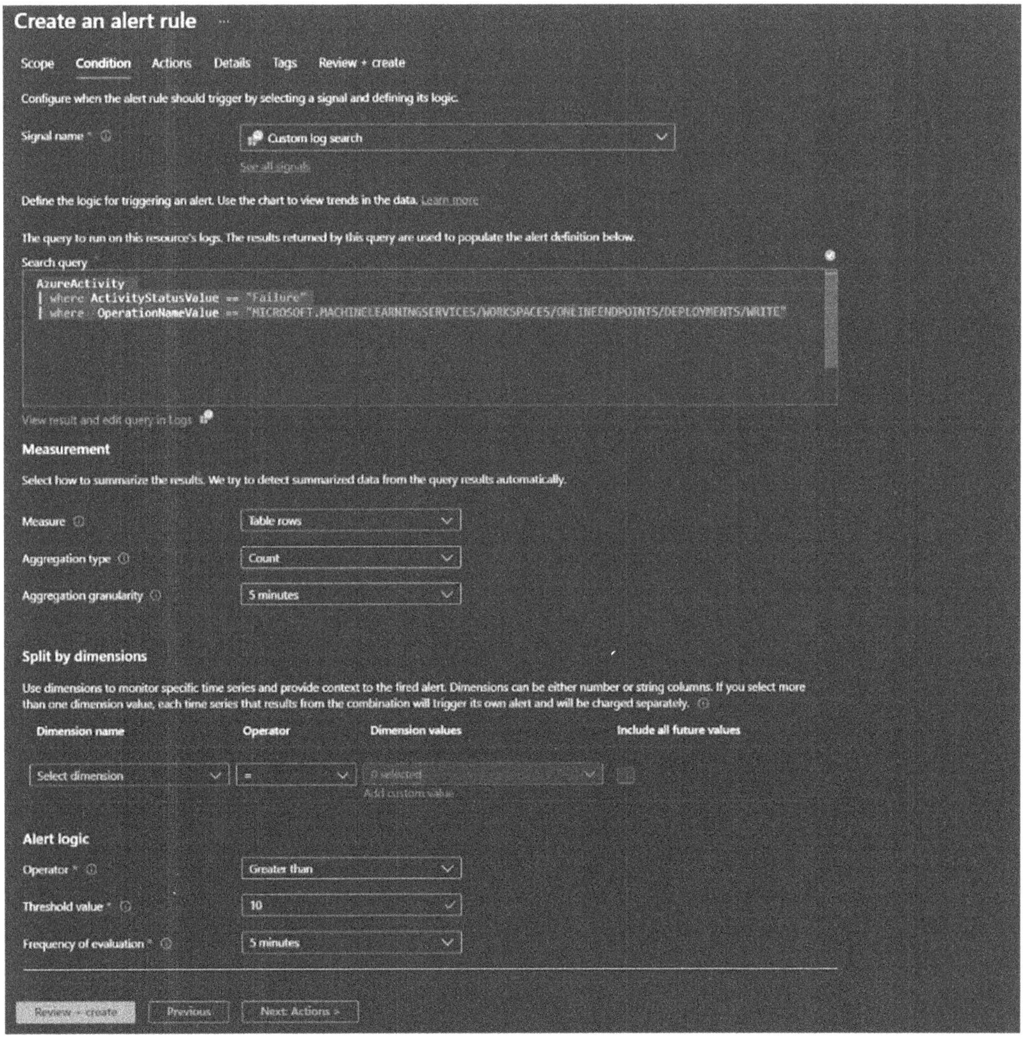

Figure 8.3 – Creating an alert on deployment failure count

Here, we define the following key elements:

- **Search query**: The query filters the logs to show only failure events for model deployments (`OperationNameValue == "MICROSOFT.MACHINELEARNINGSERVICES/WORKSPACES/ONLINEENDPOINTS/DEPLOYMENTS/WRITE"`). This helps narrow down failures specific to online endpoint model deployments.

- **Measurement**: The alert is set to count the number of failed operations over a 5-minute interval.

- **Alert logic**: An alert is triggered when the number of failed deployments exceeds 10 within a 5-minute window, notifying the relevant Ops engineers.

Once configured, this alert ensures that any significant issues in the model deployment process are caught and handled quickly.

Figure 8.4 shows a sample alert fired and delivered to the email address it was configured with. It has some important information regarding the alert, as shown, including the time, signal type, workspace name, and so on:

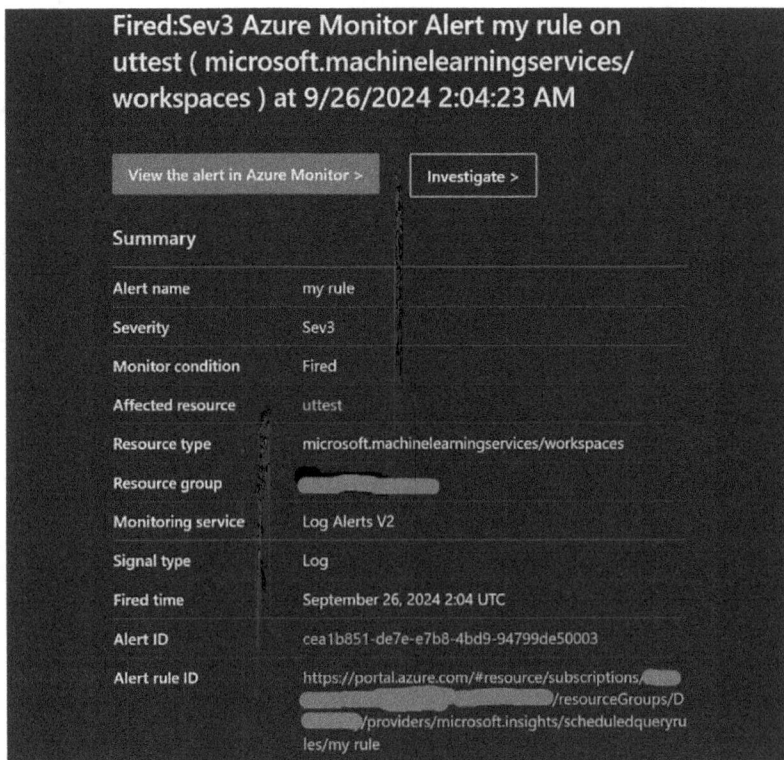

Figure 8.4 – An alert email

The alert email includes a link labeled **Investigate**. This is an important feature that provides more in-depth information. In this scenario, Azure's ML capabilities are leveraged to automatically correlate relevant data points from around the time of the alert. This feature offers a summarized view of what might have led to the issue, which serves as an excellent starting point for any Ops engineer conducting a root cause analysis.

By utilizing this feature, you can gain immediate insights into the broader context of the failure, enabling faster troubleshooting, recommendations, and resolution, as shown in *Figure 8.5*:

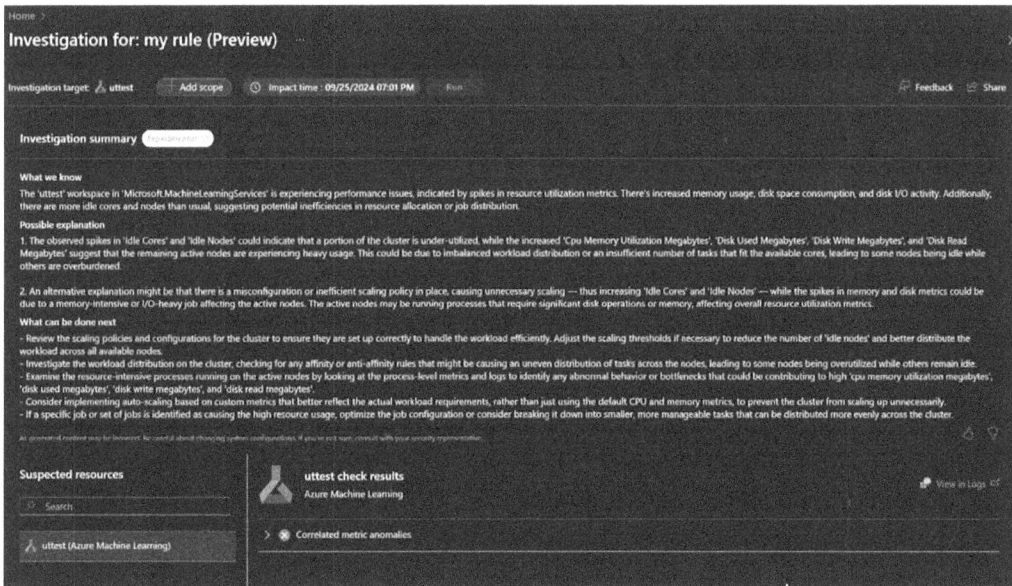

Figure 8.5 – Autocorrelation/analysis of the alert

In this section, we covered the basics of setting up alerting mechanisms in AML and demonstrated how to make them actionable through practical examples. This provides a solid foundation for monitoring key events and responding to failures. As you become more familiar with Azure's capabilities, you can extend these concepts by designing more sophisticated monitoring solutions. Depending on your alerting needs, you can craft complex KQL queries and leverage advanced logic to meet intricate monitoring requirements, ensuring robust MLOps practices.

With a solid alerting system in place for a single AML workspace, the next step is to expand this capability across multiple workspaces within your organization, enabling broader monitoring and centralized control.

Extending alerts to multiple workspaces

Having established a robust alerting system for a single AML workspace, the next logical step is to extend this setup to multiple workspaces within an organization. This is where the concept of a Log Analytics workspace becomes essential.

Introduction to Log Analytics workspaces

A **Log Analytics workspace** acts as a centralized hub for collecting, storing, and analyzing log data from various sources, including multiple AML workspaces. By consolidating events from different workspaces into a single Log Analytics workspace, you gain a unified view of your ML operations, streamlining the process of monitoring, analyzing, and responding to critical events across your organization.

In this section, we'll explore how to configure a Log Analytics workspace to collect data from multiple AML workspaces. Once the data is centralized, you can apply the same alerting logic you used for a single workspace, but with enhanced control over event aggregation and monitoring. For detailed instructions on setting up a Log Analytics workspace, refer to the official guide (`https://learn.microsoft.com/en-us/azure/azure-monitor/logs/quick-create-workspace?tabs=azure-portal`).

Configuring centralized collection

In *Figure 8.3*, we demonstrated how to set up alerts based on the outcome of a log query for a single workspace. Now, let's expand this concept to cover multiple workspaces.

The first step is to configure the export of activity logs. Navigate to **Activity log** from the left-hand navigation bar and select **Export Activity Logs**, as shown in *Figure 8.6*:

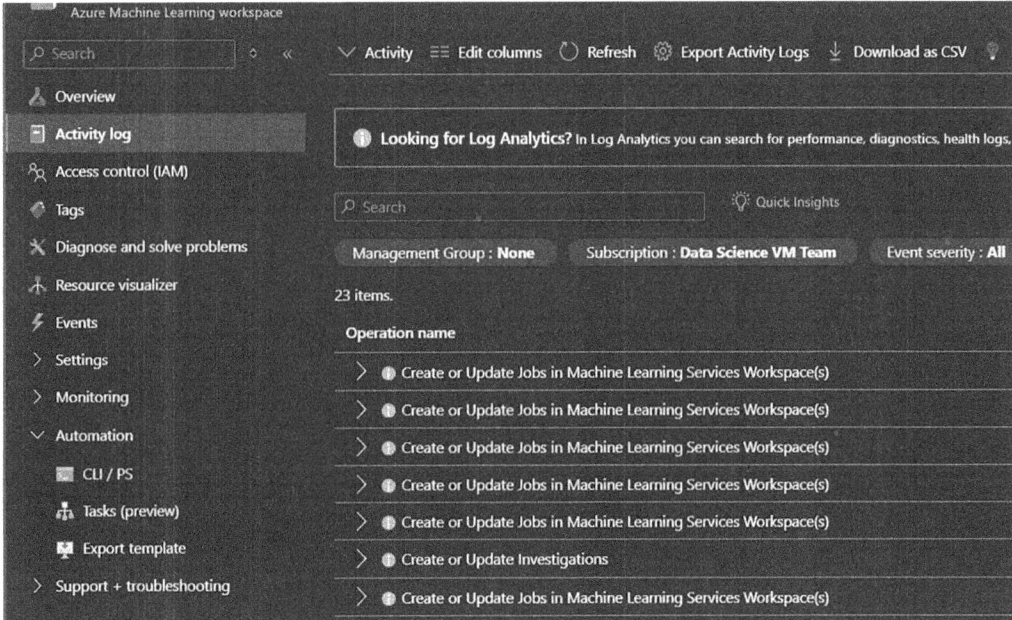

Figure 8.6 – Export Activity Logs

After selecting the export option, you'll need to specify which logs to export and their destination. *Figure 8.7* shows the configuration panel where you can select the Log Analytics workspace as your destination and choose the relevant log categories to export:

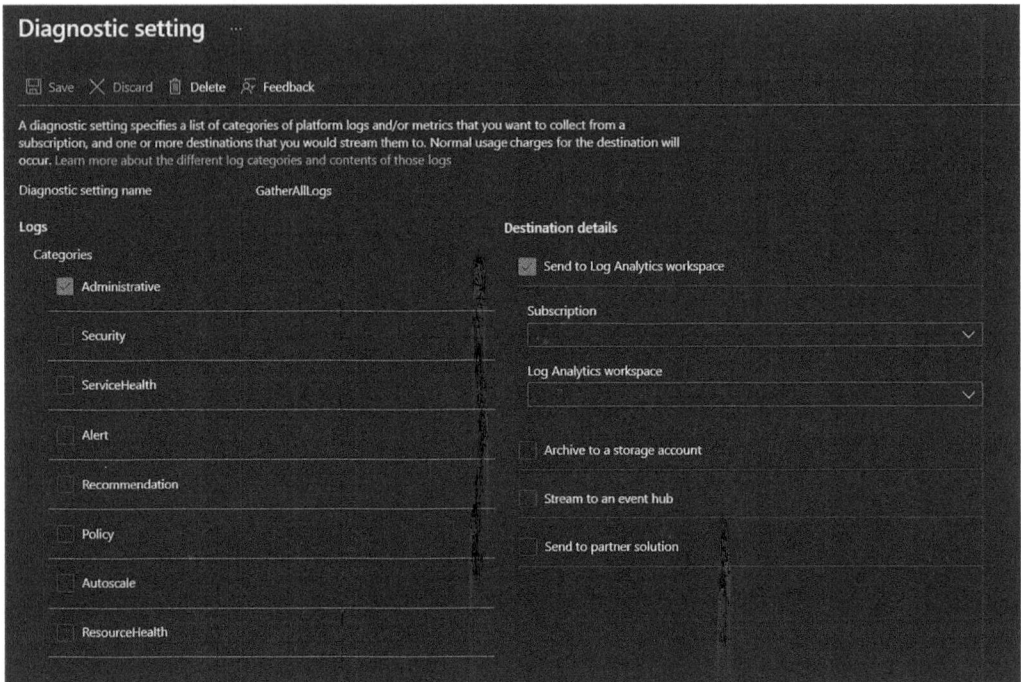

Figure 8.7 – Choosing logs and destination

The key difference here is that, previously, the alert was configured directly within an individual workspace. Now, we are sending the same logs from each workspace to a Log Analytics workspace, which is configured to aggregate logs from multiple workspaces. This setup enables centralized monitoring across all relevant workspaces, provided each workspace is configured accordingly.

Once this setup is complete, you can run the same query on the Log Analytics workspace and see aggregated logs from all connected workspaces, as shown in *Figure 8.8*:

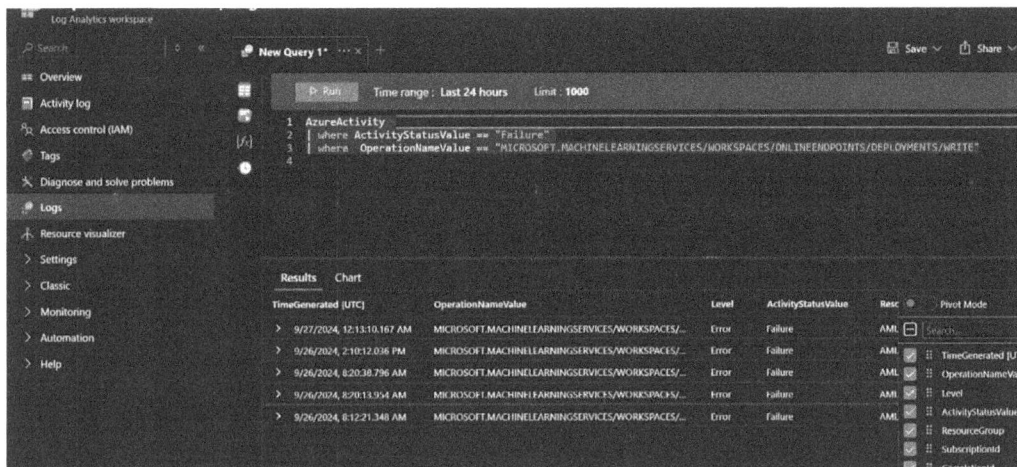

Figure 8.8 – Discovering the exported logs from the Log Analytics workspace

With the centralized collection of logs from multiple workspaces in place, let's now explore some more advanced alerting techniques.

Advanced alerting

While Azure's native alerting system provides a robust solution for monitoring ML lifecycle events across multiple workspaces, there are more advanced approaches that can further enhance your MLOps alerting strategy. These advanced solutions often involve integrating third-party providers and exporting logs and metrics, including model performance data (discussed in the previous chapter), to external systems for deeper analysis and complex alerting logic.

One such method is exporting logs to external storage, such as **Azure Blob Storage**, which enables more flexibility in how you store, analyze, and trigger alerts. By sending logs and metrics from multiple workspaces to Blob Storage, you can enable the following:

- **Advanced log analysis**: External systems or third-party analytics platforms can ingest these logs, allowing you to define more sophisticated alerting logic. This could include anomaly detection, custom thresholds, or analysis across different time periods.

- **Complex alerting logic**: You can build alerts that go beyond simple thresholds, incorporating advanced statistical models or even ML to predict failures or identify trends across multiple workspaces. These advanced alerts can help you detect unusual behavior in model training, deployment, or performance at an early stage, preventing larger operational issues.

- **Webhook integrations**: Webhooks can be used to trigger real-time alerts or automated actions based on specific events. For example, integrating with a third-party provider through webhooks allows you to send custom notifications to your incident management tool, or even trigger an automated response, such as rolling back a deployment or spinning up additional resources.

- **ML for alerting**: A more sophisticated approach involves using ML models to analyze the collected logs and trends. By leveraging ML, you can predict potential issues before they happen or identify correlations between different events in the MLOps lifecycle that traditional alerts might miss.

These advanced alerting solutions provide more granular control and deeper insights into the entire MLOps process, giving you better optics on key events and helping you proactively manage and optimize the lifecycle of your ML models.

Integrating alerts with incident management

To maximize the effectiveness of your MLOps alerting system, integrate alerts directly with your organization's incident management workflow. This integration ensures that alerts don't just notify but also trigger appropriate response processes. The integration approach includes the following:

- **Automated ticket creation**: Configure critical alerts to automatically create incidents in your **IT Service Management (ITSM)** platform (ServiceNow, Jira Service Management, etc.).

- **Escalation workflows**: Route different alert severities to appropriate teams, such as model performance issues to data science teams and infrastructure failures to DevOps teams.

- **Status page integration**: Automatically update customer-facing status pages when ML services are impacted.

- **Runbook automation**: Link alerts to automated remediation scripts or clear manual runbooks that responders can follow.

This integration transforms alerts from simple notifications into actionable incidents with clear ownership and resolution paths.

Best practices for alert management

Effective alert management is crucial for maintaining a responsive and efficient MLOps environment. However, poorly configured alerts can lead to alert fatigue, overwhelming your team with notifications and potentially causing important issues to be overlooked. This section will cover best practices for setting alert thresholds and strategies to avoid alert fatigue.

Setting appropriate alert thresholds

When configuring alert thresholds, there are several best practices to consider:

- **Understand your baseline**: Before setting thresholds, monitor your systems for a period to understand normal behavior. This baseline will help you distinguish between regular fluctuations and genuine issues.

- **Start conservative**: Begin with wider thresholds and gradually tighten them as you gain more insights into your system's behavior. This approach helps avoid an initial flood of false positives.

- **Use dynamic thresholds**: Where possible, implement dynamic thresholds that adjust based on historical data. This is particularly useful for metrics that have predictable patterns, such as model training times that vary with dataset size.

- **Consider time windows**: Instead of alerting on single data points, consider using time windows. For example, alert when a metric exceeds a threshold for 15 minutes, rather than triggering on a momentary spike.

- **Implement graduated thresholds**: Set up multiple thresholds for the same metric with different severity levels, such as the following:

    - **Warning**: Model accuracy drops below 95%

    - **Critical**: Model accuracy drops below 90%

- **Regular review and adjustment**: Periodically review your alert thresholds and adjust them based on real-world performance and feedback from your team.

While these strategies help ensure that your alerts are properly calibrated, it's also crucial to address the issue of alert fatigue.

Avoiding alert fatigue

Alert fatigue occurs when teams are bombarded with too many notifications, causing them to become desensitized and less responsive to important alerts. To prevent alert fatigue, consider implementing the following best practices:

- **Prioritize alerts**: Categorize alerts by severity and impact. Ensure that high-priority alerts stand out and are routed to the appropriate team members.

- **Implement alert correlation**: Use tools or custom logic to group related alerts. This prevents a single issue from triggering multiple notifications.

- **Use smart notifications**: Implement escalation policies that start with less intrusive notifications (e.g., Slack messages) before moving to more urgent methods (e.g., phone calls) if the issue persists.

- **Implement alert suppression**: For known issues or during maintenance windows, suppress alerts to avoid unnecessary notifications.

- **Create clear alert descriptions**: Each alert should clearly describe the problem and its potential impact, and suggest the next steps. This helps recipients quickly understand and act on the alert.

- **Establish a "no-alert" culture**: Encourage your team to question and refine alerts. If an alert consistently doesn't require action, it should be modified or removed.

- **Use runbooks**: Develop and maintain runbooks for common alerts. These step-by-step guides can help reduce response time and standardize issue resolution.

- **Implement alert analytics**: Regularly analyze your alert data to identify patterns. This can help you refine your alerting strategy and potentially address recurring issues at their root cause.

Implementing these strategies will help maintain alert effectiveness while preventing notification overload that can compromise your team's responsiveness.

Example: Refining model deployment failure alerts

Let's revisit our earlier example of alerting on model deployment failures and apply these best practices:

- **Baseline understanding**: After monitoring for a month, you notice that having one or two deployment failures per day is normal due to various non-critical reasons.

- **Graduated thresholds**:

  - **Warning alert**: More than 5 deployment failures in 24 hours

  - **Critical alert**: More than 10 deployment failures in 24 hours, or 5 failures of the same model

- **Time window**: Instead of alerting on each failure, trigger alerts based on the number of failures within a 24-hour rolling window.

- **Alert correlation**: Group alerts for failures of the same model or with similar error messages.

- **Clear description**: "Multiple model deployment failures detected. 7 failures in the last 24 hours, exceeding the warning threshold of 5. Check the attached log analysis for common error patterns."
- **Runbook link**: Include a link to a runbook with steps to investigate common deployment failure causes and resolution steps.

By applying these practices, you create a more nuanced alerting system that reduces noise while ensuring that significant issues are promptly addressed. Remember, the goal is to strike a balance between being informed of important events and not overwhelming your team with unnecessary alerts.

Regular reviews and adjustments of your alerting strategy, combined with feedback from your MLOps team, will help you maintain an effective and efficient notification system that supports your ML operations.

Summary

In this chapter, we've explored the critical role of notification and alerting in MLOps, from understanding AML lifecycle events to implementing advanced, cross-workspace alerting strategies. By leveraging Azure's capabilities and following best practices, you can build a responsive alerting system that provides actionable insights, enables quick issue resolution, and supports continuous improvement. Remember, effective alerting is about striking the right balance – staying informed without succumbing to alert fatigue. As your MLOps practices evolve, regularly refine your alerting approach to maintain operational excellence in your ML lifecycle.

As you build a responsive alerting system to maintain visibility and control, the next step is to streamline and automate your ML workflows for consistent, efficient operations. In the next chapter, we will explore how to achieve this using AML pipelines and GitHub workflows.

Part 3

MLOps and Beyond

This final part focuses on automating the ML lifecycle and translating MLOps practices into real-world business impact. You will learn how to build automated pipelines and CI/CD workflows using AML pipelines and GitHub Actions, ensuring consistent, reproducible, and scalable operations. The part then shifts to practical applications, demonstrating how to use models in production environments through case studies across Azure, AWS, and GCP, giving you insights into multi-cloud MLOps strategies. Finally, you will explore next-generation MLOps, including operationalizing large language models, preparing you to extend your MLOps expertise into cutting-edge AI deployments. This part empowers you to implement, manage, and scale MLOps in complex, production-grade environments confidently.

This part has the following chapters:

- *Chapter 9, Automating the ML Lifecycle with ML Pipelines and GitHub Workflows*
- *Chapter 10, Using Models in Real-world Applications*
- *Chapter 11, Exploring Next-Gen MLOps*

9

Automating the ML Lifecycle with ML Pipelines and GitHub Workflows

Machine learning pipelines are the backbone of efficient, reproducible, and scalable ML workflows. In this chapter, we'll dive deep into the world of ML pipelines, exploring how they can be implemented across multiple cloud platforms to create robust, end-to-end solutions. We'll build upon the concepts of components and pipelines introduced in *Chapter 3*, taking them to the next level with real-world applications and advanced CI/CD strategies.

In *Chapter 3*, we introduced the concepts of components and pipelines to build machine learning workflows, along with a few practical examples. In this chapter, we will expand on those foundations by demonstrating how to construct an end-to-end workflow that begins with data ingestion and transformation and progresses through to model deployment. We will also explore scenarios where AML pipelines may need to be complemented with GitHub Actions to enable robust CI/CD practices.

You'll learn how to automate and streamline the various phases of the ML lifecycle using AML pipelines within the Azure ecosystem. We will then move beyond AML pipelines to address more complex, real-world cases that require multi-cloud support and advanced CI/CD orchestration, illustrating how GitHub Actions can be integrated to build scalable and maintainable MLOps workflows.

By the end of this chapter, you'll be equipped to design and implement sophisticated multi-cloud ML pipelines. You'll understand how to leverage the strengths of different cloud providers such as Azure, AWS, and GCP in a single, cohesive workflow. This knowledge will enable you to build highly available, compliant, and scalable ML solutions that can meet the demands of enterprise-level applications.

These skills are essential for MLOps engineers and data scientists who want to take their ML workflows to the next level, ensuring robustness, reproducibility, and scalability across diverse cloud environments.

In this chapter, we're going to cover the following main topics:

- Implementing end-to-end AML pipelines
- Real-world scenario: Multi-cloud CI/CD for ML workflows
- Challenges and best practices

While previous chapters focused primarily on AML, this chapter expands beyond single-cloud approaches to demonstrate enterprise-grade MLOps workflows. Many organizations require multi-cloud strategies for compliance, redundancy, and avoiding vendor lock-in. We'll start with AML pipelines and progressively show how GitHub Actions enables integration across multiple cloud providers.

Implementing end-to-end AML pipelines

Pipelines in Azure Machine Learning are workflows that stitch together various ML phases, such as data ingestion, preprocessing, feature engineering, model training, evaluation, and deployment, into an inferencing endpoint. They allow you to automate these steps, ensuring that each stage is executed in a consistent and reproducible manner.

We will be focusing on two different kinds of pipelines here: an AML pipeline, which is specific to AML, and then a CI/CD pipeline, which encompasses the AML pipeline and beyond that.

AML pipeline

Here's an example of a YAML file that defines an end-to-end pipeline and schedules it using AML CLI v2. This example includes steps for data ingestion, preprocessing, model training, evaluation, and deployment to an inferencing endpoint:

```
$schema: https://azuremlschemas.azureedge.net/latest/pipelineJob.schema.
json
```

```yaml
name: ml-pipeline-job
description: End-to-end ML pipeline job
experiment_name: ml-pipeline-experiment

jobs:
  data_ingestion:
    type: command
    command: >
      python data_ingestion.py
    environment: azureml:AzureML-sklearn-0.24-ubuntu18.04-py37-cpu:1
    compute: azureml:cpu-cluster

  data_preprocessing:
    type: command
    command: >
      python data_preprocessing.py --input_data ${{inputs.data}}
    inputs:
      data:
        job_output_type: uri_file
        source: jobs.data_ingestion.outputs.output_data
    environment: azureml:AzureML-sklearn-0.24-ubuntu18.04-py37-cpu:1
    compute: azureml:cpu-cluster

  model_training:
    type: command
    command: >
      python train.py --input_data ${{inputs.preprocessed_data}}
    inputs:
      preprocessed_data:
        job_output_type: uri_file
        source: jobs.data_preprocessing.outputs.preprocessed_data
    environment: azureml:AzureML-pytorch-1.7-ubuntu18.04-py37-cpu:1
    compute: azureml:gpu-cluster

  model_evaluation:
    type: command
    command: >
```

```
        python evaluate.py --model ${{inputs.model}}
    inputs:
      model:
        job_output_type: uri_file
        source: jobs.model_training.outputs.model
    environment: azureml:AzureML-sklearn-0.24-ubuntu18.04-py37-cpu:1
    compute: azureml:cpu-cluster

  model_deployment:
    type: command
    command: >
      az ml model deploy --model ${{inputs.model}}
      --endpoint-name my-endpoint
    inputs:
      model:
        job_output_type: uri_file
        source: jobs.model_training.outputs.model
    environment: azureml:AzureML-sklearn-0.24-ubuntu18.04-py37-cpu:1
    compute: azureml:cpu-cluster

schedule:
  name: ml-pipeline-schedule
  description: Schedule for ML pipeline job
  trigger:
    type: recurrence
    frequency: day
    interval: 1
    start_time: '2024-10-19T00:00:00Z'
    time_zone: 'UTC'
```

This pipeline configuration defines five sequential jobs that execute in dependency order: data ingestion, preprocessing, training, evaluation, and deployment. Each job specifies its Python script, compute environment (CPU or GPU cluster), and data dependencies through the inputs section, which references outputs from previous jobs. The schedule section at the bottom automates daily execution at midnight UTC using a recurrence trigger.

The following Azure CLI commands demonstrate the core operations:

```
az ml job create --file pipeline.yml
az ml schedule create --file pipeline.yml
```

These commands create a model registry entry, establish an online endpoint, and deploy the model for real-time inference. The `--file` flag references additional YAML configuration files that define deployment specifications.

While AML pipelines excel at orchestrating machine learning workflows within the Azure ecosystem, there are scenarios where expanding beyond this framework becomes necessary. GitHub Actions offers a more versatile approach for complex CI/CD requirements, especially in multi-cloud or hybrid deployments. Unlike AML pipelines, which are primarily focused on ML workflows, GitHub Actions can integrate with broader application components, manage deployments across multiple cloud providers, and offer more advanced customization for notifications and security checks. GitHub Actions also provides superior version control integration and can trigger workflows based on a wider range of events. By complementing AML pipelines with GitHub Actions, organizations can create more robust, flexible, and comprehensive MLOps workflows that extend beyond the boundaries of a single cloud platform.

Expanding beyond Azure: GitHub Actions for CI/CD

While AzureML pipelines are powerful and can handle a wide range of machine learning workflows, there are certain scenarios where GitHub Actions might be needed to complement AzureML pipelines:

- **Complex CI/CD workflows**: If you need to integrate your ML pipeline with a broader CI/CD workflow that includes building, testing, and deploying other components of your application (for example, web services, databases), GitHub Actions can help orchestrate these tasks alongside your AzureML pipeline.

- **Multi-cloud or hybrid deployments**: If your deployment strategy involves multiple cloud providers or a hybrid environment, GitHub Actions can help manage and coordinate deployments across different platforms, ensuring seamless integration.

- **Custom notifications and alerts**: While AzureML provides basic notifications, GitHub Actions can offer more advanced and customizable notifications and alerts, such as sending messages to Slack, Teams, or other communication tools based on specific events in your pipeline.

- **Advanced security and compliance checks**: GitHub Actions can be used to run security and compliance checks on your code and models before they are deployed. This can include vulnerability scanning, license compliance checks, and more.

- **Integration with external tools and services**: If your workflow requires integration with external tools and services that are not natively supported by AzureML, GitHub Actions can help bridge the gap by running custom scripts and actions to interact with these services.

You can integrate GitHub Actions with AML pipelines to create an end-to-end machine learning workflow. This example will show you how to set up a GitHub Actions workflow that trains a model using Azure Machine Learning and then deploys it to an inferencing endpoint.

Create a file named `.github/workflows/azureml-pipeline.yml` in your GitHub repository with the following content:

```yaml
name: AzureML Pipeline
on:
  push:
    branches:
      - main
jobs:
  build:
    runs-on: ubuntu-latest
    steps:
    - name: Checkout repository
      uses: actions/checkout@v2
    - name: Set up Python
      uses: actions/setup-python@v2
      with:
        python-version: '3.8'
    - name: Install dependencies
      run: |
```

```
    python -m pip install --upgrade pip
    pip install azure-ai-ml azure-identity
- name: Authenticate with Azure
  uses: azure/login@v2
  with:
    creds: ${{ secrets.AZURE_CREDENTIALS }}
- name: Run AzureML Pipeline
  run: |
    az ml model create --model ./model.pkl --name model_name
--version model_version
    az ml online-endpoint create --name endpoint_name
    az ml online-deployment create --name deployment_name
--file deployment_config.yaml
```

The GitHub pipeline has two main components:

- **GitHub Actions workflow YAML:** This workflow triggers a push to the main branch. It checks out the repository, sets up Python, installs dependencies, authenticates with Azure using a service principal, and runs the AML pipeline job.

- **AML pipeline YAML:** This file defines the AML pipeline with steps for data ingestion, preprocessing, model training, evaluation, and deployment (like the one before ml-pipeline-job, except this does not have a fixed schedule; the pipeline job execution is controlled by GitHub Actions).

This GitHub Actions workflow acts as a bridge between your GitHub repository and AML services, enabling continuous integration and deployment whenever code changes are pushed to the main branch.

Each step specifies the command to run, the environment to use, and the compute target. In *Figure 9.1*, the workflow shows how GitHub Actions orchestrates the ML pipeline execution within Azure, with each step building upon the previous one's outputs.

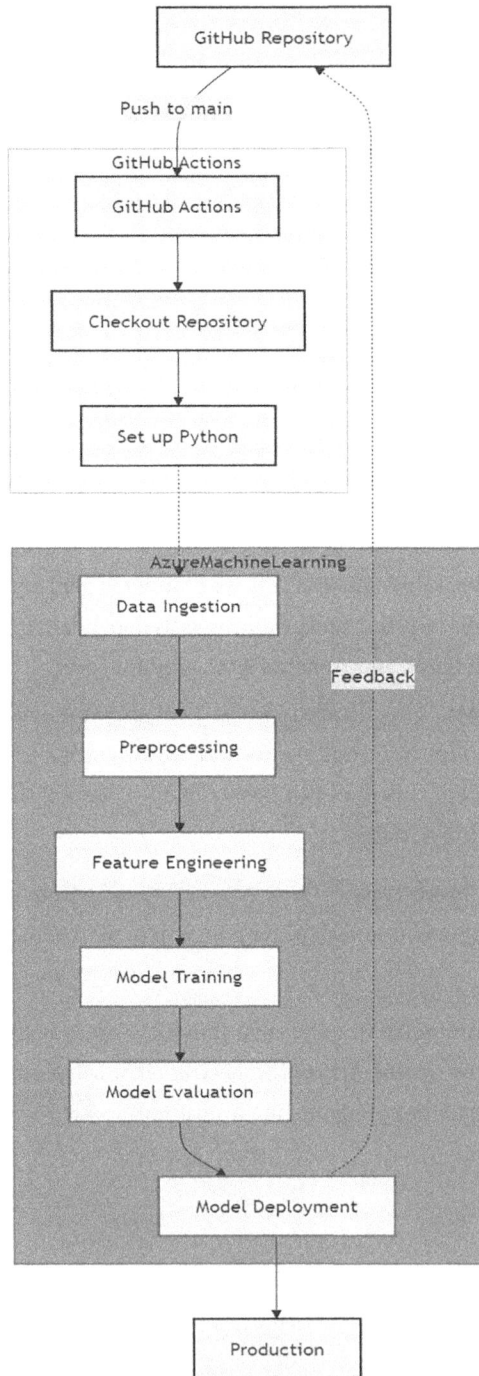

Figure 9.1 – GitHub CI/CD using AML

Now that we've explored how GitHub Actions can enhance and extend AML pipelines, let's take a step further and examine how these concepts apply in a complex, real-world scenario, as many organizations require solutions that span multiple cloud providers to meet their specific needs for scalability, compliance, and redundancy.

In the following section, we'll dive into a case study that demonstrates the power and flexibility of a multi-cloud CI/CD workflow for machine learning. This real-world example will showcase how the principles we've discussed can be applied to create a sophisticated, end-to-end ML pipeline that leverages the strengths of multiple cloud platforms.

Real-world scenario: Multi-cloud CI/CD for ML workflows

Let's consider an example of a real-world application where a CI/CD workflow was implemented for a multi-cloud environment using Azure, AWS, and GCP.

A financial services company needed to deploy its machine learning models across multiple cloud platforms (Azure, AWS, and GCP) to ensure high availability, redundancy, and compliance with various regional regulations. The company aimed to automate the entire ML lifecycle, from data ingestion to model deployment, using a CI/CD workflow that integrates with all three cloud providers.

The main expectations of this CI/CD workflow implementation were as follows:

- **Source code management**: The source code for the ML models and pipeline scripts was stored in a GitHub repository. GitHub Actions was used to trigger the CI/CD pipeline on code changes.
- **Data ingestion and preprocessing**: Data was ingested from various sources and preprocessed using Azure Data Factory, AWS Glue, and Google Cloud Dataflow. Each cloud provider's data processing service was used to ensure data locality and compliance with regional regulations.
- **Model training**: The models were trained using Azure Machine Learning, AWS SageMaker, and Google AI Platform. The training jobs were orchestrated using GitHub Actions, which triggered the respective cloud provider's training service based on the region and availability.
- **Model evaluation**: The trained models were evaluated using custom scripts that ran on Azure Batch, AWS Batch, and Google Cloud Batch. The evaluation results were stored in a centralized database accessible from all three cloud platforms.

- **Model deployment**: The evaluated models were deployed to inferencing endpoints on **Azure Kubernetes Service (AKS)**, **Amazon Elastic Kubernetes Service (EKS)**, and **Google Kubernetes Engine (GKE)**. GitHub Actions were used to automate the deployment process, ensuring that the models were deployed to the appropriate cloud platform based on the region and availability.

- **Custom notifications and alerts**: Custom notifications and alerts were set up using Slack and email. GitHub Actions was configured to send notifications to a Slack channel and email distribution list whenever a pipeline job was triggered, completed, or failed.

Here are the benefits of this workflow:

- **High availability**: By deploying models across multiple cloud platforms, the company ensured high availability and redundancy, minimizing the risk of downtime

- **Compliance**: The multi-cloud approach allowed the company to comply with various regional regulations by processing and storing data locally

- **Scalability**: The CI/CD workflow enabled the company to scale its ML operations across different cloud platforms, leveraging the strengths of each provider

- **Efficiency**: Automation of the entire ML lifecycle reduced manual intervention, improved efficiency, and ensured consistent and reliable model updates

This example demonstrates how a financial services company successfully implemented a multi-cloud CI/CD workflow using Azure, AWS, and GCP, leveraging the strengths of each cloud provider.

Create a file named `.github/workflows/multi-cloud-cicd.yml` in your GitHub repository with the following content:

```yaml
name: Multi-Cloud CI/CD Pipeline

on:
  push:
    branches:
      - main

jobs:
  data_ingestion_preprocessing:
    runs-on: ubuntu-latest

    steps:
    - name: Checkout repository
      uses: actions/checkout@v2
```

```
    - name: Set up Python
      uses: actions/setup-python@v2
      with:
        python-version: '3.8'

    - name: Install AWS CLI
      run: |
        sudo apt-get update
        sudo apt-get install awscli -y

    - name: Authenticate with AWS
      run: |
        aws configure set aws_access_key_id ${{ secrets.AWS_ACCESS_KEY_
ID }}
        aws configure set aws_secret_access_key ${{ secrets.AWS_SECRET_
ACCESS_KEY }}
        aws configure set default.region ${{ secrets.AWS_REGION }}

    - name: Run Data Ingestion and Preprocessing
      run: |
        aws s3 cp s3://your-bucket/data.csv ./data.csv
        python data_preprocessing.py --input ./data.csv
--output ./preprocessed_data.csv

    - name: Upload Preprocessed Data to S3
      run: |
        aws s3 cp ./preprocessed_data.csv s3://your-bucket/preprocessed_
data.csv

  model_training:
    runs-on: ubuntu-latest
    needs: data_ingestion_preprocessing

    steps:
    - name: Checkout repository
      uses: actions/checkout@v2

    - name: Set up Python
      uses: actions/setup-python@v2
```

```yaml
    with:
      python-version: '3.8'

  - name: Install GCP CLI
    run: |
      sudo apt-get update
      sudo apt-get install google-cloud-sdk -y

  - name: Authenticate with GCP
    run: |
      echo ${{ secrets.GCP_SERVICE_ACCOUNT_
KEY }} | gcloud auth activate-service-account --key-file=-
      gcloud config set project ${{ secrets.GCP_PROJECT_ID }}

  - name: Download Preprocessed Data from S3
    run: |
      aws s3 cp s3://your-bucket/preprocessed_data.csv ./preprocessed_
data.csv
  - name: Run Model Training
    run: |
      python train.py --input ./preprocessed_data.csv
--output ./model.pkl
  - name: Upload Model to GCS
    run: |
      gsutil cp ./model.pkl gs://your-bucket/model.pkl
model_deployment:
  runs-on: ubuntu-latest
  needs: model_training
  steps:
  - name: Checkout repository
    uses: actions/checkout@v2
  - name: Set up Python
    uses: actions/setup-python@v2
    with:
      python-version: '3.8'
    - name: Install Azure CLI
      uses: Azure/setup-cli@v2
- name: Install Azure ML CLI
run: |
az extension add -n ml
```

```
      - name: Authenticate with Azure
        uses: azure/login@v2
        with:
          creds: ${{ secrets.AZURE_CREDENTIALS }}

      - name: Download Model from GCS
        run: |
          gsutil cp gs://your-bucket/model.pkl ./model.pkl

      - name: Deploy Model to Azure ML
        run: |
          az ml model create --model ./model.pkl --name model_name
--version model_version
          az ml online-endpoint create --name endpoint_name
          az ml online-deployment create --name deployment_name
--file deployment_config.yaml
```

This comprehensive workflow orchestrates ML operations across three cloud providers in sequence. The needs keyword creates dependencies between jobs, ensuring data flows properly from AWS (preprocessing) to GCP (training) to Azure (deployment). Each job authenticates with its respective cloud provider using GitHub secrets and transfers data between platforms using cloud-native storage services (S3, GCS). This demonstrates how GitHub Actions can serve as a universal orchestrator for multi-cloud ML workflows.

If we closely look into this pipeline, it shows the following steps/stages:

1. **Data ingestion and preprocessing on AWS:** This job checks out the repository, sets up Python, installs the AWS CLI, authenticates with AWS, runs data ingestion and preprocessing, and uploads the preprocessed data to an S3 bucket.

2. **Model training on GCP:** This job depends on the data ingestion and preprocessing job. It checks out the repository, sets up Python, installs the GCP CLI, authenticates with GCP, downloads the preprocessed data from S3, runs model training, and uploads the trained model to a GCS bucket.

3. **Model deployment on AML:** This job depends on the model training job. It checks out the repository, sets up Python, installs the Azure CLI, authenticates with Azure, downloads the trained model from GCS, and deploys the model to an AML endpoint.

The following diagram illustrates the data and model flow across three cloud providers, with GitHub Actions serving as the central orchestrator, managing authentication, data transfer, and job dependencies.

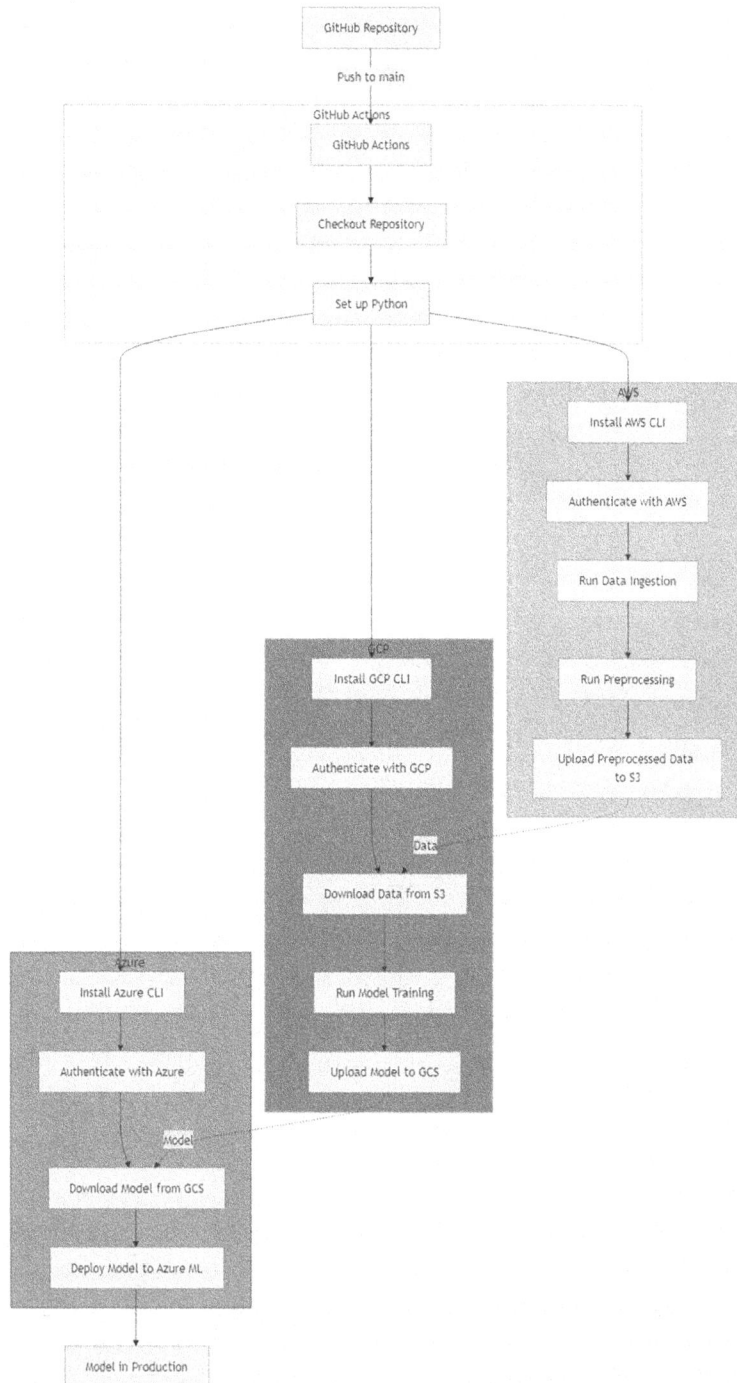

GitHub Repository

Push to main

GitHub Actions

GitHub Actions

Checkout Repository

Set up Python

AWS

Install AWS CLI

Authenticate with AWS

Run Data Ingestion

Run Preprocessing

Upload Preprocessed Data
to S3

GCP

Install GCP CLI

Authenticate with GCP

Data

Download Data from S3

Run Model Training

Upload Model to GCS

Azure

Install Azure CLI

Authenticate with Azure

Model

Download Model from GCS

Deploy Model to Azure ML

Model in Production

Figure 9.2 – GitHub CI/CD multi-cloud architecture

However, for GitHub to work in these types of scenarios, the authentication can be complex. This is an easy setup, but might need to change based on the enterprise security guidelines.

To authenticate with AWS, GCP, and Azure, you'll need to set up secrets in your GitHub repository:

1. Go to your repository on GitHub.

2. Click on **Settings | Secrets | New repository secret**.

3. Add the following secrets:

    a. **AWS_ACCESS_KEY_ID**: Your AWS access key ID.

    b. **AWS_SECRET_ACCESS_KEY**: Your AWS secret access key.

    c. **AWS_REGION**: Your AWS region.

    d. **GCP_SERVICE_ACCOUNT_KEY**: Your GCP service account key in JSON format.

    e. **GCP_PROJECT_ID**: Your GCP project ID.

    f. **AZURE_CREDENTIALS**: JSON output from the `az ad sp create-for-rbac` command.

These secrets enable secure, programmatic access to each cloud provider from GitHub Actions. The service account credentials are stored encrypted in GitHub and injected as environment variables during workflow execution. This approach follows security best practices by avoiding hardcoded credentials in your pipeline configuration files. This setup will allow you to automate the entire ML lifecycle, from data ingestion and preprocessing on AWS to model training on GCP and deployment on AML, using GitHub Actions.

Caveat

Implementing multi-cloud ML pipelines presents several challenges that require careful consideration. Key issues include maintaining data consistency across platforms, managing costs effectively, ensuring compliance with varied standards, optimizing performance across different environments, maintaining a consistent security posture, and developing cross-platform expertise within teams. To address these challenges, organizations should implement robust data synchronization tools, utilize cloud cost monitoring solutions, adopt a unified data governance framework, employ cloud-agnostic orchestration tools such as Kubernetes, implement consistent security policies, and invest in cross-cloud training for their teams. By proactively addressing these considerations, organizations can maximize the benefits of multi-cloud ML pipelines while minimizing potential pitfalls.

While this real-world workflow demonstrates the power of multi-cloud CI/CD pipelines in orchestrating end-to-end ML operations, it also highlights the practical complexities that teams encounter when managing such environments. To help you navigate these challenges effectively, let's explore the key issues to anticipate in multi-cloud ML pipelines and the best practices you can adopt to address them.

Challenges and best practices

Implementing multi-cloud ML pipelines brings significant benefits but also presents unique challenges that require careful consideration and planning.

Common challenges in multi-cloud ML pipelines

When implementing multi-cloud MLOps pipelines, there are several challenges you need to be aware of to ensure your workflows remain efficient, secure, and cost-effective:

- **Data consistency and synchronization**: Maintaining data consistency across different cloud platforms can be complex. Data formats, storage mechanisms, and access patterns vary between providers, making it challenging to ensure a seamless data flow.

- **Security and authentication**: Managing authentication across multiple cloud providers requires careful coordination of service accounts, secrets, and access policies. Each platform has different security models and best practices.

- **Cost management**: Multi-cloud deployments can lead to unexpected costs if not monitored properly. Each cloud provider has different pricing models, data transfer fees, and cost optimization strategies.

- **Vendor-specific features**: While we aim for cloud-agnostic solutions, each provider has unique strengths and APIs that may create dependencies or require platform-specific implementations.

- **Network latency and data transfer**: Moving data between cloud providers introduces latency and potential bandwidth costs that can impact pipeline performance.

While these challenges can add complexity to your multi-cloud MLOps workflows, adopting targeted best practices can help you manage them effectively and build resilient, scalable pipelines.

Best practices

To address the aforementioned challenges effectively, consider adopting the following best practices when building and managing multi-cloud MLOps pipelines:

- **Centralized secret management**: Use GitHub secrets or dedicated secret management services such as HashiCorp Vault to maintain consistent authentication across all cloud providers. Rotate credentials regularly and follow the principle of least privilege.

- **Monitoring and logging**: Implement unified monitoring across all cloud platforms. Tools such as Datadog, New Relic, or cloud-native solutions can provide centralized visibility into pipeline performance and health.

- **Cost optimization strategies**: To optimize costs in your multi-cloud MLOps pipelines, consider the following strategies:

  - Implement cloud cost monitoring tools and set up budget alerts

  - Use resource tagging strategies for better cost tracking

  - Consider data locality to minimize cross-cloud transfer costs

  - Leverage spot instances or preemptible VMs where appropriate

- **Error handling and rollback**: Design your pipelines with robust error handling and rollback mechanisms. Each stage should be able to recover gracefully from failures, with clear retry policies and fallback strategies.

- **Testing strategy**: Test your pipelines in staging environments that mirror your production multi-cloud setup. Implement comprehensive integration tests that validate data flow between cloud providers.

- **Documentation and governance**: Maintain clear documentation of data flows, dependencies, and authentication requirements across all cloud platforms. Establish governance policies for multi-cloud resource management.

By following these best practices, you can navigate the complexities of multi-cloud MLOps pipelines confidently, ensuring your workflows remain secure, cost-efficient, and resilient across diverse cloud environments.

Summary

In this chapter, we explored the power and versatility of machine learning pipelines across multiple cloud platforms. Key takeaways include the following:

- **AML pipelines**: We learned how to automate and streamline ML workflows within the Azure ecosystem

- **GitHub Actions**: We expanded beyond Azure, using GitHub Actions to create more complex CI/CD workflows

- **Multi-cloud strategy**: We implemented a sophisticated pipeline leveraging AWS, GCP, and Azure, demonstrating how to do the following:

  - Preprocess data on AWS

  - Train models on GCP

  - Deploy models on AML

- **Best practices**: We covered authentication, error handling, and modular design for robust, scalable pipelines

By mastering these concepts, you're now equipped to design and implement advanced ML pipelines that operate seamlessly across multiple cloud environments. This multi-cloud approach offers enhanced availability, scalability, and compliance – crucial skills for tackling complex, real-world ML challenges in modern organizations.

As MLOps continues to evolve, the ability to create flexible, multi-cloud pipelines will become increasingly valuable. Keep building on these foundations to stay at the forefront of ML innovation.

With this, we've completed our exploration of MLOps core concepts. In the next chapter, we'll examine three real-world case studies that demonstrate how these MLOps principles can be applied to solve practical business challenges.

10

Using Models in Real-world Applications

MLOps extends the core principles of DevOps to machine learning projects, addressing the unique challenges posed by data dependencies, model versioning, and the need for continuous monitoring and retraining. By adopting MLOps practices, organizations can streamline their machine learning workflows, improve collaboration between data scientists and operations teams, and ensure reliable and efficient deployment of models in production environments.

In this chapter, we will explore three distinct case studies that illustrate how MLOps strategies can solve various real-world problems. To showcase the strengths of different cloud providers, each case study will focus on a unique cloud platform. This offers valuable insights into the offerings of the major cloud providers, highlighting their capabilities in supporting MLOps pipelines.

In this chapter, we will be covering the following main topics:

- Recapping fundamental concepts
- Case study 1: Demand forecasting on Azure
- Case study 2: Handwriting assistance for children on Google Cloud Platform
- Case study 3: Real-time precision delivery on Amazon Web Services

Recapping fundamental concepts

Before diving into the case studies, we'll revisit the fundamental MLOps and DevOps concepts that underlie most machine learning projects. This will establish a common framework to reference as we analyze how each cloud platform handles the unique challenges posed by specific use cases.

By doing so, you'll be better equipped to understand the practical implementations of MLOps in different environments.

Figure 10.1 illustrates a cloud-agnostic MLOps/DevOps process, integrating traditional DevOps practices with machine learning-specific operations:

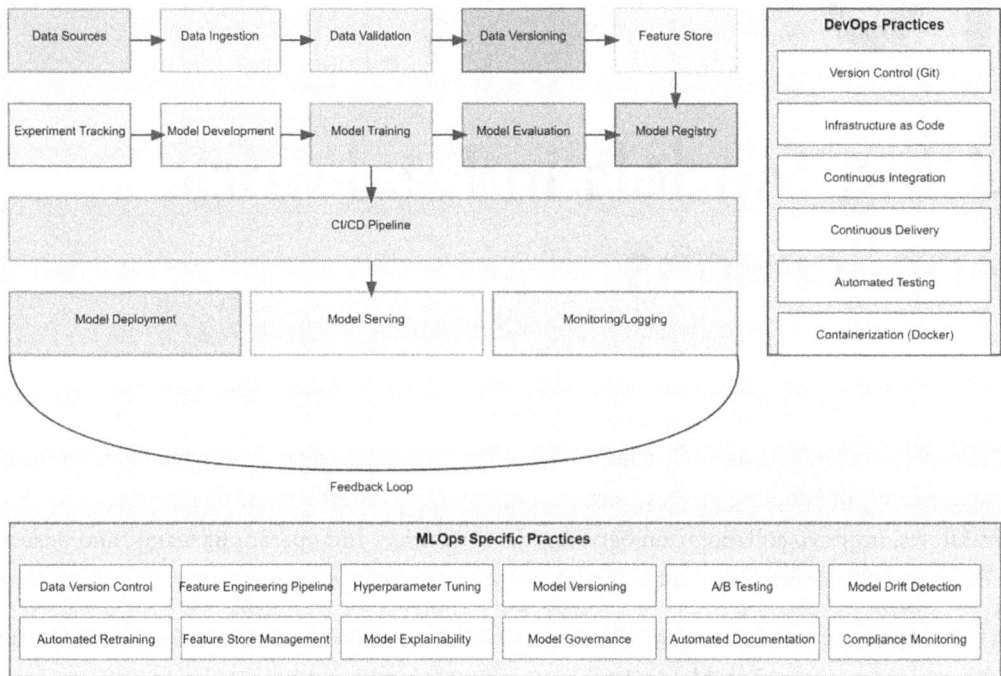

Figure 10.1 – Comprehensive MLOps process

This pipeline represents the full lifecycle of a machine learning project, from data ingestion to model deployment and monitoring. By implementing such a pipeline, organizations can enhance collaboration across teams and ensure the continuous delivery of reliable machine learning models.

In the following sections, we will examine three case studies, each showcasing the application of MLOps on different cloud platforms:

- **Demand forecasting on Azure:** We'll examine how a retail company leverages Azure's machine learning services to predict product demand, showcasing the integration of time series forecasting with cloud-native MLOps tools

- **Handwriting assistance for children on Google Cloud Platform (GCP):** This case study will explore how an educational technology company implements an MLOps pipeline on GCP to continuously improve a handwriting recognition and assistance model for young learners

- **Real-time precision delivery on Amazon Web Services (AWS)**: We'll investigate how a logistics company utilizes AWS services to deploy and manage machine learning models that optimize delivery routes and timing in real time

To systematically examine how different cloud platforms implement MLOps capabilities, each case study follows a consistent structure aligned with the MLOps lifecycle we introduced previously. We'll walk through the data pipeline, model development, deployment, monitoring, and feedback phases, examining how Azure's tools and services address each aspect. This structured approach will help us compare cloud providers' strengths and unique features while maintaining a clear focus on practical implementation challenges and solutions.

Case study 1: Demand forecasting on Azure

In this case study, we will explore how a global retail company leverages Azure's machine learning services to build and operationalize a demand forecasting system at scale. You will learn how time-series forecasting can be integrated with cloud-native MLOps tools to automate data pipelines, streamline model development, implement CI/CD for reliable deployment, and monitor model performance in production. This case study will demonstrate how adopting an end-to-end MLOps framework can transform manual forecasting processes into an automated, scalable, and accurate system that improves inventory management and enhances operational efficiency across a large retail organization.

Business context and requirements

MegaRetail, a global retail chain with over 1,000 stores, faced a significant challenge in accurately predicting product demand across its diverse product range. Misaligned forecasts had serious implications, such as the following:

- Overstocking led to increased storage costs and potential waste for perishable goods.
- Understocking resulted in lost sales and dissatisfied customers.

The company relied on manual forecasting methods, which were time-consuming and prone to errors, especially during market fluctuations or new product launches. To address these inefficiencies, MegaRetail needed an automated solution that could do the following:

- Scale across its extensive operations
- Adjust quickly to changing market dynamics
- Improve overall supply chain management

By adopting an MLOps framework on Azure, MegaRetail successfully transitioned from manual forecasting to an automated, scalable, and accurate system. This MLOps-driven transformation not only optimized their inventory management but also enhanced operational efficiency. Let's examine how MegaRetail implemented each component of its MLOps pipeline using Azure's cloud services.

Implementation architecture

To implement its MLOps solution, MegaRetail followed a systematic approach that aligned with the core MLOps lifecycle components. Each component was carefully designed to leverage Azure's native capabilities while meeting the specific demands of large-scale retail forecasting.

Data pipeline

The demand forecasting process begins with data, and MegaRetail needed a reliable, scalable pipeline for data ingestion, processing, and feature engineering:

- **Data ingestion**: MegaRetail utilized Azure Data Factory to automate data ingestion from various sources, such as **point-of-sale (POS)** systems, inventory databases, and external market data. Real-time data was streamed using Azure Event Hubs, ensuring timely updates for model training.

- **Data storage and versioning**: All datasets were versioned using Azure Data Lake Storage Gen2, which served as a central data lake offering unified storage for both raw and processed data. This ensured that model training could be reproduced with consistent data snapshots.

- **Data validation**: Azure Functions was used to perform real-time data quality checks, with alerts for anomalies.

- **Feature engineering**: MegaRetail deployed distributed data processing using Azure Databricks for large-scale feature engineering.

With this robust and scalable data pipeline in place, MegaRetail could now focus on building, tracking, and optimizing its forecasting models.

Model development pipeline

Accurate forecasting requires continuous experimentation and model refinement, and MegaRetail built a streamlined model development pipeline to support this:

- **Experiment tracking**: Using AML, data scientists were able to track experiments, compare model performance, and tune hyperparameters efficiently. AML datasets provided efficient management and versioning of training data.

- **Model development**: Automated model training pipelines were established with the AML SDK, reducing manual involvement and accelerating model iteration. The solution leveraged AML compute clusters to scale training workloads based on demand.

- **Model evaluation**: Automated evaluation scripts assessed each model's accuracy against predefined business metrics, ensuring consistent performance across different store locations and product categories.

With models being developed and evaluated seamlessly, the next step was to automate the deployment of these models across MegaRetail's vast network of stores.

CI/CD pipeline

To integrate machine learning models into their broader operations, MegaRetail implemented a CI/CD pipeline that facilitated rapid and reliable deployment. The entire pipeline was orchestrated through Azure DevOps, ensuring tight integration between model deployment and infrastructure management:

- **Continuous integration**: Application code and machine learning models were tested automatically using GitHub Actions, ensuring smooth integration between development and deployment environments.

- **Continuous delivery**: Azure Pipelines automated the deployment of models to both staging and production environments. Docker images for model-serving applications were managed through Azure Container Registry, enabling consistent deployments across environments.

- **Model versioning**: All models were versioned and tracked using an AML model registry, maintaining a clear history of model lineage and enabling quick rollbacks if needed.

With models consistently integrated and deployed, MegaRetail could now focus on how best to serve these models in production environments.

Deployment and serving

Scalable and efficient model deployment is critical for MegaRetail's forecasting system, ensuring that predictions can be served in real time across thousands of stores. The solution leveraged a combination of Azure services to balance performance, cost, and reliability:

- **Model deployment:** MegaRetail automated the deployment of models using **Azure Kubernetes Service (AKS)** for scalable inference. Models were served through AML endpoints, offering RESTful APIs for real-time predictions. For locations with lower prediction volumes, Azure Container Instances provided a cost-effective serving option.

- **A/B testing:** Azure API Management facilitated A/B testing of different models, allowing for controlled experimentation in production. This enabled MegaRetail to validate model improvements before full rollout.

- **Canary releases:** Canary deployments were implemented to gradually roll out new model versions, reducing the risk of performance degradation. This approach ensured that any issues could be detected and addressed before affecting the entire store network.

With models now live in production, MegaRetail needed continuous monitoring to ensure consistent model performance.

Monitoring and logging

Ongoing monitoring and logging were crucial for maintaining the accuracy of MegaRetail's demand forecasts. The company implemented a comprehensive monitoring strategy that combined real-time alerting with long-term performance tracking:

- **Performance monitoring:** Custom dashboards in Azure Monitor tracked system health and model performance metrics. Azure Application Insights complemented this by providing end-to-end request tracing, offering detailed insights into model serving performance and user interaction patterns.

- **Data drift detection:** Automated data drift detection, powered by AML, triggered alerts when data patterns began to deviate significantly from training data distributions. Azure Event Grid enabled event-driven monitoring and alerting, ensuring quick responses to potential issues.

- **Logging:** Centralized logging with Azure Log Analytics enabled fast troubleshooting and auditing capabilities. This unified logging approach helped MegaRetail maintain compliance requirements while facilitating quick problem resolution across its store network.

To maintain long-term accuracy, MegaRetail needed a robust feedback loop to retrain models based on new data and shifting trends.

Feedback loop

An efficient feedback loop ensured that MegaRetail's models stayed up to date with the latest market trends and customer behavior. The solution balanced automated processes with human oversight to maintain model reliability:

- **Automated retraining**: Azure Functions triggered retraining pipelines whenever performance degraded or data drift was detected. AML pipelines orchestrated the end-to-end retraining process, ensuring automation and efficiency in updates.

- **Human-in-the-loop**: Approval workflows in Azure Logic Apps were implemented for critical model updates, allowing human oversight when necessary. This ensured that significant model changes were validated before deployment to production.

The implementation of this comprehensive feedback loop, combined with the robust monitoring system, enabled MegaRetail to maintain model accuracy while adapting to changing market conditions. With the core MLOps pipeline components in place, the next crucial step was ensuring the scalability and compliance of the underlying infrastructure.

Platform-specific solution

Managing the MLOps infrastructure effectively required automation, consistency, and security. MegaRetail leveraged Azure's native capabilities to create a secure, compliant, and automated infrastructure management system:

- **Infrastructure automation: Azure Resource Manager (ARM)** templates were used to automate and standardize the deployment of infrastructure across environments. This infrastructure-as-code approach ensured consistency and reduced manual configuration errors.

- **Environment management**: AML environments helped maintain consistent dependencies and configurations across development, testing, and production. This standardization was crucial for reproducible model development and reliable deployments.

- **Security and compliance**:

    - Azure Policy enforced compliance and security standards across the MLOps infrastructure.

    - Azure Key Vault provided centralized management of secrets, credentials, and API keys.

    - **Azure role-based access control (Azure RBAC)** ensured appropriate access levels across teams.

By leveraging these Azure-specific capabilities, MegaRetail created a robust, secure, and scalable MLOps infrastructure that supported their entire demand forecasting system. This foundation proved crucial for maintaining model performance and reliability at scale.

Challenges and solutions

The implementation of MegaRetail's MLOps pipeline revealed several technical and operational challenges that required innovative Azure-based solutions. These challenges tested the system's ability to handle regional variations and maintain performance at scale.

Regional time-series forecasting

MegaRetail encountered two major challenges in implementing region-specific forecasting at scale. These challenges required innovative solutions leveraging Azure's machine learning capabilities:

- **Region-specific model optimization:** The challenge of handling diverse sales patterns across different regions was addressed through Azure Machine Learning's custom time-series algorithms and automated hyperparameter tuning. This solution improved forecast accuracy by 35% across regions while reducing model training time by 60%, enabling precise demand prediction for each market's unique characteristics.

- **Parallel training and deployment:** To manage multiple region-specific models efficiently, MegaRetail implemented parallel training pipelines using AML. This approach enabled simultaneous training of models across 20+ regions while maintaining consistent performance metrics, resulting in a 75% reduction in overall model deployment time.

Scalability and performance

As MegaRetail's operations expanded globally, the system faced significant scaling challenges that required robust solutions to maintain performance across its infrastructure:

- **Data processing and model training:** The challenge of processing massive volumes of retail data was solved through Azure Databricks' horizontal scaling capabilities and AML compute clusters. This solution successfully processed over 100 TB of historical sales data while reducing training costs by 40% through efficient resource utilization.

- **Dynamic model serving:** To handle varying demand across time zones and peak shopping periods, MegaRetail leveraged AKS for dynamic scaling. This implementation successfully served 50,000 predictions per second during peak hours while maintaining response times under 100 ms and achieving 99.9% availability.

While MegaRetail's demand forecasting demonstrated the power of MLOps in handling structured, time-series data, our next case study explores how similar principles can be applied to unstructured data in the form of handwriting samples. This shift from numerical prediction to computer vision highlights the versatility of MLOps practices across different domains.

Case study 2: Handwriting assistance for children on Google Cloud Platform

In this case study, we will explore how an educational technology company leverages **Google Cloud Platform (GCP)** and MLOps practices to build, deploy, and continuously improve a handwriting recognition and assistance system for young learners. You will learn how to design an end-to-end MLOps pipeline for unstructured data, including scalable data ingestion and preprocessing, model development with AutoML and custom TensorFlow models, CI/CD deployment strategies, and real-time serving using GCP's native tools. This case study will also demonstrate how to implement effective monitoring, logging, and feedback loops to ensure continuous model adaptation and improvement, enabling the delivery of engaging, personalized learning experiences for children while maintaining high system reliability and performance.

Business context and requirements

An educational technology company, EduLearn, sought to build a handwriting assistance application for children. The goal was to help young learners improve their handwriting skills by analyzing writing patterns and offering personalized feedback in real time. The challenge was to create a system that could handle the variability in children's handwriting, recognize different writing styles, and continuously improve the underlying model based on user feedback.

EduLearn faced several critical business challenges:

- Managing the high variability in children's handwriting styles
- Supporting continuous improvement as learners progress
- Delivering real-time, engaging feedback to maintain student interest

These requirements made traditional manual approaches inefficient and unsuitable. To solve these challenges, EduLearn turned to **Google Cloud Platform (GCP)** and MLOps practices to build a scalable, adaptive, and automated system.

To implement their MLOps solution, EduLearn followed a systematic approach that aligned with the core MLOps lifecycle components. Each component was carefully designed to leverage GCP's native capabilities while meeting the specific demands of real-time handwriting analysis.

Implementation architecture

To deliver effective handwriting assistance, EduLearn designed a comprehensive MLOps architecture that leveraged GCP's native capabilities for processing and analyzing handwriting samples. Each component was carefully structured to handle the unique challenges of computer vision processing and real-time feedback delivery.

Data pipeline

The handwriting assistance system begins with data processing, and EduLearn needed a reliable, scalable pipeline for handling unstructured image data. Their data pipeline was designed to process thousands of handwriting samples while maintaining data quality and versioning:

- **Data ingestion**: EduLearn utilized Google Cloud Storage for scalable storage of handwriting images, while the Cloud Vision API handled initial processing and feature extraction. Real-time handwriting samples were streamed directly from the application, ensuring continuous model improvement.

- **Data storage and versioning**: Cloud Storage and BigQuery managed data versioning and metadata storage. While Cloud Storage maintained raw handwriting images, BigQuery handled metadata and annotations, enabling the efficient tracking of data lineage and sample evolution.

- **Data validation**: Custom validation pipelines through Cloud Functions performed quality checks on incoming data, assessing image quality, formatting, and metadata consistency. The process monitored sample diversity across writing styles to maintain a balanced, generalizable dataset.

- **Feature engineering**: Cloud Dataflow orchestrated distributed processing of handwriting images, handling preprocessing, normalization, and feature extraction through the Cloud Vision API. The system generated training-specific features that captured essential handwriting characteristics, creating optimized formats for model training.

This robust data pipeline ensured that EduLearn could efficiently process and manage the large volume of handwriting samples needed for model training and improvement.

Model development pipeline

Accurate handwriting recognition requires continuous experimentation and adaptation to different writing styles. EduLearn built a streamlined model development pipeline to support rapid iteration and optimization of their models:

- **Experiment tracking**: Vertex AI Experiments enabled data scientists to track model parameters, performance indicators, and training datasets across different user segments. The system maintained complete reproducibility by logging all configurations and results, allowing teams to replicate successful experiments and learn from previous iterations.

- **Model development**: EduLearn implemented a two-phase approach, starting with AutoML Vision for rapid prototyping and baseline performance, followed by fine-tuning using custom TensorFlow models on Vertex AI. TPU Pods and Vertex AI Workbench accelerated the development process, enabling efficient experimentation and collaborative development.

- **Model evaluation**: Automated evaluation pipelines assessed model performance across handwriting styles, age groups, and skill levels. The system monitored recognition accuracy, real-time inference performance, and user engagement metrics to ensure consistent quality across all user segments.

With this comprehensive development pipeline in place, EduLearn could rapidly iterate on its models while maintaining rigorous quality standards. The next critical step was establishing a reliable deployment pipeline to bring these models into production.

CI/CD pipeline

EduLearn implemented an MLOps CI/CD pipeline to streamline the deployment of updated models and application code, ensuring reliable updates while maintaining system stability across their global user base:

- **Continuous integration**: Cloud Build automated the testing infrastructure, validating both model code and performance metrics. Through integration with Cloud Source Repositories, the pipeline maintained version control of code and model artifacts, ensuring thorough validation before deployment.

- **Continuous delivery**: Cloud Deploy orchestrated the automated deployment of new model versions across production environments. The system coordinated updates between inference systems and feedback mechanisms, managing region-specific deployments to maintain consistent performance for EduLearn's global user base.

- **Model versioning**: Vertex AI Model Registry served as the central hub for tracking model versions and their metadata. This versioning system enabled quick rollbacks when needed and facilitated the easy comparison of models in production, supporting continuous improvement while maintaining service quality.

With this robust CI/CD pipeline in place, EduLearn could confidently deploy model updates while ensuring consistent performance. The next critical component was establishing effective deployment and serving strategies for these models.

Deployment and serving

Low-latency, scalable model deployment was critical for delivering real-time feedback to children using the application. EduLearn needed an infrastructure that could handle varying loads while maintaining consistent response times to keep young learners engaged:

- **Model deployment**: EduLearn leveraged Vertex AI Prediction to deploy its TensorFlow models at scale, ensuring reliable and efficient serving of predictions. Through Cloud Run, the system exposed a responsive inference API that provided immediate feedback to users while seamlessly handling containerized deployment and auto-scaling based on demand.

- **Canary deployments**: To minimize risks associated with model updates, EduLearn implemented canary releases using Cloud Run and **Google Kubernetes Engine (GKE)**. This approach enabled gradual rollouts of new model versions, initially directing only a small percentage of traffic to updated models. GKE's orchestration capabilities ensured high availability during these transitions, automatically scaling resources based on traffic patterns and maintaining performance during peak usage.

With this robust deployment infrastructure in place, EduLearn successfully balanced the demands of real-time performance with the need for reliable, scalable service delivery. The next crucial component was implementing comprehensive monitoring and logging to ensure sustained quality of service.

Monitoring and logging

To ensure the system's effectiveness, EduLearn implemented real-time monitoring and logging for both model performance and user feedback. This comprehensive monitoring approach was essential for maintaining high-quality handwriting assistance:

- **Performance monitoring**: Custom dashboards in Google Cloud Monitoring tracked critical metrics, including latency, model accuracy, and user interactions. The system integrated with Vertex AI Model Monitoring to detect model drift, particularly important as children's handwriting styles evolve over time.

- **Logging**: Cloud Logging provided centralized logging management, capturing both model predictions and user feedback. This unified logging approach enabled quick debugging, performance auditing, and continuous system optimization through detailed insights into user interactions and model behavior.

With robust monitoring and logging in place, EduLearn could proactively address performance issues and ensure consistent service quality. The final component was establishing an effective feedback loop for continuous model improvement.

Feedback loop

The model needed to adapt continuously to children's evolving handwriting styles, and the feedback loop was designed to facilitate this ongoing improvement process:

- **Automated retraining**: EduLearn implemented automated retraining triggers using Vertex AI Pipelines, initiating new training cycles when performance metrics indicated degradation. The pipeline orchestrated the end-to-end retraining process, incorporating new data and updating models based on recent user interactions.

- **Human-in-the-loop**: For edge cases involving unusual handwriting patterns, the system incorporated human oversight through Cloud Functions and Cloud Tasks. This workflow automatically flagged outlier predictions for expert review, ensuring quality control while maintaining system automation.

This comprehensive feedback system enabled EduLearn's handwriting recognition models to evolve alongside their users' progress, maintaining high accuracy across diverse writing styles and skill levels.

Challenges and solutions

EduLearn's implementation of the handwriting assistance system presented unique technical challenges that required sophisticated GCP-based solutions. These challenges tested the system's ability to handle diverse input data and maintain real-time performance.

Variability in handwriting styles

EduLearn faced significant challenges in handling the diverse and inconsistent nature of children's handwriting, requiring sophisticated solutions to address both individual variation and skill progression:

- **Model generalization and adaptation**: The challenge of processing inconsistent handwriting styles across different age groups and skill levels was addressed through AutoML Vision's automated model-building capabilities. By implementing continuous fine-tuning with Vertex AI, the system achieved a 40% improvement in recognition accuracy across diverse writing styles while reducing manual intervention by 85%.

- **Learning progress tracking**: To handle the evolution of individual students' handwriting over time, EduLearn developed a progressive learning system that maintained personalized models for each student. This approach, combined with automated retraining pipelines, enabled the system to adapt to improvements in writing skills while maintaining 95% recognition accuracy for individual users.

Real-time inference performance

To deliver immediate, engaging feedback to learners, EduLearn needed to ensure that its handwriting assistance system could provide real-time predictions at scale while maintaining low latency and high reliability. This is how it handled the problem:

- **Latency management and user experience**: The critical challenge of providing instantaneous feedback was solved through Cloud Run's serverless architecture and Vertex AI Prediction's optimized inference pipeline. This solution consistently delivered feedback within 200 ms, maintaining student engagement while processing over 1,000 handwriting samples per second.

- **Scalable resource management**: To handle varying loads across different time zones and usage patterns, EduLearn implemented dynamic scaling using Cloud Run's auto-scaling capabilities. This approach successfully managed peak loads of 50,000 concurrent users while maintaining consistent response times and reducing operational costs by 30%.

Having examined MLOps in both retail forecasting and educational technology contexts, we now turn to perhaps the most demanding scenario: real-time logistics optimization. This case study demonstrates how MLOps principles can be adapted for applications requiring split-second decisions and continuous adaptation.

Case study 3: Real-time precision delivery on Amazon Web Services

In this case study, we will explore how a logistics company leverages **Amazon Web Services** (**AWS**) to build, deploy, and manage machine learning models that enable real-time precision delivery. You will learn how to design an end-to-end MLOps pipeline on AWS to handle continuous streams of geospatial and traffic data, build reinforcement learning models for route optimization, and implement scalable CI/CD pipelines for rapid model updates. This case study will also demonstrate how to deploy low-latency prediction services for real-time decision-making, monitor model and system performance, and implement effective feedback loops for continuous improvement, illustrating how MLOps practices can drive operational efficiency in high-demand, time-sensitive logistics environments.

Business context and requirements

FastRoutes, a logistics company, aimed to optimize delivery routes and timing in real time to achieve precision deliveries. The company faced complex challenges involving dynamic traffic patterns, fluctuating customer locations, and strict delivery windows. Manual route planning and static optimization methods were no longer sufficient for its growing operations and customer expectations.

The business requirements were multifaceted for FastRoutes, including the following:

- Minimize delivery delays by adapting to real-time traffic conditions
- Maximize resource utilization through optimal route and load planning
- Ensure precise delivery windows to enhance customer satisfaction

This use case presented unique challenges compared to our previous scenarios. Unlike batch-processed demand forecasting or single-user handwriting assistance, precision delivery requires split-second decisions for multiple drivers simultaneously. The system needed to process continuous streams of geospatial data, including traffic updates, driver locations, and delivery addresses. Additionally, the solution had to balance complex constraints such as vehicle capacity, driver schedules, and customer time preferences while continuously optimizing routes.

To address these challenges, FastRoutes implemented an MLOps solution on AWS, leveraging services such as Amazon Kinesis for real-time data processing, Amazon SageMaker for geospatial machine learning, and AWS IoT Core for device connectivity. This infrastructure enabled FastRoutes to make instant routing decisions while maintaining system reliability and scalability.

Implementation architecture

FastRoutes developed a comprehensive MLOps architecture on AWS to enable real-time route optimization and precision delivery. The system was designed to process streaming data from multiple sources while maintaining the agility to respond to rapidly changing conditions. Each component was carefully structured to handle the unique demands of real-time logistics optimization.

Data pipeline

FastRoutes required a robust pipeline for processing real-time data from multiple sources, including traffic updates, GPS data, and customer information. The system needed to handle continuous data streams while maintaining data quality and historical records:

- **Data ingestion**: Amazon Kinesis managed real-time data ingestion from IoT devices, GPS trackers, delivery vehicles, and customer apps. The streaming architecture ensured immediate processing of traffic updates and location data to support real-time route optimization.

- **Data storage and versioning**: Amazon S3 and AWS Glue handled data versioning and historical storage, maintaining both real-time and historical data for model training and analysis. This dual-storage approach enabled both immediate access to current data and long-term analysis of delivery patterns.

- **Data validation**: AWS Lambda implemented real-time validation checks, triggering alerts for data inconsistencies such as incorrect GPS coordinates or invalid traffic updates. This ensured clean, reliable data for the downstream optimization models.

- **Feature engineering**: Amazon EMR orchestrated large-scale feature engineering, extracting critical information such as delivery time estimates and traffic patterns. The system processed streaming data in real time to generate features that captured the dynamic nature of delivery operations.

This robust data pipeline enabled FastRoutes to process and analyze massive amounts of real-time data while maintaining historical records for continuous model improvement.

Model development pipeline

The dynamic nature of delivery optimization required frequent model updates and real-time predictions to maintain routing efficiency across changing conditions:

- **Experiment tracking**: Amazon SageMaker Experiments tracked model versions, hyperparameters, and optimization techniques, enabling FastRoutes to systematically improve their routing algorithms.

- **Model development**: Using Amazon SageMaker, FastRoutes developed reinforcement learning models for route optimization, while Amazon Elastic Inference enhanced prediction performance and cost efficiency.

> Note
>
> Amazon Elastic Inference was deprecated in April 2024. For new projects, consider using AWS Inferentia or GPU-based endpoints for efficient inference.

- **Model evaluation**: SageMaker Model Monitor evaluated real-time performance against key metrics, including delivery time accuracy and fuel efficiency, ensuring that the system maintained optimal routing decisions.

This comprehensive development pipeline enabled FastRoutes to continuously improve its routing models while maintaining consistent performance. The next step was establishing a reliable deployment pipeline to bring these models into production.

CI/CD pipeline

With frequent updates to the optimization models and software, FastRoutes implemented a seamless CI/CD pipeline to ensure reliable deployments across its delivery network:

- **Continuous integration**: AWS CodeBuild and CodeCommit automated the testing of model updates and application changes, ensuring consistent quality across all components.
- **Continuous delivery**: AWS CodePipeline managed deployments across regions, making new optimizations rapidly available to all delivery routes, while SageMaker Model Registry enabled version control and quick rollbacks when needed.

Deployment and serving

To ensure low-latency predictions for real-time route adjustments, FastRoutes implemented a scalable serving infrastructure:

- **Model deployment**: Amazon EKS provided containerized model deployment with fault tolerance, while SageMaker endpoints delivered real-time inference for route adjustments based on incoming traffic and location data.
- **Canary deployments**: AWS App Mesh enabled gradual rollouts of new model versions, while Amazon API Gateway facilitated integration with driver and customer applications, ensuring smooth transitions during updates.

With this robust deployment pipeline in place, FastRoutes could confidently update its routing models while maintaining consistent service quality. The next critical component was implementing comprehensive monitoring to ensure sustained performance.

Monitoring and logging

Ensuring real-time precision delivery required continuous monitoring of both models and system infrastructure:

- **Performance monitoring**: Amazon CloudWatch dashboards tracked key metrics, including prediction accuracy, latency, and route update effectiveness, while SageMaker Model Monitor detected drift in model performance as traffic patterns evolved.

- **Logging**: Centralized logging through CloudTrail and CloudWatch Logs provided comprehensive visibility into system operations, enabling quick identification and resolution of any delivery optimization issues.

Feedback loop

Continuous optimization was essential for maintaining precise delivery operations, requiring regular model updates based on real-world performance:

- **Automated retraining**: SageMaker Pipelines managed automated retraining workflows, triggered by significant traffic pattern changes or performance degradation. AWS Lambda handled the orchestration of these retraining events based on monitored thresholds.

- **Human-in-the-loop**: For exceptional cases such as major traffic incidents or unusual events, Amazon Mechanical Turk enabled manual intervention in route adjustments, ensuring system reliability even in unexpected situations.

Challenges and solutions

The implementation of FastRoutes' MLOps pipeline revealed critical operational challenges that required innovative AWS-based solutions. Each challenge presented unique technical hurdles that tested different aspects of the system's architecture.

Real-time processing at scale

FastRoutes faced two critical challenges in processing and responding to massive volumes of real-time data from their delivery network:

- **Data processing and response time**: Faced with processing massive streams of real-time traffic, GPS, and weather data, FastRoutes implemented a comprehensive streaming architecture using Kinesis Data Streams and Lambda. This solution, coupled with SageMaker endpoints, enabled the processing of thousands of data points per second while maintaining low-latency predictions.

- **System scalability and performance**: The challenge of maintaining consistent performance across growing delivery networks was addressed through dynamic scaling of AWS resources and distributed processing. This approach successfully handled peak loads of over 10,000 concurrent route calculations while keeping response times under 100 ms.

Complex route optimization

Beyond real-time data processing, FastRoutes needed to address the intricate challenge of optimizing delivery routes while balancing multiple operational constraints to maximize efficiency and customer satisfaction. This is how it handled the situation:

- **Multi-constraint optimization:** To handle the complex interplay of driver schedules, vehicle capacity, and delivery windows, FastRoutes developed sophisticated reinforcement learning models on SageMaker. This solution dynamically balanced multiple constraints while adapting to real-time conditions, resulting in a 15% reduction in delivery times.

- **Resource utilization and efficiency**: The challenge of optimizing both fuel consumption and delivery efficiency was solved through an EKS-deployed model that continuously adjusted routes based on real-time conditions. This approach improved vehicle utilization by 23% while maintaining high customer satisfaction scores.

These three case studies demonstrate that while each cloud platform offers unique services and capabilities, the fundamental MLOps architecture remains consistent across implementations.

Figure 10.2 illustrates how the core MLOps components—data pipelines, model development, CI/CD, deployment, monitoring, and feedback loops—form a unified framework that can be adapted to any cloud environment.

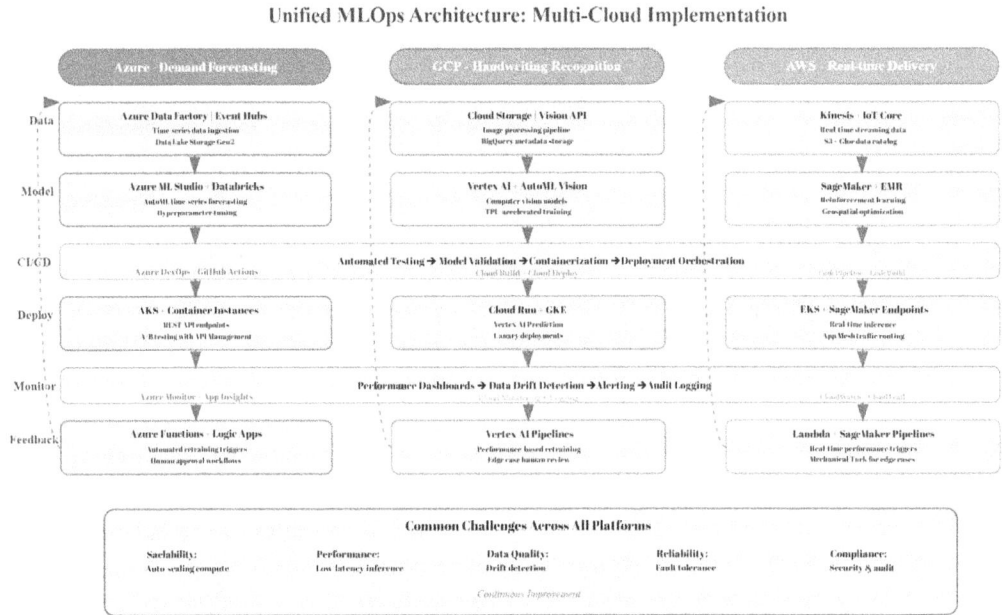

Figure 10.2 – Unified MLOps architecture: multi-cloud implementation

As *Figure 10.2* demonstrates, successful MLOps implementation follows common patterns regardless of the underlying cloud infrastructure, with each platform providing specialized tools to address similar operational challenges. This architectural consistency enables organizations to apply MLOps principles effectively across different cloud environments while leveraging platform-specific strengths.

Summary

In this chapter, we explored three real-world applications of MLOps, each implemented on a different cloud platform—Azure, GCP, and AWS. Through these case studies, we demonstrated how MLOps principles can streamline machine learning workflows across diverse industries, from retail and education to logistics.

Each cloud provider offers unique tools and services tailored to solve specific challenges. Azure was leveraged for its robust time-series forecasting capabilities and scalable data pipelines, enabling precise demand forecasting.

GCP focused on continuous model improvement and automation in an educational context, showcasing GCP's strengths in handling unstructured data and iterative learning. AWS emphasized real-time decision-making and dynamic optimization for delivery services, highlighting AWS's real-time data processing and scalability.

Despite the differences in cloud platforms and business needs, the common MLOps tasks—such as data ingestion, model development, CI/CD pipelines, deployment, monitoring, and retraining— were critical to all scenarios. By adopting MLOps strategies, organizations can not only improve operational efficiency but also ensure the scalability and reliability of machine learning models in production.

This chapter provided a practical understanding of how to implement MLOps in various cloud environments, offering insights into the competitive advantages of each platform. With these concepts in hand, you're now better equipped to tackle machine learning operations in your own projects, regardless of the cloud provider you choose.

In the next chapter (the final one), we will briefly explore how these MLOps principles extend to **large language models** (**LLMs**), examining the unique challenges and specialized practices required for operationalizing LLM applications at scale.

11

Exploring Next-Gen MLOps

Congratulations on reaching the final chapter of our MLOps journey! Having explored traditional MLOps practices throughout the previous 10 chapters, this final chapter introduces **Large Language Model Operations (LLMOps)**—a specialized evolution that addresses the unique operational challenges of **Large Language Models (LLMs)**. Rather than diving deep into all aspects, this chapter aims to familiarize you with the emerging landscape of LLMOps and prepare you for a more in-depth study. LLMOps is rapidly evolving, with unique challenges, tools, and processes, particularly in deploying and managing LLMs such as GPT-4.

As we move through this chapter, you'll gain a foundational understanding of the unique aspects of LLMOps, from its frameworks and practical applications to the challenges it presents. Also, for illustration purposes, there will be screenshots from the Azure Foundry portal (`https://ai.azure.com`). By the end of this chapter, you'll not only appreciate how LLMs differ from traditional **Machine Learning (ML)** models but also understand how to operationalize them using strategies such as **Retrieval-Augmented Generation (RAG)** and prompt engineering. You'll walk away equipped with the knowledge to navigate the complexities of deploying, monitoring, and optimizing LLMs—skills that are essential as you step into the evolving landscape of AI operations.

The chapter covers the following key areas:

- Introducing LLMs: New concepts and key differences from MLOps
- Challenges and risks in LLMOps
- Benefits and trends of LLMOps
- Practical example: Implementing LLMOps with Azure AI

Introducing LLMs: New concepts and key differences from MLOps

While sharing foundational principles with MLOps, LLMOps requires distinct methodologies, evaluation frameworks, and safety considerations that traditional ML operations don't adequately address, as shown in the following figure:

Aspect	Traditional MLOps	LLMOps
Model Development	Custom model training from scratch	Prompt engineering + fine-tuning/RAG with foundation models
Data Requirements	Structured datasets for training	Unstructured text, knowledge bases, prompt-response pairs
Iteration Process	Model retraining cycles	Prompt refinement, parameter tuning, retrieval optimization
Evaluation Metrics	Accuracy, precision, recall	Hallucination detection, safety metrics, response quality
Deployment Artifacts	Trained model binaries	Prompts, retrieval systems, orchestration workflows
Monitoring Focus	Model drift, data drift	Content safety, response quality, token usage
Risk Considerations	Performance degradation	Hallucinations, bias, security vulnerabilities
Feedback Loops	Retraining with new data	Prompt iteration, retrieval refinement

Figure 11.1 – Key differences between MLOps and LLMOps

These fundamental differences require specialized approaches, tools, and methodologies that traditional MLOps frameworks don't adequately address.

Foundational models, such as GPT-4, are pre-trained on vast amounts of data across the internet. They can take inputs in various forms, such as language, audio, and vision, and generate an output in all three formats. However, these models come with inherent limitations:

- **Lack of domain knowledge** in LLMs is a significant challenge when applying these models to specific business contexts. While LLMs possess vast general knowledge, they often lack specialized, up-to-date, or proprietary information crucial for many business applications. This limitation can lead to inaccurate or irrelevant responses when queried about company-specific processes, products, or recent developments.

- **Hallucinations and factual inaccuracies:** LLMs can generate content that appears plausible but contains factual errors or completely fabricated information, especially when asked about topics beyond their training data.

- **Temporal limitations**: These models have knowledge cutoffs and cannot access real-time information without external integrations, making them potentially outdated for time-sensitive applications.

- **Reasoning limitations**: While LLMs excel at pattern recognition, they may struggle with complex logical reasoning, mathematical problem-solving, or maintaining logical consistency across lengthy outputs.

- **Bias and fairness issues**: LLMs can perpetuate or amplify biases present in their training data, potentially leading to unfair or discriminatory outputs in business contexts.

- **Context window constraints**: LLMs have finite context windows, limiting their ability to process very long documents or maintain context across extended conversations.

Developing an effective LLM solution requires a nuanced approach that goes beyond simply selecting a base model. Successful implementation involves carefully orchestrating several key components that transform a generic LLM into a targeted, efficient solution.

To develop a business solution with an LLM, let's explore the process and then delve into Azure-specific tools that help with this. Let's first look at the components of an LLM.

Components of LLM solution development

Implementing an effective LLM solution requires more than just selecting a model. It demands a carefully orchestrated system of interconnected components working together to transform a general-purpose model into a business-specific tool. Each of these components plays a critical role in the overall solution architecture:

- **Base model**: This involves selecting an appropriate model based on the task requirements, performance, and cost considerations.

- **Custom components**: Integrating necessary packages (e.g., Python packages) or other tools (such as LangChain or Semantic Kernel) to support the application's functionality.

- **Data preparation**: This can involve either fine-tuning or RAG approaches:

  - **Fine-tuning**: This approach involves further training the model on a smaller dataset of domain-specific information, effectively teaching the model new knowledge and tailoring its responses to the specific use case. The process is to iterate fine-tuning job parameters and training data.

- **RAG**: This involves dynamically retrieving relevant information from a separate knowledge base and incorporating it into the model's generation process. RAG allows the LLM to access current and domain-specific information without retraining. Implementing RAG requires systematic experimentation—testing different indexing strategies, optimizing document chunk sizes, and evaluating various retrieval methods to find the configuration that delivers the most relevant and accurate information to the model.

- **Prompt engineering**: Crafting and refining prompts to guide the LLM's output effectively.

- **Orchestration**: Implementing tools and workflows to manage the application's components and processes.

These components must work in harmony to create an effective LLM solution. The careful selection and integration of each element determines not only the technical performance of the system but also its business value and user experience. Organizations that excel at integrating these components can transform general-purpose LLMs into powerful, domain-specific tools that address unique business challenges.

As we move from understanding the components to implementing them, it's important to recognize that LLM development follows a distinct process that differs significantly from traditional ML approaches.

Development process

Unlike traditional ML models, LLM development is inherently experimental and non-linear. Developers must continuously adjust multiple interconnected parameters to achieve the desired performance, balancing technical capabilities with business requirements and user experience. To achieve satisfactory results before deployment, developers typically iterate on the following parameters:

- **LLM-specific parameters**: These foundational settings directly control the model's generation behavior and significantly impact output quality. Fine-tuning these parameters requires understanding the trade-offs between creativity and determinism:

    - **Temperature**: Controls output randomness, with higher values (0.7-1.0) producing more creative but potentially inconsistent outputs, while lower values (0.1-0.3) generate more deterministic, focused responses

    - **Top-P (nucleus sampling)**: Defines the probability threshold for token selection, allowing developers to limit the model to higher-probability tokens without completely eliminating creative options

- **Max tokens**: Limits the length of generated text, requiring careful balancing between comprehensive responses and computational efficiency

- **Prompt design**: The engineering of effective prompts is both an art and a science, requiring systematic experimentation to achieve reliable results:

  - Prompt structure and language significantly impact model outputs, with clear instructions and consistent formatting yielding more predictable results.

  - Zero-shot versus few-shot prompting techniques offer different approaches based on task complexity. Few-shot examples provide guided learning for complex tasks, while zero-shot keeps prompts efficient for simpler queries.

  - Strategic inclusion of relevant context or examples helps ground the model's responses in domain-specific knowledge and desired output formats.

- **Data processing**: The preparation and organization of data fundamentally shapes how LLMs access and utilize information:

  - **For RAG**: Effective chunk size determination balances context preservation with retrieval granularity, while indexing strategy and embedding method selection directly impact relevance and retrieval accuracy

  - **For fine-tuning**: Careful dataset selection, preprocessing for consistency, and augmentation techniques help prevent overfitting while ensuring the model learns domain-specific patterns

- **Workflow optimization**: The architecture connecting various LLM components determines system efficiency, scalability, and maintenance complexity:

  - Integration of specialized AI agents for discrete tasks enables modular design and easier debugging while improving overall system performance

  - Thoughtful orchestration of components in the application pipeline reduces latency, minimizes computational overhead, and ensures smooth information flow between modules

- **Performance metrics**: Comprehensive evaluation frameworks must capture both technical performance and business value:

  - Accuracy, relevance, and consistency metrics should align with business objectives and use case requirements rather than generic benchmarks

- Response time and computational efficiency considerations vary by application context—user-facing applications demand low latency, while batch processing may prioritize throughput

- **User experience**: The ultimate measure of an LLM solution's success lies in its ability to meet user needs effectively:

  - The clarity and usefulness of generated responses must be evaluated through systematic user testing with representative stakeholders

  - Alignment with user expectations and domain-specific requirements ensures the solution delivers meaningful value in its intended context

The development process is inherently iterative, involving continuous testing, evaluation, and refinement through version control prompts, automated testing, and rapid deployment techniques. This iterative approach fits within a broader LLMOps lifecycle that emphasizes cyclical workflows with multiple feedback loops, unlike traditional MLOps' linear training-deployment patterns.

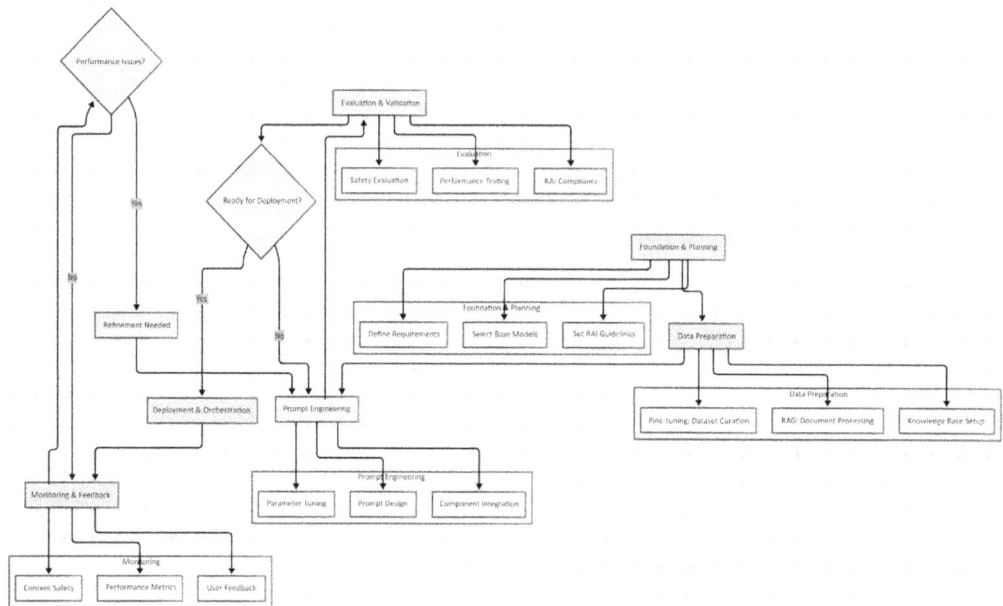

Figure 11.2 – The LLMOps lifecycle

This lifecycle depicted in *Figure 11.2* illustrates how LLMOps differs fundamentally from traditional MLOps workflows, with continuous feedback loops between prompt engineering, evaluation, and deployment phases. The iterative nature ensures that LLM solutions can adapt and improve based on real-world performance and user feedback.

Readiness for deployment

Determining when an LLM solution is ready for deployment represents a nuanced challenge that goes far beyond traditional software or ML deployment criteria. Unlike conventional applications, where performance can be measured through straightforward metrics, LLM solutions introduce multi-dimensional complexities that require holistic evaluation. These models operate in a domain of probabilistic outputs, natural language understanding, and context-dependent responses, which means *readiness* cannot be captured by a single, linear measurement. Instead, deployment preparedness becomes a sophisticated assessment involving technical performance, ethical considerations, business alignment, and user experience adaptability.

The power of LLMs comes with significant operational risks that require specialized guardrails and safety mechanisms—considerations that extend far beyond traditional MLOps risk management.

Challenges and risks in LLMOps

LLM operations present unique challenges and risks that organizations must carefully navigate:

- **Hallucinations and misinformation**: LLMs can generate convincing but incorrect information, posing significant risks in domains requiring factual accuracy, such as healthcare, finance, and legal applications.

- **Bias and fairness issues**: Models may perpetuate or amplify societal biases present in training data, potentially leading to discriminatory outputs that harm specific groups.

- **Security vulnerabilities**: LLMs can be susceptible to prompt injection attacks, data leakage, and other security concerns that traditional applications might not face.

- **Compliance and regulatory risks**: Rapidly evolving regulations around AI governance create complex compliance challenges, especially for global organizations.

- **Deployment and operational complexity**: The experimental nature of LLM development makes standardizing deployment practices difficult, potentially leading to inconsistent performance.

To address these challenges, organizations are increasingly adopting **Responsible AI (RAI)** frameworks. RAI emerges as a crucial approach to ensuring that technological advancement aligns with human values and societal well-being.

Responsible AI

RAI is a critical framework for organizations implementing AI technologies, focusing on ethical, transparent, and accountable practices. RAI is used to ensure AI systems are developed and deployed in ways that benefit society while mitigating potential risks. It's important for a multitude of reasons:

- **Trust and reputation**: RAI practices help businesses build trust with customers, stakeholders, and the public, enhancing the company's reputation and fostering long-term loyalty.

- **Risk mitigation**: RAI identifies and mitigates risks associated with AI systems, including biases, privacy concerns, and unintended consequences, preventing costly legal and regulatory issues.

- **Regulatory compliance**: With increasing global regulations for AI, businesses must adhere to RAI principles to ensure compliance and avoid penalties.

- **Innovation and value creation**: Surprisingly, RAI can improve product quality and drive innovation. A survey of company officials ranked product quality as the area receiving the most value from implementing RAI practices.

- **Ethical considerations**: RAI ensures AI systems are designed with power dynamics and ethics in mind, minimizing risks and preserving human dignity and rights.

By implementing RAI, organizations can harness AI's transformative potential while addressing inherent risks, ultimately leading to sustainable business growth and positive societal impact.

Azure RAI

Building upon RAI principles, Azure AI introduces two critical concepts:

- **Evaluation**: Evaluation encompasses a comprehensive set of metrics to assess the quality, performance, and safety of AI-generated content, including AI-assisted quality metrics, NLP-based metrics, and risk and safety evaluators. These metrics help developers gauge the accuracy, relevance, and potential risks of their AI applications.

- **Content safety**: Azure AI Content Safety complements it and provides robust tools for detecting and mitigating harmful content in text and images, offering APIs and interactive studios to identify and categorize potentially offensive, risky, or undesirable material across various severity levels.

Together, these features enable organizations to develop and deploy AI solutions that not only perform well but also adhere to ethical standards and safety guidelines.

RAI practices are integrated throughout the development lifecycle of LLM applications using Azure AI's **prompt flow**. This tool incorporates evaluation metrics and content safety checks at various stages of development. During prompt engineering, developers can use prompt flow to test and refine prompts, ensuring they adhere to ethical guidelines and produce safe, unbiased outputs. The tool allows for the automated testing of prompts against diverse datasets, helping identify potential fairness issues. Content safety filters can be applied to both inputs and outputs, mitigating risks of harmful content. Prompt flow also facilitates the continuous monitoring and evaluation of deployed models, enabling developers to track performance metrics, detect drift, and assess the model's adherence to RAI principles over time. By providing a structured workflow that emphasizes testing, monitoring, and iterative improvement, prompt flow helps developers embed RAI practices from the initial design phase through to the deployment and ongoing maintenance of LLM applications.

Figure 11.3 shows the view from Azure Foundry of a sample evaluation result. The evaluation was run on an LLM that generates images based on a prompt, and after the generation, the automated process checks for certain metrics and flags if something is not as per the expectation.

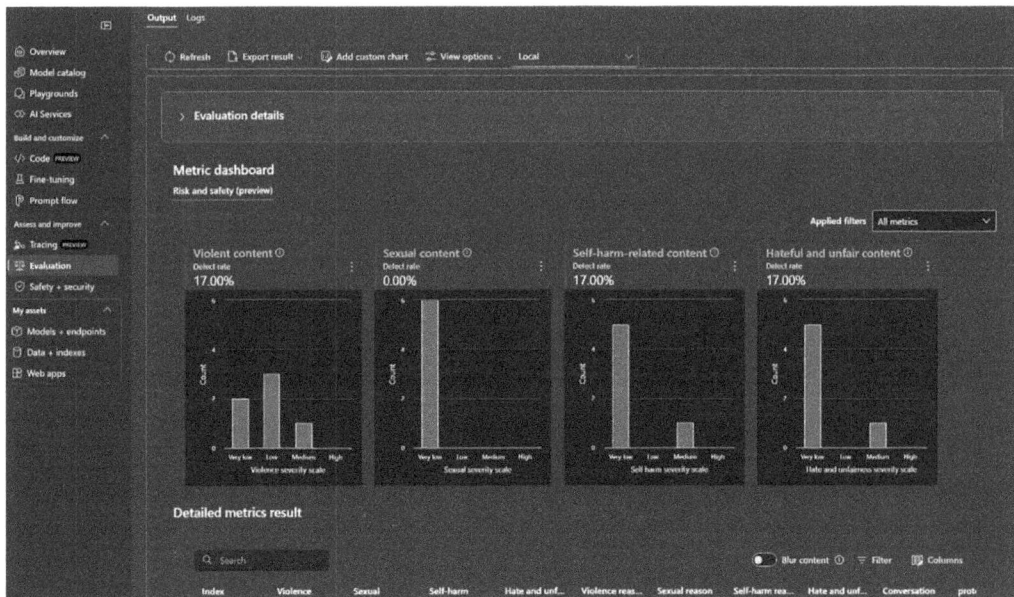

Figure 11.3 – Evaluation result of a prompt

Broadly speaking, when the LLM solution is ready—on the basis of satisfactory evaluation results in terms of both business KPIs and RAI KPIs—it can be deployed.

Deployment

The journey of an LLM solution from development to operational status is more complex than traditional software deployment. At its core, deployment transforms a carefully crafted artifact—a collection of prompts, language models, custom tools, and supporting scripts—into a live, functional system.

When a prompt developer is satisfied with the quality and performance of the solution, it transitions from an experimental prototype to an operational tool. In Azure Foundry, this process is elegantly managed through a sophisticated cloud-based development and storage ecosystem, as shown in *Figure 11.4*.

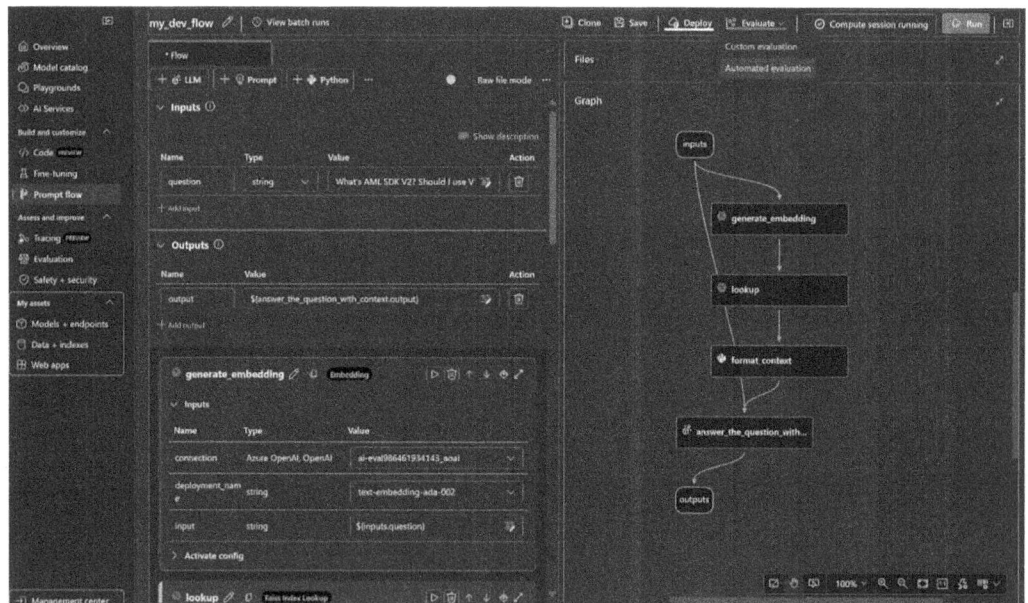

Figure 11.4 – Prompt flow development, evaluation, and deployment

The Azure AI Foundry portal provides a comprehensive interface for developing, evaluating, and deploying LLM solutions.

The **prompt flow** is not merely a static piece of code, but a dynamic entity that moves seamlessly between local development environments and cloud infrastructure. The cloud-based storage in Azure Foundry automatically generates a dedicated flow folder within the AML workspace. This folder, typically located in the Users/<username>/promptflow directory, becomes the central repository for the entire solution. The prompt flow folder structure, as shown in *Figure 11.5*, in Azure Foundry can be used to enable version control and seamless transitions between local and cloud development.

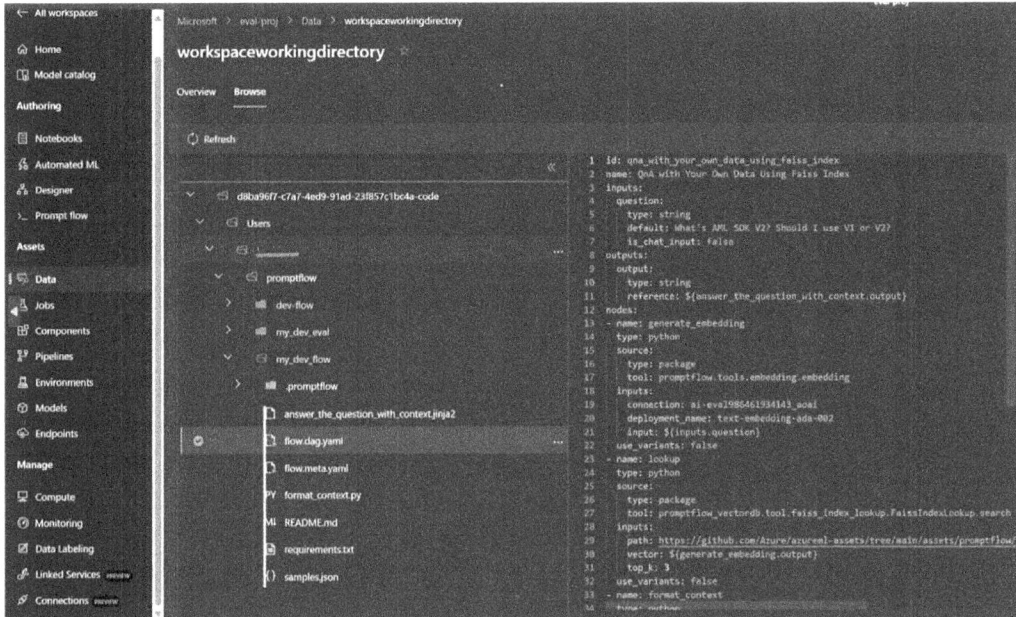

Figure 11.5 – promptflow file share backup

For teams committed to robust version control, Azure provides straightforward mechanisms for exporting and importing flow configurations. Developers can download their entire flow as a ZIP package, work on it locally using tools such as VS Code with the Prompt flow extension, and then reimport the refined version. This flexibility supports continuous development cycles, allowing teams to leverage both cloud resources and local development tools.

The integration capabilities extend to **continuous integration and continuous deployment** (**CI/CD**) pipelines. By utilizing the prompt flow CLI or SDK, teams can automate flow runs, ensuring consistent testing and deployment processes. Azure AI Studio provides a visual interface that offers transparency and accessibility throughout this journey.

Once an LLM solution is successfully deployed, the focus shifts to maintaining operational excellence through robust monitoring and alerting systems, which are crucial for ensuring ongoing performance and reliability.

Alerting and monitoring

Monitoring an LLM solution requires a comprehensive approach that goes beyond traditional performance metrics. The dynamic and generative nature of LLMs demands a nuanced set of **Key Performance Indicators** (**KPIs**) that capture the multifaceted aspects of AI service performance:

- **Request metrics** provide the first layer of insight, tracking the volume and rate of interactions with the AI service. These metrics, such as the number of HTTP requests and requests per second, offer a quantitative view of system utilization. Complementing these are token usage metrics, which provide granular visibility into the computational resources consumed by input prompts and generated outputs.

- **Performance metrics** delve deeper, measuring critical aspects such as latency and response time. These indicators are crucial for understanding the real-world responsiveness of the LLM solution. Quality metrics take this a step further, incorporating sophisticated measures such as precision, recall, and F1 score to assess the accuracy and reliability of the model's outputs.

Azure AI's monitoring ecosystem is designed to provide comprehensive visibility through multiple channels. Azure Monitor serves as a central hub for setting up alerts based on collected metrics and logs. The AI Foundry portal offers preconfigured monitoring results and visualizations, while custom thresholds can be defined to trigger specific alerts tailored to organizational requirements:

- Safety metrics represent a unique and critical dimension of LLM monitoring. By tracking the volume of blocked or potentially harmful content, organizations can ensure their AI solutions maintain ethical standards and comply with RAI principles. This goes beyond traditional performance monitoring, embedding safety directly into the operational framework.

- The notification configuration allows for real-time alerting, ensuring that any significant deviations or potential issues are immediately brought to the attention of the development team. Whether through email notifications or integrated alert systems, this approach enables proactive management of the LLM solution.

By integrating these comprehensive monitoring strategies, organizations can not only track the performance of their LLM solutions but also continuously refine and improve them, ensuring they remain effective, safe, and aligned with business objectives.

Having explored the operational aspects of LLM solutions, from development through deployment to monitoring, let's now examine the broader benefits and emerging trends that are shaping the future of LLM development.

Benefits of and trends in LLM developments

While LLMOps is still in its early stages, the benefits to organizations in implementing these practices are substantial and multifaceted:

- **Accelerated development cycles**: LLMOps frameworks reduce the time to production by standardizing development workflows, automating evaluations, and enabling rapid iteration on prompts and retrievers.

- **Enhanced model performance**: Systematic prompt engineering and evaluation methodologies lead to more reliable, accurate, and contextually appropriate model outputs that better serve business requirements.

- **Reduced operational risk**: Comprehensive monitoring, content safety filters, and RAI practices mitigate potential harms, ensuring compliance with emerging regulations and organizational governance frameworks.

- **Cost optimization**: Efficient prompt design, context window utilization, and retrieval systems minimize token usage and computational resources, significantly reducing operational expenses.

- **Knowledge integration**: RAG implementations enable organizations to leverage their proprietary data alongside general model capabilities, creating truly differentiated AI solutions that competitors cannot easily replicate.

These substantial benefits are driving rapid adoption and innovation in the LLMOps space, with several emerging trends reshaping how organizations approach LLM development and deployment.

Emerging trends transforming LLMOps

The LLMOps landscape is evolving rapidly, with several key trends emerging that will define the future of LLMOps:

- **Multimodal integration**: LLMs are rapidly evolving beyond text, with models integrating text, code, image, and audio understanding for more comprehensive applications. Systems such as GPT-4V, Claude Opus, Gemini, and DALL-E 3 demonstrate how these capabilities enable new use cases from visual reasoning to cross-modal content generation.

- **AI copilots for developers**: Tools such as GitHub Copilot, Amazon CodeWhisperer, and Microsoft Dev Center are transforming development workflows, with LLMs handling repetitive coding tasks, suggesting optimizations, and even generating test cases.

- **Explainable AI and ethical frameworks**: Organizations are implementing robust evaluation methodologies that track model reasoning, assess factuality, and detect potential biases. Projects such as Anthropic's Constitutional AI and Microsoft's Responsible AI Toolbox exemplify this trend.

- **Fine-tuning alternatives**: Techniques such as **Parameter-Efficient Fine-Tuning (PEFT)**, RAG, and prompt-engineering frameworks are emerging as cost-effective alternatives to full model fine-tuning.

- **Agentic systems and orchestration**: LLMs are increasingly being deployed as orchestrators within multi-agent systems, coordinating specialized tools to solve complex tasks. Examples include AutoGPT, LangChain, and Microsoft's Semantic Kernel framework.

- **Domain-specific optimization**: Moving beyond general-purpose models, organizations are creating domain-optimized LLM implementations for healthcare, legal, financial services, and other specialized domains requiring subject matter expertise.

- **Decentralized LLM infrastructure**: Open source models such as Llama, Mistral, and Falcon are enabling organizations to deploy LLMs on-premises, addressing data sovereignty, compliance, and cost concerns associated with API-only access.

- **Continuous learning systems**: Beyond static deployments, systems that implement ongoing learning from user interactions and feedback loops are emerging, allowing models to adapt to changing requirements and improve over time.

As the technology matures, we can anticipate the emergence of new programming paradigms and increased democratization of software development, potentially allowing individuals with limited coding experience to contribute to projects through natural language interfaces and LLM-assisted development environments.

Looking ahead, we can expect even more robust tools and best practices to emerge as LLMOps becomes a critical part of AI/ML workflows.

The current landscape of LLM app development is characterized by rapid innovation and increasing specialization. Developers are moving away from defaulting to general-purpose models such as ChatGPT and exploring open source alternatives such as Llama 2 and Mixtral. This shift allows for greater flexibility and customization, with a growing focus on fine-tuning models for specific domains such as healthcare, finance, and law. The integration of LLMs into software development workflows is also gaining traction, with enhanced code generation capabilities and natural language programming interfaces emerging as key trends.

Looking to the future, several exciting developments are on the horizon for LLM app development. **Multimodal learning** is an educational approach that integrates multiple sensory inputs and learning styles to create a more comprehensive and effective learning experience. It combines various modes of information delivery, such as visual, auditory, and kinesthetic elements, to cater to diverse learning preferences and enhance information retention.

This approach recognizes that each learner has unique strengths and preferences, offering multiple pathways to understanding and accommodating different learning needs. This mode of learning is expected to become more prevalent, with LLMs integrating text, code, and image understanding for more complex applications. The concept of LLMs as copilots for developers is gaining momentum, promising to accelerate the development process by handling repetitive tasks and suggesting innovative approaches. Additionally, there's a growing emphasis on explainable AI and ethical development practices to address concerns about bias and transparency in LLM outputs. Examples of this trend include OpenAI's development of DALL-E 3 for text-to-image generation, Anthropic's research into constitutional AI for safer model outputs, and Microsoft's integration of GitHub Copilot into development workflows. Google's Gemini and Meta's Llama have also made strides in multimodal capabilities, demonstrating how LLMs are evolving beyond text-only applications toward more comprehensive AI solutions. As the technology matures, we can anticipate the emergence of new programming paradigms and increased democratization of software development, potentially allowing individuals with limited coding experience to contribute to projects.

With these trends and benefits in mind, let's examine how these concepts are being applied in practice through a detailed case study that demonstrates the implementation of LLMOps principles using Azure AI tools.

Practical example: Implementing LLMOps with Azure AI

Case study: Revolutionizing patient triage with an AI-powered symptom assessment chatbot

Background

MedConnect, a progressive healthcare technology start-up, recognized the growing challenge of patient triage and initial medical screening. Emergency rooms and healthcare providers were overwhelmed with patients seeking initial medical advice, leading to long wait times and inefficient resource allocation. The company envisioned an AI-powered solution that could provide initial symptom assessment, offer preliminary guidance, and help patients determine the appropriate level of medical care.

Solution development

The team at MedConnect chose Azure AI as their primary platform for developing a sophisticated symptom assessment chatbot. Their goal was to create a solution that could understand patient symptoms, provide initial guidance, and route patients to the most appropriate care pathway while maintaining the highest standards of RAI.

They began by selecting a base LLM that could handle medical dialogues effectively. Initial experiments with general-purpose models revealed significant limitations in domain-specific understanding. To address this, the team implemented a RAG approach, creating a comprehensive medical knowledge base drawn from reputable medical databases and clinical guidelines.

Prompt engineering and model customization

The development process was inherently iterative. The team spent considerable time crafting prompts that could elicit precise medical information while maintaining a compassionate and clear communication style. They experimented with various prompt structures, including zero-shot and few-shot prompting techniques, to improve the model's ability to understand and respond to complex medical scenarios.

Prompt flow in Azure Foundry became instrumental in this phase. Developers could systematically test and refine prompts, ensuring that the chatbot could handle a wide range of medical scenarios while maintaining accuracy and empathy. They implemented multiple safety checks to prevent the generation of potentially harmful or misleading medical advice.

RAI implementation

Recognizing the critical nature of healthcare interactions, MedConnect placed significant emphasis on RAI principles. They used Azure AI's content safety tools to implement rigorous filters that prevented the chatbot from providing inappropriate or potentially dangerous medical recommendations. The evaluation metrics went beyond traditional performance indicators, incorporating ethical considerations and patient safety as primary concerns.

The team developed a comprehensive set of evaluation criteria that included the following:

- Medical accuracy of responses
- Clarity of communication
- Potential for misinterpretation
- Alignment with clinical guidelines
- Emotional sensitivity in communication

Deployment and monitoring

Once the initial version was developed, MedConnect deployed the chatbot through Azure AI, leveraging the platform's robust monitoring capabilities. They set up detailed alerting mechanisms to track KPIs such as request volumes, response times, and safety metric violations.

The monitoring dashboard in Azure Foundry provided real-time insights into the chatbot's performance. Custom thresholds were established to trigger alerts for any deviations from expected performance or potential safety concerns. This allowed the team to continuously refine and improve the system.

Results and impact

The deployed solution demonstrated remarkable outcomes. During initial trials, the chatbot successfully handled over 70% of initial patient inquiries, providing accurate preliminary assessments and appropriate care recommendations. Emergency room wait times for non-critical cases were reduced by an average of 45 minutes, and patients reported high satisfaction with the initial screening process.

More importantly, the chatbot consistently demonstrated adherence to RAI principles. It successfully identified scenarios requiring immediate human medical intervention and provided clear, compassionate guidance that prioritized patient safety.

Future developments

Looking ahead, MedConnect plans to expand the chatbot's capabilities by incorporating multimodal learning. Future iterations may include the ability to analyze uploaded medical images, integrate with wearable health devices, and provide more personalized health guidance.

The success of this project highlighted the transformative potential of LLMOps in healthcare, demonstrating how carefully developed AI solutions can improve patient care while maintaining the highest standards of ethical and responsible technology deployment.

Summary

This chapter has provided a strategic overview of LLMOps—a critical evolution of MLOps principles that addresses the unique challenges of operationalizing LLMs. Rather than treating LLMOps as merely an extension of traditional ML operations, we've established its distinct operational paradigm, characterized by specialized workflows, evaluation methodologies, and deployment strategies. We've examined the architectural components essential for enterprise-grade LLM implementations: from the strategic selection of foundation models to the integration of sophisticated RAG systems, the development of robust prompt engineering frameworks, and the implementation of comprehensive monitoring solutions. Each of these components demands expertise that bridges traditional software engineering with emerging AI governance principles.

The exploration of Azure's implementation showcases how enterprise platforms are evolving to accommodate the unique requirements of LLM systems. The case study of MedConnect demonstrated the practical application of these principles in high-stakes environments where performance, safety, and ethical considerations are paramount. For DevOps practitioners, cloud engineers, and SREs already versed in traditional operational paradigms, LLMOps presents both familiar patterns and novel challenges. The field demands a sophisticated understanding of model behavior, retrieval systems, and evaluation methodologies that extend well beyond conventional software metrics.

As this field continues its rapid evolution, practitioners must maintain a dual focus: implementing today's best practices while actively developing frameworks flexible enough to accommodate tomorrow's advancements. The lines between model architecture, prompt engineering, retrieval system design, and operational excellence continue to blur, creating an environment where operational expertise directly impacts model performance and business outcomes. This chapter serves as a strategic cornerstone for professionals looking to build mature LLMOps practices— establishing a framework that acknowledges the complexity of the domain while providing actionable insights for implementation. The journey from MLOps to LLMOps is not merely an incremental step but a transformative shift in how we conceptualize, implement, and govern AI systems at scale.

Stay Sharp in Cloud and DevOps — Join 44,000+ Subscribers of CloudPro

CloudPro is a weekly newsletter for cloud professionals who want to stay current on the fast-evolving world of cloud computing, DevOps, and infrastructure engineering.

Every issue delivers focused, high-signal content on topics like:

- AWS, GCP & multi-cloud architecture
- Containers, Kubernetes & orchestration
- **Infrastructure as Code (IaC)** with Terraform, Pulumi, etc.
- Platform engineering & automation workflows
- Observability, performance tuning, and reliability best practices

Whether you're a cloud engineer, SRE, DevOps practitioner, or platform lead, CloudPro helps you stay on top of what matters, without the noise.

Scan the QR code to join for free and get weekly insights straight to your inbox:

https://packt.link/cloudpro

<packt>

packtpub.com

Subscribe to our online digital library for full access to over 7,000 books and videos, as well as industry leading tools to help you plan your personal development and advance your career. For more information, please visit our website.

Why subscribe?

- Spend less time learning and more time coding with practical eBooks and Videos from over 4,000 industry professionals
- Improve your learning with Skill Plans built especially for you
- Get a free eBook or video every month
- Fully searchable for easy access to vital information
- Copy and paste, print, and bookmark content

At www.packtpub.com, you can also read a collection of free technical articles, sign up for a range of free newsletters, and receive exclusive discounts and offers on Packt books and eBooks.

Other Books You May Enjoy

If you enjoyed this book, you may be interested in these other books by Packt:

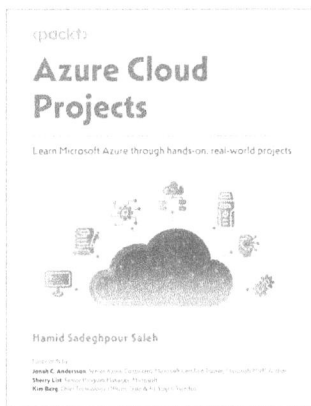

Azure Cloud Projects

Hamid Sadeghpour Saleh

ISBN: 978-1-83620-423-7

- Set up Azure and explore cloud fundamentals
- Implement Entra ID and hybrid identity solutions
- Build and secure storage with Azure Blob Storage
- Design virtual networks and configure VPN gateways
- Deploy your first web app using Azure App Service
- Automate workflows with Azure Functions
- Create CI/CD pipelines with Azure DevOps

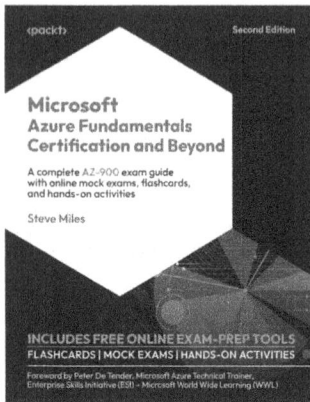

Microsoft Azure Fundamentals Certification and Beyond

Steve Miles

ISBN: 9-781-83763-059-2

- Core cloud computing concepts and how they apply to Azure
- Azure's key services, deployment methods, and management tools
- Implementation of security concepts, identity management, and governance features
- Resource deployment, monitoring, and compliance best practices
- Skills to manage and optimize Azure environments effectively

Packt is searching for authors like you

If you're interested in becoming an author for Packt, please visit authors.packt.com and apply today. We have worked with thousands of developers and tech professionals, just like you, to help them share their insight with the global tech community. You can make a general application, apply for a specific hot topic that we are recruiting an author for, or submit your own idea.

Share your thoughts

Now you've finished *Hands-On MLOps on Azure*, we'd love to hear your thoughts! Scan the QR code below to go straight to the Amazon review page for this book and share your feedback or leave a review on the site that you purchased it from.

https://packt.link/r/1836200331

Your review is important to us and the tech community and will help us make sure we're delivering excellent quality content.

Index

Download a free PDF copy of this book

Thanks for purchasing this book!

Do you like to read on the go but are unable to carry your print books everywhere?

Is your eBook purchase not compatible with the device of your choice?

Don't worry, now with every Packt book you get a DRM-free PDF version of that book at no cost.

Read anywhere, any place, on any device. Search, copy, and paste code from your favorite technical books directly into your application.

The perks don't stop there, you can get exclusive access to discounts, newsletters, and great free content in your inbox daily.

Follow these simple steps to get the benefits:

1. Scan the QR code or visit the link below:

https://packt.link/free-ebook/9781836200338

2. Submit your proof of purchase.
3. That's it! We'll send your free PDF and other benefits to your email directly.